A HANDBOOK

OF

GREEK AND LATIN
PALAEOGRAPHY

BY

EDWARD MAUNDE THOMPSON

ARES PUBLISHERS INC.
CHICAGO   MCMLXXV

481.7
T37h
109468
May 1979

Unchanged Reprint of the Edition:
London, 1901 & Chicago, 1966
ARES PUBLISHERS INC.
612 N. Michigan Avenue
Chicago, Illinois 60611
Printed in the United States of America
International Standard Book Number:
0-89005-094-5
Library of Congress Catalog Card Number:
75-21021

PREFACE

This *Handbook of Greek and Latin Palaeography* which now becomes part of the series in the *Argonaut Library of Antiquities*, needs no special introduction nor proclamation to be recognized as *the* standard reference manual on the subject available in the English language.

During the 65 years since its first edition, a parade of scholars, among whom we can readily recognize the experts of the earlier generation and our own, have learned the basics of palaeography from this book. Masterfully written by a master of the subject, as Sir Edward Maunde Thompson was, this handbook is, and will be in the future, one of the great achievements of the golden age of classical scholarship. Its absence from the list of books available to scholars was noted with regret as long as thirty years ago and it is no secret in the world of scholars that the appearance of some newer works has not made this old and tested work any the less desirable.

The same author's *Introduction to Greek and Latin Palaeography* (Oxford 1912), no doubt is more extensive and rich in references, but specialists agree that it lacks the instructive value and methodic classification of the *Handbook*. It is admitted that the *Introduction* is the only book in the English language which can stand together with *Griechische Palaeographie* by V. Gardthausen, but we feel that the *Handbook* will be more helpful in serving both teacher and student before they proceed to the others.

We should like to add a note here about the best augmented edition of the *Handbook* which appeared in 1903. It was then that the well known scholar Spyridon P. Lambros (known to many for his *Catalogue of the Greek Manuscripts on Mount Athos*, Cambridge 1895-1900, 2 vols.) published a modern Greek translation of Thompson's *Handbook* in the series "Bibliotheke Marasle." Lambros' addenda to the original and his notes were so important that Thompson himself admitted that the modern Greek edition was, even for him, virtually a new book.

The duty of the editors of the *Argonaut Library of Antiquities*, as outlined at the beginning of the series, is to provide bibliographies of other works in the field of any given book, to provide an awareness for the reader of the scholarship between the first publication and that of the first American edition. The following select bibliography will serve this purpose successfully, we hope. It is not extensive, but there have been few important contributions to the science of palaeography in recent years, so perhaps the reappearance of Thompson's *Handbook* will answer a real need.

SELECT BIBLIOGRAPHY

Bataille, A., *Pour une terminologie en paleographie grecque*. Paris 1954.

Cappelli, A., *Dizzionario di abbreviature latine ed italiane*. 5th ed. 1954.

Collomp, P., *La papyrologie*. Paris 1927.

Devreesse, R., *Introduction a l'etude des manuscrits grecs*. Paris 1954.

Foerster, H., *Abriss der lateinischen Palaeographie*. Berlin 1949.

Gardthausen, V., *Griechische Palaeographie*. 2nd ed. 1911-1913.

Kenyon, F. G., *Palaeography of Greek Papyri*. Oxford 1899.

Lehmann, P., *Lateinische Palaeographie* (in preparation).

Mallon, J., *Paleographie romaine*. Paris 1952.

Milne, H. J. M., *Greek Shorthand Manuals*. London 1934.

Minns, E. H., "Palaeography," in Whibley's *Companion to Greek Studies*. 4th ed. 1931, pp. 705-719.

d'Ors, A., *Introduccion al Estudio de los Documentos del'Egipto Romano*. Madrid 1948.

Richard, S., *Repertoire de bibliotheques et des catalogues de manuscrits grecs*. 2nd ed. 1958.

Roberts, C. H., *Greek Literary Hands*. corr. ed. 1956.

Sigalas, A., *History of Greek Writing*. Thessalonike 1934. (in Greek).

Schubart, W., *Griechische Palaeographie*. Munich 1925.

———, *Das Buch bei den Griechen und Romern*. 3rd ed. by E. Paul. 1961.

Steffans, F., *Einfuhrung in die Papyruskunde*. Berlin 1918.

———, *Lateinische Palaeographie*. 2nd ed. 1929 (repr. 1963).

Tsereteli, *Abbreviations in Greek MSS.*, St. Petersburg 1904. (in Russian).

Thompson, E. M., *Introduction to Greek and Latin Palaeography*. Oxford 1912. (repr. 1962).

Ullman, B. L., *Ancient Writing and its Influence*. London 1960.

Van Groningen, B. A., *Short Manual of Greek Palaeography*. 2nd ed. 1955.

Weitzmann, K., *Ancient Book Illumination*. Oxford 1959.

Wessely, C., *Studien zur Palaeographie und Papyruskunde*. Leipzig 1902.

PREFACE.

THIS Hand-book does not pretend to give more than an outline of the very large subject of Greek and Latin Palæography. It must be regarded as an introduction to the study of the subject, indicating the different branches into which it is divided and suggesting the lines to be followed, rather than attempting full instruction. It in no way supersedes the use of such works as the collections of facsimiles issued by the Palæographical Society and by other societies and scholars at home and abroad; but it is hoped that it will serve as an aid to the more intelligent and profitable study of them.

Our conclusions as to the course of development of the handwritings of former ages are based on our knowledge and experience of the development of modern forms of writing. Children at school learn to write by copying formal text-hands in their copy-books, and the handwriting of each child will bear the impress of the models. But as he grows up the child developes a handwriting of his own, diverging more and more from the models, but never altogether divesting itself of their first influence. Thus, at all times, we have numerous individual handwritings, but each bearing the stamp of its school and of its period; and they, in their turn, react upon and modify the writing of the next generation.

In this way have arisen the handwritings of nations

and districts, of centuries and periods, all distinguish-able from each other by the trained eye. And the faculty of distinction is not entirely, but to a very great degree, dependent on familiarity. Anyone will readily distinguish the handwritings of individuals of his own time, and will recognize his friend's writing at a glance as easily as he recognizes his face; he has more difficulty in discriminating between the individual handwritings of a foreign country. Set before him specimens of the writing of the last century, and he will confuse the hands of different persons. Take him still farther back, and he will pronounce the writing of a whole school to be the writing of one man; and he will see no difference between the hands, for example, of an Englishman, a Frenchman, and a Fleming. Still farther back, the writing of one century is to him the same as the writing of another, and he may fail to name the locality where a MS. was written by the breadth of a whole continent.

Palæographical knowledge was formerly confined to a few, chiefly to the custodians or owners of collections of manuscripts; works of reference on the subject were scarce and expensive; and facsimiles, with certain excep-tions, were of no critical value. In these days, when photography has made accurate reproduction so simple a matter, the knowledge is within the reach of all who care to acquire it. The collections of facsimiles which have been issued during the last twenty years have brought into the private study materials which the student could formerly have gathered only by travel and personal research. And more than this: these facsimiles enable us to compare, side by side, specimens from manuscripts which lie scattered in the different libraries of Europe and which could never have been brought together. There is no longer any lack of

Preface.

material for the ready attainment of palæographical knowledge.

Abroad, this attainment is encouraged in various countries by endowments and schools. In our own country, where the development of such studies is usually left to private exertion and enterprise, Palæography has received but little notice in the past. In the future, however, it will receive better recognition. In the Universities its value has at length been acknowledged as a factor in education. The mere faculty of reading an ancient MS. may not count for much, but it is worth something. The faculty of assigning a date and locality to an undated codex; of deciding between the true and the false; in a word, of applying accurate knowledge to minute points—a faculty which is only to be acquired by long and careful training—is worth much, and will give a distinct advantage to the scholar who possesses it.

I have to thank my colleague, Mr. G. F. Warner, the Assistant-Keeper of the Department of MSS., for kind help in passing this work through the press.

E. M. T.

British Museum,
   14th December, 1892.

CONTENTS.

Contents.

TABLES OF ALPHABETS.

PALÆOGRAPHY.

CHAPTER I.

THE GREEK AND LATIN ALPHABETS.

ALTHOUGH the task which lies before us of investigating
the growth and changes of Greek and Latin palæography
does not require us to deal with any form of writing till
long after the alphabets of Greece and Rome had assumed their final shapes, yet a brief sketch of the origin
and formation of those alphabets is the natural introduction to such a work as this.

The alphabet which we use at the present day has
been traced back, in all its essential forms, to the ancient
hieratic writing of Egypt of about the twenty-fifth century
before Christ. It is directly derived from the Roman
alphabet; the Roman, from a local form of the Greek;
the Greek, from the Phœnician; the Phœnician, from
the Egyptian hieratic.

The hieroglyphic records of Egypt extend through a
period of from four to five thousand years, from the age
of the second dynasty to the period of the Roman
Empire. Knowing the course through which other
primitive forms of writing have passed, we must allow
a considerable period of time to have elapsed before the
hieroglyphs had assumed the phonetic values which they
already possess in the earliest existing monuments.
Originally these signs were ideograms or pictures, either
actual or symbolical, of tangible objects or abstract

B

ideas which they expressed. From the ideograms in course of time developed the phonograms, or written symbols of sounds, first as verbal signs representing entire words, then as syllabic signs of the articulations of which words are composed. The last stage of development, whereby the syllabic signs are at length taken as the alphabetical signs representing the elementary sounds into which a syllable can be resolved, has always proved the most difficult. Some forms of writing, such as the ancient cuneiform and the modern Chinese, have scarcely passed beyond the syllabic stage. The Egyptians curiously went more than half-way in the last perfecting stage; they developed alphabetical signs, but failed to make independent use of them. A phonogram was added to explain the alphabetically-written word, and an ideogram was added to explain the phonogram. It has been truly said that this cumbrous system seems almost inconceivable to us, who can express our thoughts so easily and so surely by six-and-twenty simple signs. The fact, however, remains that the Egyptians had unconsciously invented an alphabet; and they had been in possession of these letters for more than four thousand years before the Christian era. The oldest extant hieroglyphic inscription is engraved on a tablet, now in the Ashmolean Museum at Oxford, which was erected to the memory of a priest who lived in the reign of Sent, a monarch of the second dynasty, whose period has been variously given as 4000 or 4700 B.C. In the cartouche of the king's name three of the alphabetical signs are found, one of which, *n*, has descended and finds a place in our own alphabet. The age of our first letters may thus be said to number some six thousand years. In addition, it is a moderate computation to allow a thousand years to have elapsed between the first origin of the primæval picture-writing of Egypt and the matured form of development seen in the hieroglyphic characters of the earliest monuments. We may without exaggeration allow a still longer period and be within bounds, if we carry back the invention of Egyptian writing to six or seven thousand years before Christ.

To trace the connection of the Greek alphabet with the Semitic is not difficult. A comparison of the early forms of the letters sufficiently demonstrates their common origin; and, still further, the names of the letters and their order in the two alphabets are the same. But to prove the descent of the Semitic alphabet from the Egyptian has been a long and difficult task. Firstly, in outward shape the Egyptian hieroglyphs of the monuments appear to be totally different from the Semitic letters and to have nothing in common with them. Next, their names are different. The names of the Semitic letters are Semitic words, each describing the letter from its resemblance to some particular object, as *aleph* an ox, *beth* a house, and so on. When the Greeks took over the Semitic letters, they also took over their Semitic names; by analogy, therefore, it might be assumed that in adopting the Egyptian letters the Semites would also have adopted the Egyptian names. Thirdly, the order of the letters is different. All these difficulties combined to induce scholars to reject the ancient, though vague, tradition handed down by Greek and Roman writers, that the Phœnicians had originally obtained their letters from Egypt. By recent investigation, however, the riddle has been solved, and the chain of connection between our alphabet and the ancient Egyptian hieroglyphic writing has, beyond reasonable doubt, been completed.

The number of alphabetical signs found among the inscriptions on Egyptian monuments has been reckoned at forty-five. Some of these, however, are used only in special cases; others are only alternative forms for signs more commonly employed. The total number of signs ordinarily in use may thus be reduced to twenty-five—a number which agrees with the tradition handed down by Plutarch, that the Egyptians possessed an alphabet of five-and-twenty letters. Until lately, however, these hieroglyphs had been known only in the set and rigid forms as sculptured on the monuments. In 1859 the French Egyptologist de Rougé made known the results of his study of an ancient cursive form of hieratic writing in which he had discovered the link connecting the Semitic with the Egyptian alphabet. The document which yielded the most important results was the Papyrus Prisse, which was obtained at Thebes by Mons. Prisse d'Avennes, and was given by him to the Bibliothèque Nationale. The greater part of this papyrus is occupied by a moral treatise composed by Ptah-Hotep, a prince who lived in the reign of a king of the fifth dynasty—not, however, the original, but a copy, which, having been found in a tomb of the eleventh dynasty, is anterior to the period of the Hyksos invasion, and may be assigned to the period about 2500 B.C. The old hieratic cursive character which is employed in this most ancient document is the style of writing which was no doubt made use of in Egypt for ordinary purposes at the time of the Semitic conquest, and, as de Rougé has shown, was taken by the new lords of the country as material wherewith to form an alphabet of their own. But, as has already been remarked, while adopting the Egyptian forms of letters, the Semites did not also adopt their Egyptian names, nor did they keep to their order. This latter divergence may be due to the fact that it was a selection that was made from a large-number of ideograms and phonograms, and not a complete and established alphabet that was taken over. In the table which accompanies this chapter the ancient hieratic character of the Prisse papyrus may be compared with the early Semitic alphabet of some sixteen hundred years later, and, in spite of the interval of time, their resemblance in very many instances is still wonderfully close.

This Semitic alphabet appears to have been employed in the cities and colonies of the Phœnicians and among the Jews and Moabites and other neighbouring tribes at a period not far removed from the time when the children of Israel sojourned in the land of Egypt. Bible history proves that in patriarchal times the art of writing was unknown to the Jews, but that, when they entered the promised land, they were in possession of it. All evidence goes to prove its acquisition during the Semitic occupation of the Delta; and the diffusion of the newly-formed alphabet may have been due to the retreating Hyksos when driven out of Egypt, or to Phœnician traders, or to both.[1]

The most ancient form of the Phœnician alphabet known to us is preserved in a series of inscriptions which date back to the tenth century B.C. The most important of them is that engraved upon the slab known as the Moabite stone, which records the wars of Mesha, king of Moab, about 890 B.C., against Israel and Edom, and which was discovered in 1868 near the site of Dibon, the ancient capital of Moab. Of rather earlier date are some fragments of a votive inscription engraved on bronze plates found in Cyprus in 1876 and dedicating a vessel to the god Baal of Lebanon. From these and other inscriptions of the oldest type we can construct the primitive Phœnician alphabet of twenty-two letters, as represented in the third column of the table, in a form, however, which must have passed through many stages of modification since it was evolved from the ancient cursive hieratic writing of Egypt.

The Greek Alphabet.

The Greeks learned the art of writing from the Phœnicians at least as early as the ninth century B.C.; and it is not improbable that they had acquired it even one or two centuries earlier. Trading stations and colonies of the Phœnicians, pressed at home by the advancing conquests of the Hebrews, were established in remote times in the islands and mainlands of Greece and Asia Minor; and their alphabet of two-and-twenty letters was adopted by the Greeks among whom they settled or with whom they had commercial dealings. It is not, however, to be supposed that the Greeks received the alphabet from the Phœnicians at one single place from whence it was passed on throughout Hellas; but rather at several points of contact from whence it was locally diffused among neighbouring cities and their colonies. Hence we are prepared to find that, while the

---

[1] See Isaac Taylor, *The Alphabet*, chap. ii. § 8.

Greek alphabet is essentially one and the same in all parts of Hellas, as springing from one stock, it exhibits certain local peculiarities, partly no doubt inherent from its very first adoption at different centres, partly derived from local influences or from linguistic or other causes. We cannot, then, accept the idea of a Cadmean alphabet, in the sense of an alphabet of one uniform pattern for all Greece.

Among the two-and-twenty signs adopted from the Phœnician, four, viz. *aleph, he, yod,* and *ayin,* were made to represent the vowel-sounds *a, e, i, o,* both long and short, the signs for *e* and *o* being also employed for the diphthongs *ei* and *ou.* The last sound continued to be expressed by the *omikron* alone to a comparatively late period in the history of the alphabet. The fifth vowel-sound *u* was provided for by a new letter, the *upsilon,* which may have been either a modification or "differentiation" of the Phœnician *waw,* or derived from a letter of similar form in the Cypriote alphabet. This new letter must have been added almost immediately after the introduction of the Semitic signs, for there is no local Greek alphabet which is without it. Next was felt the necessity for distinguishing long and short *e,* and in Ionia, the aspirate gradually falling into disuse, the sign H, *eta,* was adopted to represent long *e,* probably before the end of the seventh century B.C. About the same time the long *o* began to be distinguished by various signs, that used by the Ionians, the *omega,* Ω, being apparently either a differentiation of the *omikron,* or, as has been suggested, taken from the Cypriote alphabet. The age of the double letter Φ and of X and Ψ, as they appear in the Ionian alphabet, must, as is evident from their position, be older than or at least coeval with *omega.*

With regard to the sibilants, their history is involved in great obscurity. The original Semitic names appear to have become confused in the course of transmission to the Greeks and to have been applied by them to the wrong signs. The name *zeta* appears to correspond to the name *tsade,* but the letter appears to be taken from the letter *zayn*. *Xi*, which seems to be the same word as *shin*, represents the letter *samekh*. *San*, which is probably derived from *zayn*, represents *tsade*. *Sigma*, which may be identified with *samekh*, represents *shin*. But all these sibilants were not used simultaneously for any one dialect or locality. In the well-known passage of Herodotus (i. 139), where he is speaking of the terminations of Persian names, we are told that they "all end in the same letter, which the Dorians call *san* and the Ionians *sigma*." There can be little doubt that the Dorian *san* was originally the M-shaped sibilant which is found in the older Dorian inscriptions, as in Thera, Melos, Crete, Corinth and Argos.[2] This sibilant is now known to have been derived from the Phœnician letter *tsade*. In a Greek abecedarium scratched upon a small vase discovered at Formello, near Veii, this letter is seen to occupy the eighteenth place, corresponding to the position of *tsade* in the Phœnician alphabet. In the damaged Greek alphabet similarly scrawled on the Galassi vase, which was found at Cervetri in 1836, it is formed more closely on the pattern of the Phœnician letter. In the primitive Greek alphabet, therefore, *san* existed (representing *tsade*) as well as *sigma* (representing *shin*), but as both appear to have had nearly the same sibilant sound, the one or the other became superfluous. In the Ionian alphabet *sigma* was preferred.

But the disuse of the letter *san* must date far back, for its loss affected the numerical value of the Greek letters. When this value was being fixed, the exclusion of *san* was overlooked, and the numbers were calculated as though that letter had not existed. The preceding letter *pi* stands for 80; the *koppa* for 90, the numerical value of the Phœnician *tsade* and properly also that of *san*. At a later period the obsolete letter was re-adopted as the numerical sign for 900, and became the modern *sampi* (i.e. *san* + *pi*), so called from its partial resemblance, in its late form, to the letter *pi*.

[2] It has also been identified with a T-shaped sign which was used for a special sound on coins of Mesembria, and at Halicarnassus in the fifth century B.C.

With regard to the local alphabets of Greece, different states and different islands either adopted or developed distinctive signs. Certain letters underwent gradual changes, as *eta* from closed ⊟ to open H, and *theta* from crossed ⊗ to the dotted circle ⊙, which forms were common to all the varieties of the alphabet. The most ancient forms of the alphabet are found in Melos, Thera, and Crete, which moreover did not admit the double letters. While some states retained the *digamma* or the *koppa*, others lost them; while some developed particular differentiations to express certain sounds, others were content to express two sounds by one letter. The forms ⌐ for *beta* and Ɓ for *epsilon* are peculiar to Corinth and her colonies; the Argive alphabet is distinguished by its rectangular *lambda* Ⱶ; and the same letter appears in the Bœotian, Chalcidian, and Athenian alphabets in the inverted form Ʌ.

But while there are these local differences among· the various alphabets of ancient Greece, a broad division has been laid down by Kirchhoff, who arranges them in two groups, the eastern and the western. The eastern group embraces the alphabet which has already been referred to as the Ionian, common to the cities on the western coast of Asia Minor and the neighbouring islands, and the alphabets of Megara, Argos, and Corinth and her colonies ; and, in a modified degree, those of Attica, Naxos, Thasos, and some other islands. The western group includes the alphabets of Thessaly, Eubœa, Phocis, Locris, and Bœotia, and of all the Peloponnese (excepting the states specified under the other group), and also those of the Achæan and Chalcidian colonies of Italy and Sicily.

In the eastern group the letter Ξ has the sound of *x*; and the letters X, Ψ, the sounds of *kh* and *ps*. (In Attica, Naxos, etc., the letters Ξ and Ψ were wanting, and the sounds *x* and *ps* were expressed by XΣ, ΦΣ). In the western group the letter Ξ is wanting, and X, Ψ have the values of *x* and *kh*; while the sound *ps* was expressed by ΠΣ or ΦΣ, or rarely by a special sign Ж. In a word, the special test-letters are :—

Eastern : **X**=*kh.*   **Ψ**=*ps.*
Western : **X**=*x.*   **Ψ**=*kh.*

How this distinction came about is not known, although several explanations have been hazarded. It is unnecessary in this place to do more than state the fact.

As the Semitic languages were written from right to left, so in the earliest Greek inscriptions we find the same order followed. Next came the method of writing called *boustrophedon,* in which the written lines run alternately from right to left and from left to right, or *vice versâ,* as the plough forms the furrows. Lastly, writing from left to right became universal. In the most ancient tomb-inscriptions of Melos and Thera we have the earliest form of writing. *Boustrophedon* was commonly used in the sixth century B.C. A notable exception, however, is found in the famous Greek inscription at Abu Simbel—the earliest to which a date can be given. It is cut on one of the legs of the colossal statues which guard the entrance of the great temple, and records the exploration of the Nile up to the second cataract by certain Greek, Ionian, and Carian mercenaries in the service of Psammetichus. The king here mentioned may be the first (B.C. 654—617) or the second (B.C. 594—589) of the name. The date of the writing may therefore be roughly placed about 600 B.C. The fact that, besides this inscription, the work of two of the soldiers, the names of several of their comrades are also cut on the rock, proves how well established was the art of writing even at this early period.

The Latin Alphabet.

Like the local alphabets of Greece, the Italic alphabets varied from one another by the adoption or rejection of different signs, according to the requirements of language. Thus the Latin and Faliscan, the Etruscan, the Umbrian, and the Oscan alphabets are sufficiently distinguished in this way ; but at the same time the common origin of all can be traced to a primitive or so-called Pelasgian alphabet of the Chalcidian type. The period of the introduction of writing into Italy from the great trading and colonizing city of Chalcis must be carried back to the time when the Greeks wrote from right to left. A single Latin inscription[3] has been found which is thus written; and in the other Italic scripts this ancient system was also followed. We may assume, then, that the Greek alphabet was made known to the native tribes of Italy as early as the eighth or ninth century B.C., and not improbably through the ancient Chalcidian colony of Cumæ, which tradition named as the earliest Greek settlement in the land. The eventual prevalence of the Latin alphabet naturally followed the political supremacy of Rome.

The Latin alphabet possesses twenty of the letters of the Greek western alphabet, and, in addition, three adopted signs. Taking the Formello and Galassi abecedaria as representing the primitive alphabet of Italy, it will be seen that the Latins rejected the letter *san* and the double letters *theta*, *phi*, and *chi* (Ψ), and disregarded the earlier sign for *xi*.[4] In Quintilian's time letter X was the "ultima nostrarum" and closed the alphabet. The sound *z* in Latin being coincident with the sound *s*, the letter *zeta* dropped out. But at a later period it was restored to the alphabet, as Z, for the purpose of transliteration of Greek words. As, however, its original place had been meanwhile filled by the new letter G, it was sent down to the end of the alphabet. With regard to the creation of G, till the middle of the third century B.C. its want was not felt, as C was employed to represent both the hard *c* and *g* sounds,[5] a

---

[3] On a small vase found in Rome in 1880. See *L'Inscription de Duenos* in the *Mélanges d'Archéologie et d'Histoire* of the École Française de Rome, 1882, p. 147.

[4] Some of these letters are generally accepted as the origin of certain of the symbols used for the Latin numerals. But a different origin has been lately proposed by Professor Zangemeister: *Entstehung der römischen Zahlzeichen* (Sitzber. d. k. Preuss. Akad., 1887).

[5] The sound represented by C in Latin no doubt also gradually, but at a very early period, became indistinguishable from that represented by K. Hence the letter K fell into general disuse in

survival of this use being seen in the abbreviations C. and Cn. for Gaius and Gnæus; but gradually the new letter was developed from C and was placed in the alphabet in the position vacated by *zeta*. The *digamma* had become the Latin F, and the *upsilon* had been transliterated as the Latin V; but in the time of Cicero *upsilon*, as a foreign letter, was required for literary purposes, and thus became again incorporated in the Latin alphabet—this time without change of form, Y. Its position shows that it was admitted before Z.

writing, and only survived as an archaic form in certain words, such as *kalendæ*.

CHAPTER II.

OF the various materials which have been used within the memory of man to receive writing, there are three, viz. papyrus, vellum, and paper, which, from their greater abundance and convenience, have, each one in its turn, displaced all others. But of the other materials several, including some which at first sight seem of a most unpromising character, have been largely used. For such a purpose as writing, men naturally make use of the material which can be most readily procured, and is, at the same time, the most suitable. If the ordinary material fail, they must extemporize a substitute. If something more durable is wanted, metal or stone may take the place of vellum or paper. But with inscriptions on these harder materials we have, in the present work, but little to do. Such inscriptions generally fall under the head of epigraphy. Here we have chiefly to consider the softer materials on which handwriting, as distinguished from monumental engraving, has been wont to be inscribed. Still, as will be seen in what follows, there are certain exceptions; and to some extent we shall have to inquire into the employment of metals, clay, potsherds, and wood, as well as of leaves, bark, linen, wax, papyrus, vellum, and paper, as materials for writing. We will first dispose of those substances which were of more limited use.

Leaves.

It is natural to suppose that, in a primitive state of society, leaves of plants and trees, strong enough for the purpose, would be adopted as a ready-made material provided by nature for such an operation as writing. In various parts of India and the East the leaves of palm-trees have been in use for centuries, and continue to be employed for this purpose, and form an excellent and enduring substance. Manuscripts written on palm-leaves have been of late years found in Nepaul, which date back many hundreds of years. In Europe leaves of plants are not generally of the tough character of those which grow in the tropics ; but there can be no doubt that they were used in ancient Greece and Italy, and that the references by classical writers to their employment are not merely fanciful. There is evidence of the custom of πεταλισμός, or voting for ostracism with olive-leaves, at Syracuse, and of the similar practice at Athens under the name of ἐκφυλλοφορία.[1] Pliny, *Nat. Hist.* xiii. 11, writes : " Antea non fuisse chartarum usum : in palmarum foliis primo scriptitatum, deinde quarundam arborum libris."

Bark.

Better adapted for writing purposes than leaves was the bark of trees, *liber,* which we have just seen named by Pliny, and the general use of which caused its name to be attached to the book (i.e. the roll) which was made from it. The inner bark of the lime-tree, φιλύρα, *tilia,* was chosen as most suitable. Pliny, *Nat. Hist.* xvi. 14, describing this tree, says : "Inter corticem et lignum tenues tunicæ sunt multiplici membrana, e quibus vincula tiliæ vocantur tenuissiu.æ earum philyræ." It was these delicate shreds, *philyræ,* of this inner skin or bark which formed the writing material. In the enumeration of different kinds of books by Martianus Capella, ii. 136, those consisting of lime-bark are quoted, though as rare : " Rari vero in philyræ cortice subnotati." Ulpian

---

[1] The olive-leaf, used in this ceremony, is also mentioned, φύλλον ἐλαίας, as the material on which to inscribe a charm.—*Cat. Gk. Papyri in Brit. Mus.* pap. cxxi. 213 ; and a bay-leaf is enjoined for the same purpose in Papyrus 2207 in the Bibliothèque Nationale.

also, *Digest.* xxxii. 52, mentions "volumina . . . in philyra aut in tilia." But not only was the bark of the lime-tree used, but tablets also appear to have been made from its wood—the "tiliæ pugillares" of Symmachus, iv. 34; also referred to by Dio Cassius, lxxii. 8, in the passage: "δώδεκα γραμματεῖα, οἶά γε ἐκ φιλύρας ποιεῖται." It seems that rolls made from lime-bark were co-existent at Rome with those made from papyrus, after the introduction of the latter material; but the home-made bark must soon have disappeared before the imported Egyptian papyrus, which had so many advantages both in quantity and quality to recommend it.

Linen.

Linen cloth, which is found in use among the ancient Egyptians to receive writing, appears also as the material for certain rituals in Roman history. Livy, x. 38, refers to a book of this character, "liber vetus linteus," among the Samnites; and again, iv. 7, he mentions the "lintei libri" in the temple of Moneta at Rome. Pliny, *Nat. Hist.* xiii. 11, names "volumina lintea" as in use at an early period for private documents, public acts being recorded on lead. Martianus Capella, iii. 136, also refers to "carbasina volumina"; and in the *Codex Theodos.* xi. 27, 1, "mappæ linteæ" occur.

Clay and Pottery.

Clay was a most common writing material among the Babylonians and Assyrians. The excavations made of late years on the ancient sites of their great cities have brought to light a whole literature impressed on sun-dried or fire-burnt bricks. Potsherds came ready to the hand in Egypt, where earthenware vessels were the most common kind of household utensils. They have been found in large numbers, many inscribed in Greek with such ephemeral documents as tax and pay receipts, generally of the period of the Roman occupation.[2] To such inscribed potsherds has been given the title of *ostraka*, a term which will recall the practice of Athenian ostracism

---

[2] See autotypes of some specimens in *Pal. Soc.* ii. pl. 1, 2.

in which the votes were recorded on such fragments.[3]
That such material was used in Greece only on such
passing occasions or from necessity is illustrated by the
passage in Diogenes Laertius, vii. 174, which narrates
that the Stoic Cleanthes was forced by poverty to write
on potsherds and the shoulder-blades of oxen. Tiles
also, upon which alphabets or verses were scratched with
the stilus before baking, were used by both Greeks and
Romans for educational purposes.[4]

Wall-spaces.

It is perhaps straining a term to include the walls of
buildings under the head of writing materials; but the
graffiti or wall-scribblings, discovered in such large
numbers at Pompeii,[5] hold such an important place in
the history of early Latin palæography, that it must not
be forgotten that in ancient times, as now, a vacant wall
was held to be a very convenient place to present appeals
to the public, or to scribble idle words.

Metals.

The precious metals were naturally but seldom used
as writing materials. For such a purpose, however, as
working a charm, an occasion when the person specially
interested might be supposed not to be too niggard in his
outlay in order to attain his ends, we find thin plates or
leaves of gold or silver recommended,[6] a practice which is
paralleled by the crossing of the palm of the hand with

---

[3] Votes for ostracism at Athens were probably recorded on
fragments of broken vases which had been used in religious
services, and which were given out specially for the occasion.
Only two such voting ostraka appear to be known: the one is
described by Benndorf, *Griech. und sicilische Vasenbilder*, tab.
xxix. 10; the other, for the ostracism of Xanthippos, the father
of Pericles (see Aristotle, *Const. Athens*, p. 61), is noticed by
Studniczka, *Antenor und archaische Malerei* in *Jahrbuch des kais.
Deutschen Arch. Instituts*, bd. ii. (1887), 161.

[4] Facsimiles in *Corp. Inscr. Lat.* iii. 962.

[5] *Ibid.* iv.

[6] *Cat. Gk. Papyri in Brit. Mus.*, pap. cxxi. 580; also papyri
in the Bibl. Nationale, 258, 2705, 2228.

a gold or silver coin as enjoined by the gipsy fortune-teller.

Lead.

Lead was used at an ancient date. Pliny, *Nat. Hist.* xiii. 11, refers to "plumbea volumina" as early writing material. Pausanias, ix. 31, 4, states that at Helicon he saw a leaden plate (μόλιβδος) on which the Ἔργα of Hesiod were inscribed. At Dodona tablets of lead have been discovered which contain petitions to the oracle, and in some instances the answers.[7] Lenormant, *Rhein. Museum*, xxii. 276, has described the numerous small leaden pieces on which are written names of persons, being apparently *sortes judiciariæ*, or lots for selection of judges, of ancient date. *Diræ*, or solemn dedications of offending persons to the infernal deities by, or on behalf of, those whom they had injured, were inscribed on this metal. These maledictory inscriptions, called also *defixiones* or κατάδεσμοι and καταδέσεις, appear to have been extensively employed. An instance is recorded by Tacitus, *Annal.* ii. 69, in his account of the last illness and death of Germanicus, in whose house were found, hidden in the floor and walls, remains of human bodies and "carmina et devotiones et nomen Germanici plumbeis tabulis insculptum." Many have been found at Athens and other places in Greece, and some in Italy; others again in a burial-ground near Roman Carthage.[8] Several were discovered at Cnidus which have been assigned to the period between the third and first centuries B.C.; [9] and recently a collection was found near Paphos in Cyprus, buried in what appears to have been a malefactors' common grave.[1] These Cnidian and Cyprian examples are now in the British Museum. Charms and incantations were also inscribed on thin leaves of lead.[2]

[7] Carapanos, *Dodone et ses Ruines* (1878), p. 68, pl. xxxiv.-xl.; *Corp. Inscr. Lat.* i. 818, 819.

[8] *Bulletin de Corresp. Hellénique*, 1888, p. 294.

[9] Newton, *Discov. at Halicarnassus* (1863), ii. 719–745; and Collitz and Bechtel, *Griech. Dialekt-Inschriften*, iii. 233.

[1] *Soc. Biblical Archæology*, Proceedings, vol. xiii. (1891), pt iv.

[2] Leemans, *Papyri Græci Mus. Lugdun.* 1885; Wessely, *Griech. Zauber Papyri*, 1888; *Cat. Gk. Papyri in Brit. Mus.* pp. 64 sqq.

Montfaucon, *Palæogr. Græca,* 16, 181, mentions and gives an engraving of a leaden book, apparently connected with magic. In 1880 an imprecatory leaden tablet was dug up at Bath, the inscription being in Latin : a relic of the Roman occupation.[3] Of later date is a tablet found in a grave in Dalmatia, containing a charm against evil spirits, in Latin, inscribed in cursive letters of the sixth century.[4] Several specimens which have been recovered from mediæval graves prove that the custom of burying leaden inscribed plates with the dead was not uncommon in the middle ages.[5] The employment of this metal for such purposes may have been recommended by its supposed durability. But lead is in fact highly sensitive to chemical action, and is liable to rapid disintegration under certain circumstances. For the ancient *diræ* it was probably used because it was common and cheap. For literary purposes it appears to have been to some extent employed in the middle ages in Northern Italy, leaden plates inscribed with historical and diplomatic records connected with Venice and Bologna being still in existence, apparently of the fourteenth and fifteenth centuries.[6]

Bronze.

Bronze was used both by Greeks and Romans as a material on which to engrave votive inscriptions, laws, treaties, and other solemn documents. These, however, do not come under present consideration, being strictly epigraphical monuments. The only class which we need notice is that of the Roman military diplomas, those portable *tabulæ honestæ missionis,* as they have been called, which were given to veteran soldiers and conferred upon them rights of citizenship and marriage. Fifty-eight such documents, or portions of them, issued under the emperors, from Claudius to Diocletian, have been recovered.[7] They are interesting

---

[3] *Hermes* xv.; *Journ. Brit. Arch. Assoc.* xlii. 410.
[4] *Corp. Inscr. Lat.* iii. 961.
[5] Wattenbach, *Schriftw.* 42–44.
[6] *Archæologia,* xliv. 123.
[7] *Corp. Inscr. Lat.* iii. 843 sqq.

both palæographically, as giving a series of specimens of the Roman rustic capital letters, and also for the form which they took, exactly following that observed in the legal documents preserved in waxen tablets (see below). They were, in fact, *codices* in metal. The diploma consisted of two square plates of the metal, hinged with rings. The authentic deed was engraved on the inner side of the two plates, and was repeated on the outside of the first plate. Through two holes a threefold wire was passed and bound round the plates, being sealed on the outside of the second plate with the seals of the witnesses, whose names were also engraved thereon. The seals were protected by a strip of metal, attached, which was sometimes convex to afford better cover. In case of the outer copy being called in question, reference was made to the deed inside by breaking the seals, without the necessity of going to the official copy kept in the temple of Augustus at Rome.

The repetition of the deed in one and the same diploma is paralleled in some of the Assyrian tablets, which, after being inscribed, received an outer casing of clay on which the covered writing was repeated.

Wood.

Wooden tablets were used in very remote times. In many cases they were probably coated, if not with wax, with some kind of composition, the writing being scratched upon them with a dry point; in some instances we know that ink was inscribed upon the bare wood. The ancient Egyptians also used tablets covered with a glazed composition capable of receiving ink.[8] Wooden tablets inscribed with the names of the dead are found with mummies. They were also used for memoranda and accounts, and in the Egyptian schools; specimens of tablets inscribed with receipts, alphabets, and verses having survived to the present day.[9] One of the

---

[8] Wilkinson, *Anc. Egyp.* ii. 183.

[9] Reuvens, *Lettres,* iii. 111; *Transac. Roy. Soc. Lit.,* 2nd series, x. pt. 1; Leemans, *Mon. Egypt.* ii. tab. 236. Several specimens of Egyptian inscribed tablets are in the British Museum.

earliest specimens of Greek writing is a document inscribed in ink on a small wooden tablet now in the
British Museum (5849, C.) ; it refers to a money trans-
action of the thirty-first year of Ptolemy Philadelphus
(B.C. 254 or 253).[1] In the British Museum there is also
a small wooden board (Add. MS. 33,293), painted white
and incribed in ink with thirteen lines from the Iliad (iii.
273—285), the words being marked off and the syllables
indicated by accents, no doubt for teaching young
Greek scholars. It was found in Egypt, and is probably
of the third century. There is also a miscellaneous set
of broken tablets (Add. MS. 33,369) inscribed in ink
on a ground of drab paint, with records relating to the
recovery of debts, etc., at Panopolis, the modern Ekhmim,
in the Thebaid; probably of the seventh century. In
the records of ancient Greece we have an instance of
the employment of wooden boards or tablets. In
the inventory of the expenses of rebuilding the
Erechtheum at Athens, B.C. 407, the price of two
boards, on which the rough accounts were first entered,
is set down at two drachmas, or $9\frac{3}{4}d$. each : " σανίδες δύο
ἐς ἃς τὸν λόγον ἀναγράφομεν." [2] And again a second
entry of four boards at the same price occurs. In some
of the waxen tablets lately recovered at Pompeii, the
pages which have been left in the plain wood are inscribed in ink.[3] Wooden tablets were used in schools
during the middle ages.[4] In England the custom of
using wooden tallies, inscribed as well as notched, in the
public accounts lasted down to the present century.

Waxen and other Tablets.

But we may assume that as a general rule tablets
were coated with wax [5] from the very earliest times in

---

[1] See *Revue Égyptologique,* ii., Append., p. 51; *Pal. Soc.* ii. pl. 142.
[2] Rangabé, *Antiq. Hellén.* 56; Egger, *Note sur le prix de
papier,* etc., in *Mém. d' Hist. Ancienne* (1863).
[3] *Pal. Soc.* i. pl. 159.
[4] Wattenbach, *Schriftw.* 78.
[5] κηρός, cera, or μάλθη, μάλθα. Pollux, *Onomast.* x. 57, in his
chapter περὶ βιβλίων names the composition : " ὁ δὲ ἐνὼν τῇ πινακίδι

Greece and Rome. Such waxen tablets were single, double, triple, or of several pieces or leaves. In Greek they were called πίναξ, πινακίς, δέλτος, δελτίον, δελτίδιον, πυκτίον, πυξίον, γραμματεῖον;[6] in Latin, ceræ, tabulæ, tabellæ. The wooden surface was sunk to a slight depth, leaving a raised frame at the edges, after the fashion of a child's school-slate of the present day, and a thin coating of wax, usually black, was laid over it. Tablets were used for literary composition,[7] school exercises,[8] accounts, or rough memoranda. They were sometimes fitted with slings for suspension. Two or more put together, and held together by rings acting as hinges, formed a *caudex* or *codex.* Thus Seneca, *De brev. vit.* 13: " Plurium tabularum contextus caudex apud antiquos vocabatur; unde publicæ tabulæ codices dicuntur."

When the codex consisted of two leaves it was called δίθυροι, δίπτυχα, *diptycha, duplices;* of three, τρίπτυχα, *triptycha, triplices;* and of more, πεντάπτυχα, *penta-ptycha, quintuplices,* πολύπτυχα, *polyptycha, multiplices.*[9] In Homer we have an instance of the use of a tablet in the death-message of King Prœtus, "graving in a folded tablet many deadly things."[1] And Herodotus tells us (vii. 239) how Demaratus conveyed to the Lacedæmonians secret intelligence of Xerxes' intended invasion of Greece, by means of a message written on the wooden surface of a tablet (δελτίον δίπτυχον) from which the wax had been previously scraped but was afterwards renewed to cover the writing. On Greek vases of the fifth and fourth centuries B.C., tablets, generally triptychs, are represented, both open in the hands of the goddess

---

κηρὸς, ἢ μάλθη, ἢ μάλθα. Ἡρόδοτος μεν γὰρ κηρὸν εἴρηκε, Κρατίνος δὲ ἐν τῇ Πυτίνῃ μάλθην ἔφη." Μάλθα appears to have been wax mixed with tar. Cf. Aristoph. *Fragm.* 206: "τὴν μάλθαν ἐκ τῶν γραμματείων ἤσθιον."

[6] See Pollux, *Onomasticon,* x. 57.

[7] Quintilian, *Instit. orator.* x. 3, 31, recommends the use of waxen tablets: " Scribi optime ceris, in quibus facillima est ratio."

[8] Horace, *Sat.* I. vi. 74, " Lævo suspensi loculos tabulamque lacerto."

[9] Martial, xiv. 4, 6.

[1] *Iliad,* vi. 169: " γράψας ἐν πίνακι πτυκτῷ θυμοφθόρα πολλά."

Athena or other persons, and closed and bound round with strings, hanging from the wall by slings or handles.[2]

Tablets in the codex form would be used not only as mere note-books, but especially in all cases where the writing was to be protected from injury either for the moment or for a long period. Hence they were used for legal documents, conveyances and wills, and for correspondence. When used for wills, each page was technically called *cera*, as in Gaius, ii. 104 : "Hæc, ita ut in his tabulis cerisque scripta sunt, ita do lego."[3] They were closed against inspection by passing a triple thread, λίνον, *linium*, through holes in the boards, and sealing it with the seals of the witnesses, as will presently be more fully explained. As to correspondence, small tablets, *codicilli* or *pugillares*, were employed for short letters ; longer letters, *epistolæ*, were written on papyrus. Thus Seneca, *Ep.* 55, 11, makes the distinction : "Adeo tecum sum, ut dubitem an incipiam non epistulas sed codicillos tibi scribere." The tablets were sent by messengers, *tabellarii*, as explained by Festus :[4] "Tabellis pro chartis utebantur antiqui, quibus ultro citro, sive privatim sive publice opus erat, certiores absentes faciebant. Unde adhuc tabellarii dicuntur, et tabellæ missæ ab imperatoribus."[5] The answer to the letter was inscribed on the same set of tablets and returned. Love-letters appear to have been sometimes written on very small tablets ;[6] Martial, xiv. 8, 9, calls them *Vitelliani*. Tablets containing

---

[2] See Gerhard, *Auserlesene Vasenbilder*, iii. 239 ; iv. 244, 287, 288, 289, 296 ; Luynes, *Vases*, 35.

[3] Cf. Horace, *Sat.* II. v. 51 :
    "Qui testamentum tradet tibi cunque legendum
     Abnuere, et tabulas a te removere memento ;
     Sic tamen, ut limis rapias quid prima secundo
     Cera velit versu."

[4] *De Verborum Signif.*, ed. Müller, p. 359.

[5] Compare St. Jerome, *Ep.* viii.: "Nam et rudes illi Italiæ homines, ante chartæ et membranarum usum, aut in dedolatis e ligno codicillis aut in corticibus arborum mutuo epistolarum alloquia missitabant. Unde et portitores eorum tabellarios et scriptores a libris arborum librarios vocavere."

[6] See the drawing in *Museo Borbonico*, i. 2.

letters were fastened with a thread, which was sealed.[7]
The materials for letter-writing are enumerated in the
passage of Plautus, *Bacchides*, iv. 714 : "Ecfer cito . . .
stilum, ceram et tabellas, linum"; and the process of
sealing in line 748 : "cedo tu ceram ac linum actutum
age obliga, opsigna cito." In Cicero, *Catil.* iii. 5, we have
the opening of a letter : "Tabellas proferri jussimus.
. . . Primo ostendimus Cethego signum ; cognovit; nos
linum incidimus ; legimus. . . . Introductus est Statilius ;
cognovit et signum et manum suam:"

The custom of writing letters on tablets survived for
some centuries after classical times. In the 5th century
St. Augustine in his epistle to Romanianus (Migne,
Patrolog. Lat. xxxiii. 80) makes reference to his tablets
in these words :—"Non hæc epistola sic inopiam chartæ
indicat, ut membranas saltem abundare testetur. Tabellas eburneas quas habeo avunculo tuo cum litteris
misi. Tu enim huic pelliculæ facilius ignosces, quia
differri non potuit quod ei scripsi, et tibi non scribere
etiam ineptissimum existimavi. Sed tabellas, si quæ ibi
nostræ sunt, propter hujusmodi necessitates mittas peto."
St. Hilary of Arles likewise has the following passage
in his Life of Honoratus (Migne, *Patrol. Lat.* l. 1261) :
—"Beatus Eucherius cum ab eremo in tabulis, ut assolet,
cera illitis, in proxima ab ipso degens insula, litteras ejus
suscepisset : 'Mel,' inquit, 'suum ceris reddidisti.'"
Both these passages prove that the custom was general
at the period. Even as late as the year 1148 a letter
"in tabella" was written by a monk of Fulda.[8]

It will be noticed that St. Augustine refers to his tablets
as being of ivory. The ancient tablets were ordinarily
of common wood, such as beech, or fir, or box, the
"vulgaris buxus" of Propertius (iii. 23) ; but they were
also made of more expensive material. Two of Martial's
apophoreta are "pugillares citrei" and "pugillares
eborei." Propertius (*l.c.*) refers to golden fittings :
"Non illas fixum caras effecerat aurum." The large

---

[7] Clay, *cretula*, was originally used : γῆ σημάντρις, Herod. ii. 38;
ῥύπος, Aristoph. *Lysis.* 1200, Pollux, *Onomast.* x. 58.
[8] Wattenbach, *Schriftw.* 48.

consular diptychs, as we know from existing specimens, were of ivory, often most beautifully carved.

The employment of waxen tablets lasted for certain purposes through the middle ages in countries of Western Europe. Specimens inscribed with money accounts of the thirteenth and fourteenth centuries have survived to the present day in France[9]; and municipal accounts on tablets of the fourteenth and fifteenth centuries are still preserved in some of the German towns. They also exist in Italy,[1] dating from the thirteenth or fourteenth century; they were used in England; and specimens are reported to have been found in Ireland. It is said that quite recently sales in the fish-market of Rouen were noted on waxen tablets.[2]

Greek Waxen Tablets.

Ancient Greek waxen tablets have survived in not many instances. In the British Museum are some which have been found in Egypt. The most perfect is a book (Add. MS. 33,270), perhaps of the third century, measuring nearly nine by seven inches, which consists of seven tablets coated on both sides with black wax and two covers waxed on the inner side, inscribed with documents in shorthand, presumably in Greek, and with shorthand signs written repeatedly, as if for practice, and with notes in Greek; in one of the covers a groove is hollowed for the reception of the writing implements. Another smaller book, of about seven by four inches, formed of six tablets (Add. MS. 33,368), is inscribed, probably by some schoolboy of the third century, with grammatical exercises and other notes in Greek, and also with a rough drawing, perhaps meant for a caricature of the schoolmaster. There are also two tablets

---

[9] A tablet of accounts, of about the year 1300, from Cîteaux Abbey, is in the British Museum, Add. MS. 33, 215. Four tablets, of the 14th century, found at Beauvais, are in the Bibliothèque Nationale—*Acad. des Inscriptions, Comptes Rendus,* 1887, p. 141.

[1] See Milani, *Sei Tavolette cerate,* in *Pubbl. del R. Istituto di Studi Superiori,* 1877.

[2] Wattenbach, *Schriftw.* 74.

inscribed with verses in Greek uncial writing, possibly
some literary sketch or a school exercise.[3]　Two others
of a similar nature have been recently acquired, the one
containing a writing exercise, the other a multiplication
table.　The Bodleian Library has also lately purchased
a waxen tablet. (Gr. Inscr. 4) on which is a writing
exercise.　Others are at Paris ; some containing scribbled
alphabets and a contractor's accounts, which were found
at Memphis.[4]　In New York is a set of five tablets, on
which are verses, in the style of Menander, set as a copy
by a writing-master and copied by a pupil.[5]　Other
specimens of a similar character are at Marseilles, the
date of which can be fixed at the end of the 3rd or
beginning of the 4th century ;[6] and the last leaf of a
document found at Verespatak, where so many Latin
tablets have been discovered, is preserved at Karls-
burg.[7]

Latin Waxen Tablets.

Extant Latin tablets are more numerous, but have only
been found in comparatively recent years.　Twenty-four,
containing deeds ranging in date from A.D. 131 to 167,
were recovered, between the years 1786 and 1855, from
the ancient mining works in the neighbourhood of Alburnus Major, the modern Verespatak, in Dacia.　In 1840
Massmann published the few which had at that time
been discovered, in his *Libellus Aurarius ;* but the ad-
mission into his book of two undoubtedly spurious documents cast suspicion on the rest, which were accordingly
denounced until the finding of other tablets proved their
genuineness.　The whole collection is given in the
Corpus Inscriptionum Latinarum of the Berlin Academy, vol. iii.

During the excavations at Pompeii in July, 1875, a box

[3] See *Verhandl. der Philologen-Versamml. zu Würzburg,* 1869,
p. 239.
[4] *Revue Archéol.* viii. 461, 470.
[5] *Proceedings of the American Acad. of Arts and Sciences,* iii. 371.
[6] *Annuaire de la Soc. Fran. de Numism. et d'Archéol.* iii.
lxxi.– lxxvii.
[7] *Corpus Inscr. Lat.* iii. 933.

containing 127 waxen tablets was discovered in the house
of L. Cæcilius Jucundus. They proved to be *perscrip-*
tiones and other deeds connected with sales by auction
and receipts for payment of taxes.[8]

The recovery of so many specimens of Latin tablets
has afforded ample means of understanding the mechani-
cal arrangement of such documents among the Romans.
Like the military *tabulæ honestæ missiónis*, they contained the deed under seal and the duplicate copy open
to inspection. But most of them consist of three leaves:
they are triptychs, the third leaf being of great service
in giving cover to the seals. The Pompeian and Dacian
tablets differ from one another in some particulars; but
the general arrangement was as follows. The triptych
was made from one block of wood, cloven into the
three required pieces, or leaves, which were fastened by
strings or wires passing through two holes near the edge
and serving for hinges. In the Pompeian tablets, one
side of each leaf was sunk within a frame, the hollowed
space being coated with wax in such a way that, of the
six sides or pages, nos. 2, 3, 5 were waxen, while 1, 4, 6
were of plain wood. The first and sixth sides were not
used; they formed the outside. On the sides 2 and 3
was inscribed the deed, and on 4 the names of the
witnesses were written in ink and their seals sunk into
a groove cut down the centre, the deed being closed
by a string of three twisted threads, which passed
through two holes, one at the head and the other at the
foot of the groove, round the two leaves and under the
wax of the seals, which thus secured it. An abstract
or copy of the deed was inscribed on page 5. The
Dacian tablets differed in this respect, that page 4 was
also waxen, and that the copy of the deed was commenced on that page in the space on the left of the
groove, the space on the right being filled with the

---

[8] *Atti della R. Accademia dei Lincei*, ser. ii. vol. iii. pt. 3,
1875-76, pp. 150—230; Hermes, vol. xii. 1877, pp. 88–141; and
Overbeck, *Pompeji*, 4th ed. by Mau, 1884, pp. 489 sqq. The
whole collection is to be edited by Prof. Zangemeister in the
Corpus Inscr. Lat. See *Pal. Soc.* i. pl. 159.

witnesses' names. The following diagram shows the arrangement of a Dacian triptych :—

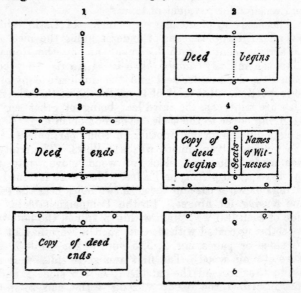

It will be noticed that, although the string which closed the deed (as indicated by dotted lines) passed through the holes of only two of the leaves, yet the third leaf (pages 5 and 6) is also perforated with corresponding holes. This proves that the holes were first pierced in the solid block, before it was cloven into three, in order that they might afterwards adjust themselves accurately.[9] In one instance the fastening threads and seals still remain.[1]

[9] See *Corp. Inscr. Lat.* iii. 922.
[1] *Ibid.* 938.

CHAPTER III.

WE now have to examine the history of the more common writing-materials of the ancient world and of the middle ages, viz. papyrus, vellum, and paper.

Papyrus.

The papyrus plant, *Cyperus Papyrus*, which supplied the substance for the great writing material of the ancient world, was widely cultivated in the Delta of Egypt. From this part of the country it has now vanished, but it still grows in Nubia and Abyssinia. Theophrastus, *Hist. Plant.* iv. 10, states that it also grew in Syria, and Pliny adds that it was native to the Niger and Euphrates. Its Greek name πάπυρος, whence Latin *papyrus*, was derived from one of its ancient Egyptian names, *P-apa*. Herodotus, our most ancient authority for any details of the purposes for which the plant was employed, always calls it βύβλος, a word no doubt also taken from an Egyptian term. Theophrastus describes the plant as one which grows in the shallows to the height of six feet, with a triangular and tapering stem crowned with a tufted head; the root striking out at right angles to the stem and being of the thickness of a man's wrist. The tufted heads were used for garlands in the temples of the gods; of the wood of the root were made various utensils; and of the stem, the pith of which was also used as an article of food, a variety of articles, including writing material, were manufactured: caulking yarn, ships' rigging, light skiffs, shoes, etc. The cable with which Ulysses bound

the doors of the hall when he slew the suitors was
ὅπλον βύβλινον (*Odyss.* xxi. 390).

As a writing material papyrus was employed in Egypt
from the earliest times. Papyrus rolls are represented
on the sculptured walls of Egyptian temples; and rolls
themselves exist of immense antiquity. The most
ancient papyrus roll now extant is the Papyrus Prisse,
at Paris, which contains the copy of a work composed in
the reign of a king of the fifth dynasty and is itself of
about the year 2500 B.C. or earlier. The dry atmosphere
of Egypt has been specially favourable to the preservation of these fragile documents. Buried with the dead,
they have lain in the tombs or swathed in the folds of
the mummy-cloths for centuries, untouched by decay,
and in many instances remain as fresh as on the day
when they were written.

Among the Greeks the papyrus material manufactured for writing purposes was called χάρτης (Latin
charta) as well as by the names of the plant itself.
Herodotus, v. 58, refers to the early use of papyrus rolls
among the Ionian Greeks, to which they attached the
name of διφθέραι, "skins," the writing material to which
they had before been accustomed. Their neighbours,
the Assyrians, were also acquainted with it.[1] They
called it "the reed of Egypt." An inscription relating
to the expenses of the rebuilding of the Erechtheum at
Athens in the year 407 B.C. shows that papyrus was
used for the fair copy of the rough accounts, which
were first inscribed on tablets. Two sheets, χάρται δύο,
cost at the rate of a drachma and two obols each, or a
little over a shilling of our money.[2]

The period of its first importation into Italy is not
known. The story of its introduction by Ptolemy, at

---

[1] In the Assyrian wall-sculptures in the British Museum there
are two scenes (Nos. 3 and 84) in which two couples of scribes
are represented taking notes. In each case, one of the scribes
is using a folding tablet (the hinges of one being distinctly
represented), and the other a scroll. The scroll may be either
papyrus or leather.

[2] See above, p. 19.

the suggestion of Aristarchus, is of suspicious authenticity.[3] We know, however, that papyrus was plentiful in Rome under the Empire. In fact, it was the common writing material among the Romans at that period, and became so indispensable that, on a temporary failure of the supply in the reign of Tiberius, there was danger of a popular tumult.[4] Pliny also, *Nat. Hist.* xiii. 11, refers to its high social value in the words: "papyri natura dicetur, cum chartæ usu maxime humanitas vitæ constet, certe memoria," and again he describes it as a thing "qua constat immortalitas hominum."

It is probable that papyrus was imported into Italy already manufactured; and it is doubtful whether any native plant grew in that country. Strabo says that it was found in Lake Trasimene and other lakes of Etruria; but the accuracy of this statement has been disputed. Still, it is a fact that there was a manufacture of this writing material carried on in Rome, the *charta Fanniana* being an instance; but it has been asserted that this industry was confined to the re-making of imported material. The more brittle condition of the Latin papyri, as compared with the Greek papyri, found at Herculaneum, has been ascribed to the detrimental effect of this re-manufacture.

At a later period the Syrian variety of the plant was grown in Sicily, where it was probably introduced during the Arab occupation. It was seen there by the Arab traveller, Ibn-Haukal, in the tenth century, in the neighbourhood of Palermo, where it throve in great luxuriance in the shallows of the Papireto, a stream to which it gave its name. Paper was made from this source for the use of the Sultan; but in the thirteenth century the plant began to fail, and it was finally extinguished by the drying up of the stream in 1591. It is still, however, to be seen growing in the neighbourhood of Syracuse, but was probably transplanted thither at a later time, for no mention of it

---

[3] See below, p. 36.
[4] Pliny, *Nat. Hist.* xiii. 13, " Sterilitatem sentit hoc quoque, factumque jam Tiberio principe inopia chartæ, ut e senatu darentur arbitri dispensandæ : alias in tumultu vita erat."

iu that place occurs earlier than 1674. Some attempts
have been made in recent years to manufacture a writing
material on the pattern of the ancient *charta* from this
Sicilian plant.

The manufacture of the writing material, as practised
in Egypt, is described by Pliny, *Nat. Hist.* xiii. 12. His
description applies specially to the system of his own day ;
but no doubt it was essentially the same that had been
followed for centuries. His text is far from clear, and
there are consequently many divergences of opinion on
different points. The stem of the plant was cut longitu-
dinally into thin strips (*philyræ*) [5] with a sharp cutting
instrument described as a needle (*acus*). The old idea
that the strips were peeled off the inner core of the stem
is now abandoned, as it has been shown that the plant,
like other reeds, contains a cellular pith within the rind,
which was all used in the manufacture. The central strips
were naturally the best, being the widest. The strips
thus cut were laid vertically upon a board, side by side,
to the required width, thus forming a layer, *scheda*,
across which another layer of shorter strips was laid at
right angles. Pliny applies to this process the phrase-
ology of net or basket making. The two layers formed a
" net," *plagula*, or " wicker," *crates*, which was thus
" woven," *texitur*. In this process Nile water was used
for moistening the whole. The special mention of this
particular water has caused some to believe that there
were some adhesive properties in it which acted as a paste
or glue on the material ; others, more reasonably, have
thought that water, whether from the Nile or any other
source, solved the glutinous matter in the strips and thus
caused them to adhere. It seems, however, more probable
that paste was actually used. [6] The sheets were finally

[5] Birt, *Antikes Buchwesen*, 229, prefers to apply the word *schedæ*
or *schidæ* to the strips. But Pliny distinctly uses the word *philyræ*,
although he elsewhere describes the inner bark of the lime tree by
this name. Another name for the strips was *inæ*.

[6] Birt, 231, points out, in regard to Pliny's words, " turbidus
liquor vim glutinis præbet," that " glutinis " is not a genitive
but a dative, Pliny never using the word " gluten," but
" glutinum."

pressed and dried in the sun. Rough or uneven places were rubbed down with ivory or a smooth shell.[7] Moisture lurking between the layers was to be detected by strokes of the mallet. Spots, stains, and spongy strips (*tæniæ*) in which the ink would run, were defects which also had to be encountered.[8]

The sheets were joined together with paste to form a roll, *scapus*, but not more than twenty was the prescribed number. There are, however, rolls of more than twenty sheets, so that, if Pliny's reading *vicinæ* is correct, the number was not constant in all times. The outside of the roll was naturally that part which was more exposed to risk of damage and to general wear and tear. The best sheets were therefore reserved for this position, those which lay nearer the centre or end of the roll not being necessarily so good. Moreover, the end of a roll was not wanted in case of a short text, and might be cut away. A protecting strip of papyrus was often pasted down the edge at the beginning or end of a roll, in order to give additional strength to the material and prevent it tearing.[9] The first sheet of a papyrus roll was called the πρωτόκολλον, a term which still survives in diplomacy ; the last sheet was called the ἐσχατοκόλλιον. Among the Romans the protocol was marked with the name of the Comes largitionum, who had the control of the manufacture, and with the date and name of the place where it was made. The portion thus marked was in ordinary practice cut away; but this curtailment was forbidden in legal documents by the laws of Justinian.[10] After their conquest of Egypt in the seventh century, the Arabs continued the manufacture and marked the

---

[7] Martial, xiv. 209 :
   "Levis ab æquorea cortex Mareotica concha
    Fiat; inoffensa currit harundo via."
   [8] Pliny, *Epist.* viii. 15 : "quæ (chartæ) si scabræ bibulæve sint," etc.
   [9] Wilcken, in *Hermes*, xxiii. 466.
   [10] "Tabelliones non scribant instrumenta in aliis chartis quam in his quæ protocolla habent, ut tamen protocollum tale sit, quod habeat nomen gloriosissimi comitis largitionum et tempus quo charta facta est."—*Novell.* xliv. 2.

protocol in Arabic. An instance of an Arab protocol thus marked is found in a bull of Pope John VIII. of 876, now in the Bibliothèque Nationale, Paris.

With regard to the width of papyrus rolls, those which date from the earliest period of Egyptian history are narrow, of about six inches; later they increase to nine, eleven, and even above fourteen inches. The width of the early Greek papyri of Homer and Hyperides in the British Museum runs from nine to ten inches. From Pliny we learn that there were various qualities of writing material made from papyrus and that they differed from one another in width. It has however been found that extant specimens do not tally with the figures that he gives; but an ingenious explanation has been lately proposed,[1] that he refers to the breadth of the individual sheets which together make up the *length* of the roll, not to the height of the sheets which forms its *width*. The best kind, formed from the broadest strips of the plant, was originally the *charta hieratica,* a name which was afterwards altered to *Augusta* out of flattery to the emperor Augustus. The *charta Livia,* or second quality, was named after his wife. The *hieratica* thus descended to the third rank. The *Augusta* and *Livia* were 13 digits, or about 9½ inches, wide; the *hieratica* 11 digits or 8 inches. The *charta amphitheatrica,* of 9 digits or 6½ inches, took its title from the principal place of its manufacture, the amphitheatre of Alexandria. The *charta Fanniana* was apparently a variety which was re-made at Rome, in the workshops of a certain Fannius, from the *amphitheatrica,* the width being increased by about an inch through pressure. The *Saitica* was a common variety, named after the city of Sais, being of about 8 digits or 5¾ inches. Finally, there were the *Tæniotica*—which was said to have taken its name from the place where it was made, a tongue of land (ταινία) near Alexandria—and the common packing-paper, *charta emporetica,* neither of which was more than 5 inches wide. Mention is made by Isidore, *Etymol.* vi. 10, of a

---

[1] Birt, 251 sqq.

quality of papyrus called *Corneliana,* which was first
made under C. Cornelius Gallus when prefect of Egypt.
But the name may have disappeared from the vocabulary
when Gallus fell into disgrace.² Another kind was
manufactured in the reign of Claudius, and on that account was named *Claudia.* It was a made-up material,
combining the *Augusta* and *Livia,* to provide a stout substance. Finally, there was a large-sized quality, of a
cubit or nearly 18 inches in width, called *macrocollon.*
Cicero made use of it (*Epp. ad Attic.* xiii. 25; xvi. 3).

Varro, repeated by Pliny, xiii. 11, makes the extraordinary statement that papyrus writing material was
first made in Alexander's time. He may have been
misled from having found no reference to its use in præ-
Alexandrine authors; or he may have meant to say that
its first free manufacture was only of that date, as it was
previously a government monopoly.

Papyrus continued to be the ordinary writing material
in Egypt to a comparatively late period.³ Greek documents of the early centuries of our era have been found
in considerable numbers in the Fayoum and other districts. In Europe also, long after vellum had become
the principal writing material, especially for literary
purposes, papyrus continued in common use, particularly
for ordinary documents, such as letters. St. Jerome,
Ep. vii., mentions vellum as a material for letters, "if
papyrus fails"; and St. Augustine, *Ep.* xv., apologizes
for using vellum instead of papyrus. A fragmentary
epistle of Constantine V. to Pepin le Bref, of 756, is
preserved at Paris. A few fragments of Greek literary
papyri of the early middle ages, containing Biblical
matter and portions of Græco-Latin glossaries, have also
survived.

For purely Latin literature papyrus was also occa-

---

² *Ibid.* 250.
³ The middle of the tenth century is the period when it has
been calculated the manufacture of papyrus in Egypt ceased.—
Karabacek, *Das arabische Papier,* in *Mittheilungen aus der
Sammlung der Papyrus Erzherzog Rainer,* bd. ii.-iii. (1887),
p. 98.

sionally used in the early middle ages. Examples, made up in book form, sometimes with a few vellum leaves incorporated to give stability, are found in different libraries of Europe. They are: The Homilies of St. Avitus, of the 6th century, at Paris; Sermons and Epistles of St. Augustine, of the 6th or 7th century, at Paris and Genoa; works of Hilary, of the 6th century, at Vienna; fragments of the Digests, of the 6th century, at Pommersfeld; the Antiquities of Josephus, of the 7th century, at Milan; an Isidore, of the 7th century, at St. Gall. At Munich, also, is the register of the Church of Ravenna, written on this material in the 10th century. Many papyrus documents in Latin, dating from the 5th to the 10th century, have survived from the archives of Ravenna; and there are extant fragments of two imperial rescripts written in Egypt, apparently in the 5th century, in a form of the Latin cursive alphabet which is otherwise unknown. In the papal chancery papyrus appears to have been used down to a late date in preference to vellum. A few papal bulls on this material have survived; the earliest being one of Stephen III. of the year 757; the latest, one of Sergius IV. of 1011.[4] In France papyrus was in common use in the sixth century.[5] Under the Merovingian kings it was used for official documents; several papyrus deeds of their period, dated from 625 to 692, being still preserved in the French archives.

Skins.

The skins of animals are of such a durable nature that it is no matter for surprise to find that they have been appropriated as writing material by the ancient nations of the world. They were in use among the Egyptians as early as the time of Cheops, in the 4th dynasty, documents written on skins at that period being referred to or copied in papyri of later date.[6] Actual specimens of skin rolls from Egypt still exist. In the British Museum is a

[4] *Rapport de M. Delisle*, in *Bulletin du Comité des Travaux hist. et scient.*, 1885, No. 2.
[5] Gregory of Tours, *Hist. Franc.* v. 5.
[6] Wilkinson, *Anc. Egypt.*, ed. Birch, ii. 182.

ritual on white leather (Salt, 256) which may be dated
about the year 2000 B.C. The Jews followed the same
custom, and to the present day continue it in their syna-
gogue rolls. It may be presumed that their neighbours
the Phœnicians also availed themselves of the same kind
of writing material. The Persians inscribed their history
upon skins.[7] The use of skins, διφθέραι, among the
Ionian Greeks is referred to by Herodotus, v. 58, who
adds that in his day many foreign nations also wrote on
them.

Parchment and Vellum.

After what has been here stated regarding the early
use of skins, the introduction of parchment, or vellum as
it is now more generally termed, that is to say, skins
prepared in such a way that they could be written upon
on both sides, cannot properly be called an invention; it
was rather an extension of, or improvement upon, an old
practice. The common story, as told by Pliny, *Nat. Hist.*
xiii. 11, on the authority of Varro, runs that Eumenes II.
of Pergamum (B.C. 197—158), wishing to extend the
library in his capital, was opposed by the jealousy of the
Ptolemies, who forbade the export of papyrus, hoping
thus to check the growth of a rival library. The
Pergamene king, thus thwarted, was forced to fall back
again upon skins; and thus came about the manufacture
of vellum: "Mox æmulatione circa bibliothecas regum
Ptolemæi et Eumenis, supprimente chartas Ptolemæo,
idem Varro membranas Pergami tradit repertas."[8]
Whatever may be the historical value of this tradition, at least it points to the fact that Pergamum
was the chief centre of the vellum trade. The name
διφθέραι, *membranæ*, which had been applied to the

[7] Diodorus, ii. 32: "ἐκ τῶν βασιλικῶν διφθέρων, ἐν αἶς οἱ Πέρσαι τὰς
παλαιὰς πράξεις εἶχον συντεταγμένας."
[8] St. Jerome, *Ep.* vii., also refers to the place of its origin:
"Chartam defuisse non puto, Ægypto ministrante commercia.
Et si alicubi Ptolemæus maria clausisset, tamen rex Attalus
membranas a Pergamo miserat, ut penuria chartæ pellibus
pensaretur. Unde et Pergamenarum nomen ad hunc usque
diem, tradente sibi invicem posteritate, servatum est."

earlier skins, was extended also to the new manufacture. The title *membrana Pergamena* is comparatively late, first occurring in the edict of Diocletian, A.D. 301, *de pretiis rerum*, vii. 38; next in the passage in St. Jerome's epistle, quoted in the footnote. The Latin name was also Græcized as μεμβράναι, being so used in 2 Tim. iv. 13: "μάλιστα τὰς μεμβράνας." The word σωμάτιον, which afterwards designated a vellum MS. as opposed to a papyrus roll, had reference originally to the contents, such a MS. being capable of containing an entire work or *corpus.*[9]

As to the early use of vellum among the Greeks and Romans, no evidence is to be obtained from the results of excavations. No specimens have been recovered at Herculaneum or Pompeii, and none of sufficiently early date in Egypt. There can, however, be little doubt that it was imported into Rome under the Republic. The general account of its introduction thither—evidently suggested by Varro's earlier story of the first use of it—is that Ptolemy, at the suggestion of Aristarchus the grammarian, having sent papyrus to Rome, Crates the grammarian, out of rivalry, induced Attalus of Pergamum to send vellum.[1] References to the *pages* of certain municipal deeds seem to imply that the latter were inscribed in books, that is, in vellum MSS., not on papyrus rolls.[2] When Cicero, *Epp. ad Attic.* xiii. 24, uses the word διφθέραι, he also seems to refer to vellum. The advantages of the vellum book over the papyrus roll are obvious: it was in the more convenient form of the *codex;* it could be re-written; and the leaves could receive writing on both sides. Martial enumerates, among his *Apophoreta*, vellum MSS. of Homer (xiv. 184), Virgil (186), Cicero (188), Livy (190), and Ovid (192).[3]

---

[9] Birt, *Ant. Buchw.*, 41.

[1] Boissonade, *Anecd.* i. 420.

[2] Mommsen, *Inscr. Neapol.* 6828; *Annali del Inst.* (1858) xxx. 192; Marquardt, *Privatleben der Römer*, 796.

[3] Pliny, *Nat. Hist.* vii. 21, mentions a curiosity: "In nuce inclusam Iliadem Homeri carmen in membrana scriptum tradit Cicero."

Vellum tablets began to take the place of the *tabulæ cerætæ,* as appears in Martial, xiv. 7 : "Esse puta ceras, licet hæc membrana vocetur : Delebis, quotiens scripta novare voles." Quintilian, x. 3, 31, recommends the use of vellum for drafts of their compositions by persons of weak sight: the ink on vellum was more easily read than the scratches of the stilus on wax.[4] Horace refers to it in *Sat.* ii. 3 : " Sic raro scribis ut toto non quater anno Membranam poscas "; and in other places.

From the dearth of classical specimens and from the scanty number of early mediæval MSS. of secular authors which have come down to us, it seems that vellum was not a common writing material under the first Roman emperors. There are no records to show its relative value in comparison with papyrus.[5] But the latter had been so long the recognized material for literary use that the slow progress of vellum as its rival may be partly ascribed to natural conservatism. It was particularly the influence of the Christian Church that eventually carried vellum into the front rank of writing materials and in the end displaced papyrus. As papyrus had been the principal material for receiving the thoughts of the pagan world, vellum was to be the great medium for conveying to mankind the literature of the new religion.

The durability of vellum recommended it to an extent that fragile papyrus could in no way pretend to. When Constantine required copies of the Scriptures for his new churches, he ordered fifty MSS. on vellum, " πεντήκοντα σωμάτια ἐν διφθέραις," to be prepared.[6] And St. Jerome, *Ep.* cxli., refers to the replacement of damaged volumes in the library of Pamphilus at Cæsarea by MSS. on vellum : " Quam [bibliothecam] ex parte corruptam

---

[4] So also Martial, xiv. 5 : "Languida ne tristes obscurent lumina ceræ, Nigra tibi niveum littera pingat ebur."

[5] Birt, *Ant. Buchwesen,* has attempted to prove that vellum was a comparatively worthless commodity, used as a cheap material for rough drafts and common work. His conclusions, however, cannot be accepted. For example, few probably will agree with him that a copy of Homer's *Batrachomyomachia* on papyrus was a gift of equal value with the Iliad on vellum.

[6] Eusebius, *Vit. Constant.,* iv. 36.

Acacius dehinc et Euzoius, ejusdem ecclesiæ sacerdotes, in membranis instaurare conati sunt."

As to the character and appearance of vellum at different periods, it will be enough to state generally that in the most ancient MSS. a thin, delicate material may usually be looked for, firm and crisp, with a smooth and glossy surface. This is generally the character of vellum of the fifth and sixth centuries. Later than this period, as a rule, it does not appear to have been so carefully prepared; probably, as the demand increased, a greater amount of inferior material came into the market.[7] But the manufacture would naturally vary in different countries. In Ireland and England the early MSS. are generally on stouter vellum than their contemporaries abroad. In Italy a highly polished surface seems at most periods to have been in favour; hence in this country and neighbouring districts, as the South of France, and again in Greece, the hard material resisted absorption, and it is often found that both ink and paint have flaked off in MSS. of the middle ages. In contrast to this are the instances of soft vellum, used in England and France and in northern Europe generally, from the thirteenth to the fifteenth century, for MSS. of the better class. In the fifteenth century the Italian vellum of the Renaissance is often of extreme whiteness and purity. Uterine vellum, taken from the unborn young, or the skins of new-born animals were used for special purposes. A good example of this very delicate material is found in Add. MS. 23,935, in the British Museum, a volume containing in as many as 579 leaves a corpus of liturgical church service books, written in France in the 13th and 14th centuries.

Vellum was also of great service in the ornamentation of books. Its smooth surfaces showed off colours in all their brilliancy. Martial's vellum MS. of Virgil (xiv. 186) is adorned with the portrait of the author: "Ipsius

---

[7] Instances, in MSS. of the seventh and tenth centuries, of vellum which was too thin or badly prepared, and therefore left blank by the scribes, are noticed in *Cat. of Anc. MSS. in the Brit. Museum*, Pt. ii. 51; and in Delisle, *Mélanges*, p. 101.

voltus prima tabella gerit." Isidore, *Orig.* vi. 11, 4,
describing this material, uses the words : " Membrana
autem aut candida aut lutea aut purpurea sunt. Candida naturaliter existunt. Luteum membranum bicolor
est, quod a confectore una tingitur parte, id est, crocatur.
De quo Persius (iii. 10), ' Jam liber et positis bicolor
membrana capillis.' " This quotation from Persius refers
to the vellum wrapper which the Romans were in the
habit of attaching to the papyrus roll : the φαινόλης,
pænula, literally a travelling cloak. The vellum was well
suited, from its superior strength, to resist constant
handling. It was coloured of some brilliant hue, generally
scarlet or purple, as in Lucian [8] : " πορφυρᾶ δι᾽ ἔκτοσθεν
ἡ διφθέρα." Ovid finds a bright colour unsuited to his
melancholy book, *Trist.* I. i. 5 : " Nec te purpureo velent
vaccinia fuco." Martial's *libellus,* viii. 72, is "nondum
murice cultus " ; and again he has the passages, iii. 2 :
" et te purpura delicata velet " ; and x. 93 : " carmina,
purpurea sed modo suta toga," the *toga* being another
expression for the wrapper. In Tibullus III. i. 9, the
colour is orange : "Lutea sed niveum involvat membrana libellum." The strip of vellum, σίλλυβος (or
σίττυβος), *titulus, index,* which was attached to the
papyrus roll and was inscribed with the title of the work
therein contained, was also coloured, as appears from
the passages in Martial, iii. 2 : " Et cocco rubeat super-
bus index," and in Ovid, *Trist.* I. i. 7 : " nec titulus minio
nec cedro charta notetur."

We do not know how soon was introduced the extra-
vagant practice of producing sumptuous volumes written
in gold or silver upon purple-stained vellum.[9] It was a

---

[8] Περὶ τῶν ἐπὶ μισθῷ συνόντων, 41.

[9] In the first edition of this book, an early reference to MSS.
of this description was quoted from D'Achery, *Spicileg.* xii. 549,
as existing in a letter of Theonas, bishop of Alexandria, who,
writing to the imperial chamberlain Lucian, directs him how he
may favourably dispose the emperor (Diocletian) towards the
Christians, and advises him, in regard to the imperial library, to
have the books ornamented "non tantum ad superstitios
sumptus quantum ad utile ornamentum : itaque scribi in

MS. of this description which Julius Capitolinus, early in the fourth century, puts into the possession of the younger Maximin: "Cum grammatico daretur, quædam parens sua libros Homericos omnes purpureos dedit, aureis litteris scriptos." Against luxury of this nature St. Jerome directed his often-quoted words in his preface to the Book of Job: "Habeant qui volunt veteres libros vel in membranis purpureis auro argentoque descriptos vel uncialibus, ut vulgo aiunt, litteris, onera magis exarata quam codices"; and again in his *Ep.* xviii., to Eustochium: "Inficiuntur membranæ colore purpureo, aurum liquescit in litteras, gemmis codices vestiuntur, et nudus ante fores earum [i.e. wealthy ladies] Christus emoritur."

The art of staining or dyeing vellum with purple or similar colour was practised chiefly in Constantinople, and also in Rome; but MSS. of this material, either entirely or in part, seem to have been produced in most of the civilized countries of Europe at least from the sixth century, if we may judge from surviving examples which, though not numerous, still exist in fair numbers. Of these the best known are:—Portion of the Book of Genesis, in Greek, in the Imperial Library at Vienna, written in silver letters and illustrated with a series of coloured drawings of the greatest interest for the history of the art of the period; of the 6th century.[1] A MS. of the Gospels, in Greek, in silver, leaves of which are in the British Museum, at Vienna, Rome, and in larger numbers at Patmos, whence the others were obtained; also of the 6th century.[2] The Codex Rossanensis, lately discovered at Rossano in South Italy, which contains the

---

purpureis membranis et litteris aureis totos codices, nisi specialiter Princeps demandaverit, non effectet." It has, however, been pointed out (*Deutsche Litteraturzeitung*, 1893, col. 782) that this letter of Theonas has been proved to be a forgery.

[1] See a facsimile of one of the pages in *Pal. Soc.* i., pl. 178; and of one of the paintings in Labarte, *Hist. des Arts industr. du Moyen Age* (1864), album ii., pl. 77.

[2] Edited by Tischendorf, *Mon. Sacr. Ined.*; see also Westwood, *Palæogr. Sacra Pict.*, "Purple Greek MSS."

Gospels in Greek, of the 6th century, written also in silver and having a series of drawings illustrative of the Life of Christ.[3] The Greek Psalter of Zürich, of the 7th century, in silver letters.[4] The famous Codex Argenteus of Upsala, containing the Gothic Gospels of Ulfilas' translation, of the 6th century.[5] The Latin Evangeliarium of Vienna, originally from Naples, of the same period, in silver uncials; a single leaf of the MS. being in Trinity College, Dublin.[6] The Latin Psalter of St. Germain (who died A.D. 576) at Paris, also in silver uncials.[7] The Metz Evangeliarium at Paris, of the same style and period. Of later date are the MSS. which were produced in the Carlovingian period, when a fresh impetus was given to this kind of ornamental luxury. Such are:—The Latin Gospels at Paris, said to have been written for Charlemagne by Godescalc in letters of gold.[8] A similar MS. at Vienna.[9] The Latin Gospels of the Hamilton collection of MSS. lately at Berlin, which appears to have once belonged to our king Henry VIII., is probably also of this period.[1] And lastly may be mentioned the Latin Psalter in the Douce collection in the Bodleian Library, written in golden Caroline minuscules and ornamented with miniatures.[2] Other specimens of purple

---

[3] Edited, with outline tracings of the drawings, by von Gebhardt and Harnack, *Evangeliorum Codex Græcus purpureus Rossanensis*, 1880.

[4] Edited by Tischendorf, *Mon. Sacr. Ined. Nova Coll.* iv.

[5] See an autotype in *Pal. Soc.* i., pl. 118.

[6] Ed. Tischendorf, 1847. A facsimile of the Dublin leaf is in *Par Palimpsest. Dublin*, ed. Abbott, 1880.

[7] Silvestre, *Univ. Palæogr.* (English ed.), pl. 110.

[8] Westwood, *Pal. Sacr. Pict.*, "Evangelistarium of Charlemagne."

[9] *Denkschrifte der kais. Akad. der Wissensch.*, xiii. 85.

[1] See "Die Handschr. der Hamiltonschen Sammlung," by Prof. Wattenbach, in *Neues Archiv.* viii. 329. Prof. Wattenbach would identify this MS. with the famous purple codex " de auro purissimo in membranis depurpuratis coloratis" which Wilfrid, archbishop of York, caused to be made and presented to the monastery of Ripon in the latter half of the 7th century.

[2] Douce MS. 59.

MSS. are cited in different palæographical works and catalogues.[3]

The practice of inserting single leaves of purple-stained vellum for the ornamentation of MSS. was not uncommon in the eighth and ninth centuries. A beautiful example is seen in the fragmentary Latin Gospels from Canterbury (Brit. Mus., Royal MS. 1. E. vi.), a large folio volume, in which there still remain some leaves dyed of a rich deep rose colour and decorated with ornamental initials and paintings, the remnant of a larger number; of the latter part of the 8th century.[4] But more generally, for such partial decoration, the surface of the vellum was coloured, sometimes on only one side of the leaf, or even on only a part of it, particularly in MSS. of French or German origin of the tenth and eleventh centuries.[5] At the period of the Renaissance there was some attempt at reviving this style of book ornamentation, and single leaves of stained vellum are occasionally found in MSS. of the fifteenth century. Other colours, besides purple, were also employed; and instances occur in MSS. of this late time of leaves painted black to receive gold or silver writing. Such examples are, however, to be considered merely as curiosities.

A still more sumptuous mode of decoration than even that by purple-staining seems to have been occasionally followed. This consisted in gilding the entire surface of the vellum. But the expense of such work must have been so great that we cannot suppose that more than a very few leaves would ever have been thus treated in any MS., however important. Fragments of two vellum leaves, thus gilt and adorned with painted designs, are preserved in the British Museum, Add. MS. 5111. They originally formed part of Greek tables of the Eusebian

[3] See references in Wattenbach, *Schriftw.* 110–113.

[4] *Cat. of Ancient MSS. in the Br. Mus*, Pt. ii. (1884) 20; Westwood, *Pal. Sacr. Pict.*, and *Facs. of Miniatures and Ornaments of A.-Saxon and Irish MSS.* pll. 14, 15.

[5] An instance of this superficial colouring occurs in a page of the Cotton MS. Vesp. A. viii., the foundation charter of Newminster, Winchester, A.D. 966. The Harley MS. 2821, written in Germany in the 11th century, contains many leaves of this kind.

Canons, no doubt prefixed to a copy of the Gospels, of the 6th century.[6]

Paper.

Paper, manufactured from fibrous substances, appears to have been known to the Chinese at a most remote period. Its introduction into Europe is due to the agency of the Arabs, who are said to have first learnt its use at Samarkand, which they captured A.D. 704. Its manufacture spread through their empire ; and it received one of its mediæval titles, *charta Damascena*, from the fact of Damascus being one of the centres of paper commerce. A comparatively large number of early Arabic MSS. on paper still exist, dating from the ninth century ; the earliest is of the year 866.[7]

This oriental paper, becoming known in Europe at a time when the Egyptian papyrus, although not in actual common use, still was not yet forgotten, was called by the same names, *charta* and *papyrus*. It was also known in the middle ages as *charta bombycina, gossypina, cuttunea, Damascena,* and *xylina,* and in Greek as ξυλοχάρτιον or ξυλότευκτον. It has in recent times also been generally known as cotton-paper, that is, paper made from the wool of the cotton plant. It is usually stout, of a yellowish tinge, and with a glossy surface. This last quality seems to have gained for it one of its titles, *charta serica.* Imported through Greece into Europe, it is referred to by Theophilus, a writer of the twelfth century (*Schedula diversarum artium,*[8] i. 24) as Greek parchment, *pergamena Græca ;* and he adds, " quæ fit ex lana ligni." But it does not appear to have been used to any great extent even in Greece before the middle of the thirteenth century, if one may judge from the very few extant Greek MSS. on paper of that time.

Paper-making in Europe was first established by the Moors in Spain and by the Arabs in Sicily ; and their

[6] *Cat. Anc. MSS.* Pt. i. (1881) 21.
[7] See facsimiles of several in the *Oriental Series* of the Palæographical Society.
[8] Ed. R. Hendrie, 1847, p. 28.

paper was at first still the same oriental paper above described. In Spain it was called *pergameno de panno,* cloth parchment, a title which distinguished it from the *pergameno de cuero,* or vellum; and it is so described in the laws of Alphonso, of 1263. On the expulsion of the Moors, an inferior quality was produced by the less skilled Christians. From Sicily the manufacture passed over into Italy.

Here we must pause a moment to revert to the question of the material of which oriental paper was made. As already stated, its early European names point to the general idea that it was made of cotton. But recent investigations have thrown doubts on the accuracy of this view; and a careful analysis of many early samples has proved that, although cotton was occasionally used, no paper that has been examined is entirely made of that substance, hemp or flax being the more usual material.[9] An ingenious solution of this difficulty has been recently offered, that the term χάρτης βομβύκινος, *charta bombycina,* is nothing more than an erroneous reading of χάρτης βαμβύκινος, *charta bambycina,* that is, paper made in the Syrian town of Bambyce, Βαμβύκη, the Arab Mambidsch.[1] The question of material is not, however, of any particular importance for our present purpose; and it is only the distinction which has been made between oriental paper and European paper, as being the one of cotton and the other of linen rag, that requires it to be noticed. A more satisfactory means of distinguishing the two kinds of paper is afforded by the employment of water-marks in European paper, a practice which was unknown to the oriental manufacturer.

Several examples survive of oriental paper, or paper

---

[9] C. M. Briquet, *Recherches sur les Premiers Papiers du Xe au XIVe Siècle,* in the *Mémoires de la Soc. Nat. des Antiquaires de France,* tome xlvi; and a review of the same by C. Paoli, *Carta di Cotone e Carta di Lino,* in the *Archivio Storico Italiano,* 1885, p. 230. Karabacek, *Das arabische Papier,* in *Mittheilungen aus der Sammlung der Papyrus Erzherzog Rainer,* bd. ii.-iii. 87.

[1] Karabacek, *Neue Quellen zur Papiergeschichte,* in *Mittheilungen (ut supr.)* bd. iv. 117.

made in the oriental fashion, used for European documents and MSS. The oldest recorded document was a deed of King Roger of Sicily of the year 1102, and others of other Sicilian kings of the 12th century are also mentioned. At Genoa there are extant letters of Greek emperors, of 1188-1202. The oldest known imperial deed is a charter of Frederic II. to the nuns of Goess, in Styria, of 1228.[2] The same emperor forbade, in 1231, the use of paper for public deeds. A Visigothic paper MS. of the 12th century, from Silos, near Burgos, is now in the Bibliothèque Nationale of Paris (Nouv. Acq. Lat. 1296);[3] a paper notarial register at Genoa dates from 1154; in the British Museum there is a paper MS. (Arundel 268), written in Italy, of the first half of the 13th century; and at Munich the autograph MS. of Albert de Beham, 1238-1255, is also on the same kind of paper. In several cities and towns of Italy there exist registers on paper dating back to the thirteenth century.[4] Letters addressed from Castile to Edward I. of England, in 1279 and following years, are on the same material; and a register of the hustings court of Lyme Regis, now in the British Museum, which begins with entries of the year 1309, is on paper which was probably imported from Spain or Bordeaux, such as that employed for the Bordeaux customs register of the beginning of the reign of Edward II., now in the Record Office.[5]

The earliest reference to the material of paper made in Europe appears to be that in the tract of Peter, abbot of Cluny (A.D. 1122-1150), "adversus Judæos," cap. 5, in which among the various kinds of books he mentions those made *ex rasuris veterum pannorum.*[6] There appears

[2] J. G. Schwandner, *Charta Linea,* 1788.

[3] Delisle, *Mélanges,* 109.

[4] Cited by Professor Paoli, *La Storia della Carta secondo gli ultimi studi,* in *Nuova Antologia,* vol. xviii. (1888), p. 297.

[5] See also Rogers, *Hist. Agricult. and Prices,* i, 644.

[6] "Quales quotidie in usu legendi habemus, utique ex pellura arietum, hircorum, vel vitulorum, sive ex biblis vel juncis orientalium paludum, aut ex rasuris veterum pannorum, seu ex qualibet alia forte viliore materia compactos."

to have certainly been an extensive manufacture in Italy in the first half of the thirteenth century. There is evidence of a paper trade at Genoa as early as 1235.[7] But the place from which we have the earliest known water-mark, on paper which was used in 1293, is Fabriano, in the marquisate of Ancona, where the industry was established certainly before the year 1276, and probably much earlier. The jurist Bartolo, in his treatise *De insigniis et armis*, mentions the excellent paper made there in the fourteenth century. Other centres of early manufacture were Colle, in Tuscany, Padua, where a factory was established at least as early as 1340, Treviso, Venice, Pignerol and Casella in Piedmont, Florence, Bologna, Parma, Milan, and other places. From the northern towns of Italy a trade was carried on with Germany, where also factories were rapidly founded in the fourteenth century. France borrowed the art of paper-making from Spain, whence it was introduced, it is said, as early as 1189, into the district of Hérault. The north of Europe, at first supplied from the south, gradually took up the manufacture. England drew her supplies, no doubt, at first from such trading ports as Bordeaux and Genoa ; but even in the fourteenth century it is not improbable that she had a rough home-manufacture of her own, although it is said that the first English mill was set up in Hertford not earlier than the sixteenth century.

Paper was in fairly general use throughout Europe in the second half of the fourteenth century ; at that time it began to rival vellum as a material for books ; in the course of the fifteenth century it gradually superseded it. MSS. of this later period are sometimes composed of both vellum and paper, a sheet of vellum forming the outer leaves of a quire, the rest being of paper : a revival of the old practice observed in certain papyrus books in which vellum leaves protected and gave strength to the leaves of papyrus.

A knowledge of the appearance of paper and of water-

[7] Briquet, *Papiers et Filigranes des Archives de Gênes*, 1888, p. 36.

marks of different periods is of great assistance in assigning dates to undated paper MSS. In the fourteenth
century European paper is usually stout, and was made
in frames composed of thick wires which have left
strongly defined impressions. In the next century the
texture becomes finer. The earliest known water-mark,
as already stated, is on paper used in the year 1293. At
first the marks are simple, and being impressed from
thick wires are well defined. In process of time they
become finer and more elaborate, and, particularly in
Italian paper, they are enclosed within circles. Their
variety is almost endless : animals, heads, birds, fishes,
flowers, fruits, domestic and warlike implements, letters,
armorial bearings, and other devices are used; some
being peculiar to a country or district, others apparently
becoming favourites and lasting for comparatively long
periods, but constantly changing in details. For example,
the glove, a common mark of the sixteenth century develops a number of small modifications in its progress;
and of the pot or tankard, which runs through the
latter part of the sixteenth century and the early part
of the seventeenth century, there is an extraordinary
number of different varieties. The names of makers were
inserted as water-marks quite at the beginning of the
fourteenth century; but this practice was very soon
abandoned, and was not revived until after the middle of
the sixteenth century. The insertion of the name of
place of manufacture and of the date of manufacture
is a modern usage.

CHAPTER IV.

The Stilus, Pen, etc.

OF writing implements the στῦλος, γραφεῖον, γραφις, γραφίδιον, *stilus, graphium,* made of iron, bronze, or other metal, ivory, or bone, was adapted for writing on waxen tablets, the letters being scratched with the sharp point. The other end was fashioned into a knob or flat head, wherewith the writing could be obliterated by smoothening the wax, for correction or erasure: hence the phrase *vertere stilum,*[1] "to correct." Among the Roman antiquities found in Britain, now deposited in the British Museum, there are several specimens of the *stilus,* in ivory, bronze, etc. Many of them are furnished with a sharp projection, at right angles to the shaft, near the head, for the purpose of ruling lines on the wax. The passage in Ovid, *Metam.* ix. 521, thus describes the action of the writer :—

> "Dextra tenet ferrum, vacuam tenet altera ceram.
> Incipit, et dubitat, scribit damnatque tabellas.
> Et notat et delet, mutat, culpatque probatque."

Here the stilus is simply *ferrum.* In another place, *Amor.* I. xi. 23, Ovid gives its title of *graphium* : "Quid digitos opus est graphio lassare tenendo ?"

This riddle on the stilus also occurs :—

> "De summo planus, sed non ego planus in imo.
> Versor utrimque manu; diversa et munera fungor:
> Altera pars revocat quidquid pars altera fecit."[2]

The case in which such implements were kept was the

---

[1] Horace, *Sat.* I. x. 72: "Sæpe stilum vertas."
[2] Riese, *Anthol. Lat.* I. no. 286.

γραφιοθήκη, *graphiarium;* as in Martial, xiv. 21, "armata suo graphiaria ferro."

For writing on papyrus the reed, κάλαμος, δόναξ γραφεύς, σχοῖνος, *calamus, canna,* was in use.[3] Suitable reeds came chiefly from Egypt, as referred to by Martial, xiv. 38 : "Dat chartis habiles calamos Memphitica tellus "; or from Cnidus, as in Ausonius, *Ep.* vii. : "Nec jam fissipedis per calami vias Grassetur Cnidiæ sulcus arundinis." Parallel with our use of steel pens is that of the ancient metal reeds, of which a few specimens, in bronze, have been found in Italy, and one in England.[4] The case in which reeds were kept was the καλαμοθήκη, καλαμίς, *calamarium, theca calamaria;* as in Martial, xiv. 19 : "Sortitus thecam, calamis armare memento." In Diocletian's edict, *De pretiis rerum venalium,* the reed-case appears as made of leather.

Reeds continued in use to some extent through the middle ages. In Italy they appear to have survived into the fifteenth century.[5]

The κονδίλιον, *peniculus, penicillus,* was the brush with which writing in gold was applied.[6]

The pen, *penna,* is first mentioned by an anonymous historian who tells us that, to enable the unlettered Ostrogoth Theodoric to write his name, he was provided with a stencil plate, through which he drew with a pen the strokes which formed the first four letters of his name : "ut, posita lamina super chartam, per eam penna duceret et subscriptio ejus tantum videretur."[7] Isidore, *Orig.* vi. 13, describes the pen thus : "Instrumenta scribæ calamus

---

[3] Pliny, *Nat. Hist.* xvi. 36 : "Chartisque serviunt calami." Some specimens of ancient reeds cut like a pen (Ausonius, "fissipes calamus") are in the Egyptian gallery, British Museum.

[4] See *Bulletino dell' Instituto,* 1849, p. 169 ; 1880, pp. 68, 69, 150. The one found in England is preserved among the Romano-British antiquities in the British Museum.

[5] For detailed information, see Wattenbach, *Schriftw.* 186.

[6] Theophilus, *De diversis artibus,* iii. 96, mentions the reed for this purpose : "Atque rogo pariter, calamo cum ceperit aurum, Illum commoveat, pulchre si scribere quærit."

[7] In the *Excerpta* printed at the end of Gronovius's edition of Ammianus Marcellinus, 1693, p. 512.

E

et penna. Ex his enim verba paginis infiguntur ; sed calamus arboris est, penna avis, cujus acumen dividitur in
duo, in toto corpore unitate servata." But, although no
earlier mention of the quill pen than these has been
found, it can scarcely be supposed that, as soon as
vellum came into general use, so obviously convenient an
implement, always ready to hand, could have been long
overlooked, particularly in places where reeds of a kind
suitable for writing could not be had. The hard surface
of the new material could bear the flexible pressure of
the pen which in heavy strokes might have proved too
much for the more fragile papyrus.

Inks, etc.

Black ink, the ordinary writing fluid of centuries,
μέλαν, or more exactly γραφικὸν μέλαν, μελάνιον, *atramentum*, or *atramentum librarium* to distinguish it from
blacking used for other purposes, later ἔγκαυστον, *incaustum*, differs in tint at various periods and in different
countries. In early MSS. it is either pure black or
slightly brown ; in the middle ages it varies a good deal
according to age and locality. In Italy and Southern
Europe it is generally blacker than in the north, in
France and Flanders it is generally darker than in
England ; a Spanish MS. of the 14th or 15th century
may usually be recognized by the peculiar blackness
of the ink. Deterioration is observable in the course
of time. The ink of the fifteenth century particularly
is often of a faded, grey colour.

The ancients used the liquid of the cuttle fish, as in the
lines of Persius, iii. 12 :—

> " Tunc queritur crassus calamo quod pendeat humor,
> Nigra quod infusa vanescat sepia lympha,
> Dilutas queritur geminet quod fistula guttas."

Pliny, *Nat. Hist.* xxxv. 6, mentions soot and gum as the
ingredients of writing ink. Other later authors add
gall-apples. Metallic infusions seem also to have been
used at an early period. In the midde ages vitriol was
an ordinary ingredient. Theophilus, in his work *De*

diversis artibus, written probably early in the twelfth century, gives a recipe (i. 40) for the manufacture of ink from thorn wood boiled down and mingled with wine and vitriol.

Inks of other colours are also found in MSS. of the middle ages: green, yellow, and others, but generally only for ornamental purposes, although volumes written entirely in coloured ink are still extant. Red, either in the form of a pigment or fluid ink, is of very ancient and common use. It is seen on the early Egyptian papyri; and it appears in the earliest extant vellum MSS., either in titles or the first lines of columns or chapters. The Greek term was μελάνιον κόκκινον; Latin *minium, rubrica.* A volume written entirely in red ink, of the 9th or 10th century, is in the British Museum, Harley MS. 2795. The purple ink, κιννάβαρις, *sacrum incaustum*, reserved at Byzantium for the exclusive use of the emperors, seems to have originally been of a distinct kind. Later the same term, κιννάβαρις, appears as a synonymous-term with *minium.*

The ink-pot, μελανδόχον, μελανδόχη, μελανδοχεῖον, *atramentarium*, used by the ancients, was generally, as appears from surviving examples, a small cylindrical jar or metal box, the cover often pierced with a hole to admit the insertion of the reed. In paintings on the walls of Pompeii double ink-pots, with hinged covers, are depicted, the two receptacles being probably for black and red ink.[8] Throughout the middle ages the ink-horn was in common use.

Gold was used as a writing fluid at a very early period. In a papyrus at Leyden, of the third or fourth century, there is a recipe for its manufacture.[9] Something has already been said on its use in connection with purple-stained vellum. Ordinary white vellum MSS. were also written in gold, particularly in the ninth and tenth centuries, in the reigns of the Carlovingian kings. In most of the large national

[8] *Museo Borbonico*, i. pl. 12.
[9] Leemans, *Papyri Graeci Mus. Lugd. Bat.*, tom. ii. (1885) p. 218.

E 2

libraries examples are to be found.[1] The practice passed
from the continent to England, and was followed to
some considerable extent in this country, not only for
partial decoration, but also for the entire text of MSS.
The record of a purple MS. written in gold, by order
of Wilfrid of York, late in the 7th century, has already
been noticed (p. 41, note 1); but the way in which this
volume is referred to: " Inauditum ante seculis nostris
quoddam miraculum " proves that such sumptuous MSS.
were not known in England before that time. St.
Boniface, writing in A.D. 735 to Eadburg, abbess of St.
Mildred's, Thanet, asks her to get transcribed for him in
gold the Epistles of St. Peter.[2] But the existing English
examples are of later date.[3] Gold writing as a practice
died out in the thirteenth century, although a few isolated
instances of later date are found. State letters of the
Byzantine emperors were also sometimes written in
gold, and the same was used for imperial charters in
Germany, as appears from extant examples of the
twelfth century, and for similar documents in other
countries.[4]

Writing in silver appears to have ceased contemporaneously with the disuse of stained vellum. This metal
would not show to advantage on a white ground.

[1] Such MSS. in the British Museum are Harl. MS. 2788, the
"Codex Aureus," a copy of the Gospels, in uncial letters, of the
9th century; Harl. MS. 2797, also a copy of the Gospels, in
minuscule writing, late in the 9th century, from the monastery of
St. Geneviève, Paris. The Cottonian MS., Tiberius A. ii., which
was sent as a present to king Æthelstan by the emperor Otho,
also contains some leaves written in gold.

[2] " Sic et adhuc deprecor .... ut mihi cum auro conscribas
epistolas domini mei Sancti Petri apostoli, ad honorem et
reverentiam sanctarum scripturarum ante oculos carnalium in
prædicando, et quia dicta ejus qui me in hoc iter direxit maxime
semper in præsentia cupiam habere."—Jaffé, *Monumenta Mogun-
tina*, iii. 99.

[3] The foundation charter of Newminster, Winchester, granted
by king Edgar in 966, in Cotton. MS. Vesp. A. viii., is written
in gold. The Benedictional of Æthelwold, bishop of Winchester,
A.D. 963–984, also contains a page in gold.

[4] Wattenbach, *Schriftw.* 214–217.

Various Implements.

For ruling papyri, a circular plate of lead, κυκλοτερὴς μόλιβος, τροχόεις μόλιβδος, κυκλομόλιβδος, was used. Ink was removed with the sponge. Papyrus would scarcely bear scraping with the knife. If the ink was still wet, or lately applied, its removal was of course easy. Martial, iv. 10, sends a sponge with his newly-written book of poems, wherewith the whole of his verses might be cleaned off.[5] Augustus effaced his half-completed tragedy of Ajax, with the remark : " Ajacem suum in spongiam incubuisse."[6] With vellum MSS. the knife or eraser, *rasorium* or *novacula*, came into use. While wet the ink could still be sponged away; but when it was hard and dry, and for erasure of single letters and words without obliterating also the surrounding text, it was scraped off.

The penknife was the σμίλη, γλύφανον, γλυπτήρ, or γλυφίς, *scalprum librarium*, the mediæval *scalpellum*, *cultellus*, or *artavus ;* the ruler was the κανών, *canon*, *norma*, *regula*, *linearium ;* the pricker or compass for spacing off the ruled lines was διαβάτης, *circinus*, or *punctorium ;* and lastly, the office of the modern pencil was performed by the pointed piece of lead, μόλυβδος, *plumbum*, or plummet.

" Dum novus est rasa nec adhuc mihi fronte libellus,
    Pagina dum tangi non bene sicca timet,
I, puer, et caro perfer leve munus amico,
    Qui meruit nugas primus habere meas.
Curre, sed instructus : comitetur Punica librum
    Spongia; muneribus convenit illa meis.
Non possunt nostros multæ, Faustine, lituræ
    Emendare jocos; una litura potest."
[6] Suetonius, *Aug.* 85.

CHAPTER V.

The Roll.

AMONG the Greeks the ordinary terms for a book (that is, a roll) were βίβλος and its diminutive βιβλίον.[1] Earlier forms of these words were βύβλος and, more rarely, βυβλίον, which were clearly derived from the material, the βύβλος or papyrus, of which books were made. The corresponding word *liber* of the Latin people, in like manner, was adopted as a term for a book, primitively made of the bark or inner rind of the lime or other tree. Such bark-books, however, disappeared in presence of the more convenient and more plentiful papyrus imported from Egypt; but' the old name was not unfitly transferred to a book made of the new substance, which in texture and general appearance was not unlike the old.[2]

A diminutive of the word *liber* was *libellus*, which, as a literary title, specially referred to a book of poems, a sense in which it is constantly used by the Roman poets. It came at length to be used as an equivalent of *liber*, and to express a book in general.

The old form of a book was the roll, the Latin *volumen*. The Greeks do not appear to have had any parallel expression at an early date; the word κύλινδρος being comparatively late. Another term was ἐνείλημα

---

[1] βιβλίον also meant a letter, and is used in this sense by Herodotus. Suidas in his Lexicon explains βιβλίον as ἐπιστολή.

[2] For instances of confusion of material, see Wattenbach, *Schriftw.* 89.

or ἐξείλημα; more rare were εἰλητάριον, εἴλητον. A mediæval Latin term is *rotulus.*

Again, a later Greek term was τόμος (originally a cutting of papyrus), applicable to a roll containing a portion of a collection or of a great work. Neither this term nor βιβλίον, nor *liber* nor *libellus,* could be applied in the singular number to more than a single roll or volume. A work consisting of many volumes, or several divisions, must be described by the plural forms βιβλία, τόμοι, *libri,* etc. On the other hand, the several books of a work, if written on one roll, counted only for one βιβλίον or *liber.* Thus Ulpian, *Digest.* xxxii. 52, lays down: "Si cui centum libri sint legati, centum volumina ei dabimus, non centum quæ quis ingenio suo metitus est. . . . ut puta, cum haberet Homerum totum in uno volumine, non quadraginta octo libros computamus, sed unum Homeri volumen pro libro accipiendum est."

For subdivisions such terms as λόγος, σύγγραμμα, σύνταγμα also were used.

The word τεῦχος, in the sense of a literary work in several volumes, was employed at a late period. Originally it seems to have been applied to the chest or vessel in which the several rolls of such work were kept, and came in course of time to refer to the contents.[3] Xenophon, *Anab.* vii. 6, 14, mentions books ἐν ξυλίνοις τεύχεσι. In like manner the terms *pandectes* and *bibliotheca,* originally referring to a work in several rolls kept together in their chest, were afterwards used specially to mean a MS. of the entire Bible.[4] *Bibliotheca* continued to bear this meaning down to the close of the fourteenth century, if not later.[5]

To distinguish a work contained in the compass of a single roll, there was the title μονόβιβλος or μονόβιβλον.

There can be no doubt that the convenience of subdividing the lengthy works of authors into rolls of

[3] Birt, *Ant. Buchw.* 89.
[4] *Bibliotheca* was used in this sense by St. Jerome. Others, as Cassiodorus, Bede, Alcuin, preferred *Pandectes.*
See examples in Wattenbach, *Schriftw.* 126–129.

moderate size must have been appreciated in the earliest period of the publication of Greek literature; and, although the authors themselves may not originally have divided their writings into separate portions to suit the ordinary length of a conveniently-sized roll, yet the practice of the scribe would eventually react on the author. Thus we find the works of Homer divided into books of a length which could be contained in an ordinary roll; and we know that in course of time authors did regularly adapt the divisions of their works to the customary length of the βιβλία and *volumina*.

The roll was rolled on a stick, ὀμφαλός or *umbilicus*, to which the last sheet of the papyrus, ἐσχατο-κόλλιον, was attached. Many of the rolls found at Herculaneum had a mere central core of papyrus. A knob or button, usually of bone or wood, was affixed to each end of the stick, the name of which, ὀμφαλός, *umbilicus*, appears to have been also extended to these ornamental additions. Porphyrion, commenting on Horace, *Epod.* xiv. 8, says: "in fine libri umbilici ex ligno aut osse solent poni." Or, instead of the simple knob or button, there was a tip, κέρας, *cornu*, of ivory or some such ornamental material; and either might be plain or coloured.[6] The edges, *frontes*, of the roll were cut down and smoothed with pumice,[7] and sometimes coloured. The wrapper of an ordinary roll might be of common papyrus, *charta emporetica*; in case of a more valuable work, a vellum cover, stained with colour,[8] was used as a protection—the φαινόλης or φαιλόνης, *pænula* (the travelling cloak), as it was commonly called.[9] Lucian, *Adv. indoctum*, 7, refers to an ornamental work thus:

[6] Tibullus, III. i. 13: "Atque inter geminas pingantur cornua frontes." Martial, iii. 2, 9, "picti umbilici"; v. 6, 15, "nigri umbilici."

[7] Ovid, *Trist.* I. i. 11, "Nec fragili geminæ poliantur pumice frontes"; Catullus, xxii. 8, "pumice omnia æquata."

[8] See above, p. 39.

[9] The "cloak" (φαιλόνης) which St. Paul left at Troas (2 Tim. iv. 13), and which Timothy was to bring together with the books and parchments, may have been in fact a book-cover. See Birt, 65.

" ὁπόταν τὸ μὲν βιβλίον ἐν τῇ χειρὶ ἔχῃς πάγκαλον,
πορφυρᾶν μὲν ἔχον τὴν διφθέραν, χρυσοῦν δὲ τὸν ὀμφαλόν ";
and Martial, i. 66, has the lines:—

> " Sed pumicata fronte si quis est nondum
> Nec umbilicis cultus atque membrana,
> Mercare: tales habeo."

For preservation against moths, etc., cedar oil was
rubbed on the papyrus.[1] A good poem was worthy of
this protection : " cedro digna locutus" (Persius, i. 42);
"cedro nunc licet ambules perunctus" (Martial, iii. 2, 7).
But it imparted a yellow tint: " quod neque sum cedro
flavus " (Ovid, *Trist.* III. i. 13).

The chest or box in which the rolls were kept was the
κίστη, κιβωτός, *capsa, cista, forulus, nidus, puteus,* or
scrinium. To tie bundles of rolls together was a
destructive process, as the papyrus was injured; so
Petronius, *Satyricon,* cii. : " Chartæ alligatæ mutant figu-
ram." Extensive works were arranged in their *capsæ*
in decades, triads, or other sets, as we know from the
examples of the works of Livy, Dio Cassius, Varro, and
others.

For convenience of reference when the roll was placed
in a box or on a shelf, a vellum label, σίλλυβος or σίττυβος,[2] πιττάκιον, also γλῶσσα, γλωσσάριον, *titulus, index,*
was attached to the edge of the roll and inscribed with
the title of the work,[3] and, for distinction, was also
coloured.[4] Such *tituli* are perhaps the "lora rubra" of
Catullus, xxii. 7. Cicero, writing to Atticus, iv. 4, gives
both Greek and Latin names : ."Etiam velim mihi mittas
de tuis librariolis duos aliquos, quibus Tyrannio utatur

---

[1] " Ex cedro oleum, quod cedreum dicitur, nascitur, quo reliquæ
res unctæ, uti etiam libri, a tineis et carie non læduntur."—
Vitruvius, ii. 9, 13.

[2] Marquardt, *Privatl. der Römer,* 794.

[3] See an engraving, copied from a sculpture, in Schwarz, *De
ornamentis librorum* (1756), tab. ii., wherein are represented series
of rolls placed on shelves, like bottles in a wine-bin, with the *tituli*
depending in front; also an engraving of a *capsa,* with rolls
enclosed, on the title-page of Marini, *Papiri Diplom.;* and
Museo Borbonico, tav. xii.

[4] See above, p. 39.

glutinatoribus, ad cetera administris, iisque imperes ut
sumant membranulam, ex qua indices fiant, quos vos
Græci, ut opinor, σιλλύβους appellatis." And the lines
of Tibullus, III. i. 9, may be quoted as describing the
outward appearance of the roll :—

> " Lutea sed niveum involvat membrana libellum,
> 　　Pumex cui canas tondeat ante comas ;
> 　Summaque prætexat tenuis fastigia chartæ,
> 　　Indicet ut nomen, littera facta, puer."

The text was written in columns, σελίδες, *paginæ*.
The term σελίς (originally the gangway between the
rowing benches of a ship) was first applied to the space
between two columns, and then to the column itself.
Other terms were the diminutive σελίδιον and κατα-
βάτον. The lines of the columns ran parallel with the
length of the roll ;[1] and lead was used for drawing the
ruled lines. Such ruling, however, was not always, and
perhaps not generally, employed, for the horizontal fibre
of the papyrus itself was a sufficient guide for the lines
of writing ; and the fact that the marginal line of the
columns frequently trends away out of the perpendicular
proves that in such instances there were no ruled lines
to bound the columns laterally. These were generally
narrow, at least in the texts which were written by
skilled scribes for the market ; and occasionally we find
the letters made smaller at the end of a line in order to
accommodate words to the available space. An example
of writing in wide columns is seen in the papyrus of
Aristotle on the Constitution of Athens—a MS. which
was written for private use and not for sale.

The title of the work was written at the end.

The reader unrolled the book with the right hand ;
with the left hand he rolled up what he had read.[2] To
unroll a book was ἐξειλεῖν, ἀνειλεῖν, ἀνελίσσειν, ἐλίσσειν,

---

[1] Before the time of Julius Cæsar, official despatches appear to
have been written "transversâ chartâ," that is, with the lines
parallel with the breadth of the roll. Suetonius, *Jul. Cæs.* 56.

[2] See an engraving, from a sculptured sarcophagus, in Darem-
berg and Saglio's *Dict. des Antiquités*, s. v. "Bibliotheca," in
which a man is represented reading from an open roll.

εἴλειν or εἰλεῖν, evolvere, revolvere, volvere, explicare.
The book read to the end was "explicitus usque ad sua
cornua" (Martial, xi. 107), or "ad umbilicum," as in
Horace, *Epod.* xiv. 8 :—

> "Deus nam me vetat
> Inceptos, olim promissum carmen, iambos
> Ad umbilicum adducere ; "

and in Martial, iv. 89 :—

> " Ohe, jam satis est, ohe libelle,
> Jam pervenimus usque ad umbilicos."

From the term " explicitus " came the mediæval " explicit," formed, no doubt, as a pendant to "incipit."
The term to roll up a book was *plicare.* The beginning
of the roll was held under the chin while the hands were
employed in turning the *umbilici.* Hence Martial, i.
66, refers to "virginis . . . . chartæ, quæ trita duro
non inhorruit mento " ; and again, x. 93, he has : " Sic
nova nec mento sordida charta juvat."

The inconvenience of writing on the back of the roll is
obvious, and this practice was probably very seldom, if
ever, followed in the case of works intended for sale.
Authors' copies, however, were often *opisthograph,* as in
Juvenal, *Sat.* i. 4 :—

> "Impune diem consumpserit ingens
> Telephus, aut summi plena jam margine libri
> Scriptus et in tergo needum finitus Orestes ? "

The younger Pliny also, *Epist.* iii. 5, 17, in reference
to his uncle's numerous works, uses the words : "Com-
mentarios clx. mihi reliquit, opisthographos quidem et
minutissime scriptos."

In the same manner worthless scribbling is referred
to by Martial, viii. 62, as written on the back of the
charta :—

> " Scribit in aversa Picens epigrammata charta
> Et dolet, averso quod facit illa deo."

Rough draughts or temporary pieces, or children's or
scholars' exercises might also be so written. Martial,
iv. 86, threatens his *libellus* with the fate of waste paper

to be utilized for such purposes, if his verses fail to please:—

> " Si damnaverit, ad salariorum
> Curras scrinia protinus licebit,
> Inversa pueris arande charta."

A most important instance of a scholar's exercise, written on the back of a papyrus, is found in the early copy of the *Epitaphios* of Hyperides in the British Museum.

After the establishment of the book-shape in general use, the roll form was almost entirely abandoned for literary purposes in the middle ages. It survived, however, for some of the Greek liturgies, for mortuary rolls, for pedigrees, for certain brief chronicles in which historical genealogies form a principal feature, and in a few other instances, as in the "Exultet" rolls of Italy, in which it was found convenient. But in all these the writing was parallel with the breadth, not with the length, of the roll. For records, however, the roll form has been continued throughout the middle ages to our own days, particularly in England, where not only public documents relating to the business of the country, but also proceedings of private manorial courts and bailiffs' accounts, were almost invariably entered on rolls.

The Codex or Book.

The earliest form of the book, in our modern sense of the word, that is, as a collection of leaves of vellum, paper, or other material, bound together, existed, as we have seen,[7] in the case of waxen tablets, when two or more were fastened together and made a *caudex* or *codex*. Hence vellum books, following the same arrangement, were also called *codices*. Similarly, by usage the title *liber*, which had been transferred from the original bark roll to the papyrus roll, was also passed on to the vellum book. So too the Greek terms βίβλος, βιβλίον and other words, which had been employed to designate the earlier rolls, were transferred in the same way. The vellum

---

[7] See above, p. 20.

codex came into general use when it was found how conveniently it could contain a large work in a much smaller space than could the papyrus roll. In the words of Isidore, *Origg.* vi. 13, 1 : " Codex multorum librorum est, liber unius voluminis."

That vellum MSS. existed in the classical period at Rome we know from Martial's *Apophoreta.* But these must have been few in number and articles of luxury. It was the requirements of the lawyers which necessitated the casting of the great law-books into a convenient form for reference; and the vellum MS., more durable than papyrus and adapted for receiving writing on both sides of the leaves, satisfied those requirements in the most perfect manner. Hence the term σωμάτιον, a name for the vellum MS., expressive of the bulk of the contents; and hence, conversely, the title of *codex* which was given to great compilations, such as those of Theodosius and Justinian.

Again, the Bible, the book which before all others became the great work of reference in the hands of the early Christians, could only be consulted with convenience and despatch in the new form. From the writings of St. Jerome and others it is evident that Bibles in codex form existed at a very early date. When once this form of multiplying texts was adopted by the Church, its rapid diffusion became a matter of certainty through the medium of monastic institutions. The form adopted for the Bible would naturally become the model for theological and ecclesiastical books of all kinds. Thus the vellum codex was destined to be the recipient of Christian literature, as the papyrus roll had been that of the pagan world.

Still, however, for the older literature the papyrus continued to some extent to hold its ground;[8] although even in this department the codex began at once to make inroads. For, as regards the works of great standard authors, such as Homer in Greek and Cicero in Latin, there is evidence that even in the earliest centuries of our era the codex form was not uncommon.[9] In St.

[8] Birt, 109.   [9] *Ibid.* 113.

Jerome's days vellum MSS. of the classics appear to have
been in ordinary use, for his library of vellum codices
included works of profane literature.[1] In the end, the
book form became so general that even papyrus was
put together in leaves and quires in the same way as
vellum. Several specimens of such papyrus books still
exist, as has been already noticed.[2]

Gatherings or Quires.

The earliest MSS. on vellum are usually of the broad
quarto size, in which the width equals, or nearly equals,
the height. The quires of which they are composed
consist, in most instances, of eight leaves, that is, of
four folded sheets, τετράς or τετράδιον, *quaternio* (whence
our word *quire*), and this number continued in general
favour for all sizes of volumes throughout the middle
ages. Quires of three sheets or six leaves, of five sheets
or ten leaves, and of six sheets or twelve leaves, are also
met with. For example, the famous Codex Vaticanus
of the Greek Bible is made up of ten-leaved quires.
Each quire was actually numbered or *signed,* to use the
technical word, either at the beginning, in the upper
margin, or, more generally at the end, in the lower inner
corner. In the Codex Alexandrinus the signatures
are at the beginnings of the quires, in the centre of the
upper margin. The numbers were frequently, in Latin
MSS., accompanied with the letter Q (for *quaternio*).
The practice of numbering the leaves of the quires, *e.g.*
A. i., A. ii., A. iii., etc., dates from the fourteenth century.
Catch-words, *exclamantes*, to connect the quires together,
first appear, but rarely, in the eleventh century; from
the twelfth century they become common.

In putting together the sheets for the quire, care was
generally taken to lay them in such a way that hair-
side faced hair-side, and flesh- (or inner) side faced
flesh-side. Thus, when the book was opened, the
two pages before the reader had the same appearance,
either the yellow tinge of the hair-side or the whiter

---

[1] *Ibid.* 115.   [2] Above, p. 34.

surface of the flesh-side. In Greek MSS. the arrangement of the sheets was afterwards reduced to a system:
the first or lowest sheet being laid with the flesh-side
downwards so that when the sheets were folded that side
always formed the first page of the quire.[3] In the Codex
Alexandrinus, however, the first page of a quire is the
hair-side of the skin. In Latin MSS. also the hair-side
appears to have generally begun the quire.

To the folded sheet was given the title *diploma;*
a barbarous mediæval name for it was *arcus.*[4] The leaf
was χαρτίον, φύλλον, *folium.* The line of writing was
στίχος, *versus, linea,* and *riga.*

Ruling.

In the earlier centuries of the middle ages, the ruled
lines of vellum MSS. were drawn with a hard-pointed
instrument, a blunt bodkin or stilus, on one side of the
leaf, the lines being impressed with sufficient force to
cause them to stand out in relief on the other side. The
ruling was almost invariably on the hair- (or outer) side of
the skin. Marginal lines were drawn to bound the text
laterally. The distances of the horizontal lines from one
another were marked off with pricks of the compass in
vertical order down the page. In earlier MSS. these
prickings are often found near the middle of the leaf, or
at least within the space occupied by the text, and the
lines are drawn right across the sheet and not confined
within the vertical boundaries. It was afterwards the
custom to prick off the spaces close to the margin and to
keep the ruled lines within limits; and eventually the
prickings often disappeared when the edges were shorn
by the binder. Each sheet should be ruled separately;
but two or more sheets were not infrequently laid and
ruled together, the lines being so deeply drawn on the
upper sheet that the lower sheets also received the
impressions. In rare instances lines are found ruled on
both sides of the leaf, as in some parts of the Codex

[3] C. R. Gregory, *Les Cahiers des MSS. Grecs.* in the *Comptes
Rendus* of the Acad. des Inscriptions, 1885, p. 261.
[4] Watterbach, *Schriftw.* 153.

Alexandrinus. In this MS. also, and in some other early codices, ruling was not drawn for every line of writing, but was occasionally spaced so that some lines of the text lay in the spaces while others stood on the ruled lines. Ruling with the lead point or plummet came into ordinary use in the twelfth century; coloured ink was also used for ruled lines in the fifteenth century.

Arrangement of the Text.

The text, which in early MSS. was written continuously without separation of words, might be written across the face of the page; and in some cases, as in poetical works, no other arrangement could well be followed. But, continuing the system observed in the papyrus rolls, the arrangement in columns was usual. The superior convenience of the column over the long line is obvious, particularly when a small character was the type of writing. The number of columns in a page was ordinarily two; but three and even four were also allowed. The Codex Sinaiticus of the Greek Bible has four columns in a page, so that the open book presents a series of eight columns to the reader, which, it has been observed, would forcibly recall the long row of *paginæ* of the papyrus roll.[5] The Codex Vaticanus has three columns in a page in the portion containing the Old Testament; and other early MSS. or fragments of MSS. exhibit the same arrangement, *e.g.* the Vatican fragments of Sallust, the Latin Pentateuch of Lyons, and others in the libraries of Rome, Milan, etc.[6] But the tri-columnar system appears to have been generally abandoned after the sixth century. The Utrecht Psalter, written at the beginning of the 9th century, in triple columns, is not an instance which counts for late usage, the MS. being only an exact copy of an

[5] The phrase of Eusebius, *Vita Const.* iv. 37, "ἐν πολυτελῶς ἠσκημένοις τεύχεσι τρισσὰ καὶ τετρασσά," probably refers to the number of columns. See Wattenbach, *Schriftw.* 149.

[6] See Wattenbach, *Schriftw.* 149. It may also be noted that the most ancient *dated* MS. in existence, the Syriac MS. of A.D. 411, containing the Recognitions of Clement of Rome (Brit. Mus. Add. MS. 12,150), is written in triple columns.

older codex.[7] Usually the later examples are the result
of necessity, as in the case of Psalters in parallel versions or languages.[8] A late instance, however, of a text
written in this fashion, without any compelling causes,
occurs in the Latin Bible of the 9th century, Add. MS.
24,142, in the British Museum.

With regard to the breaking up of the text into
paragraphs, and more particularly into the short sentences known as στιχοί, the reader is referred to what
is said below under the heads of Punctuation and
Stichometry.

As already noticed, the text of early MSS. was generally written continuously without separation of the
words; and this practice continued as a rule down
to about the ninth century. But even when the scribes
had begun to break up their lines into words, it still
continued to be the fashion to attach short words,
e.g. prepositions, to those which immediately followed
them. It was hardly before the eleventh century that
a perfect system of separately-written words was established in Latin MSS. In Greek MSS. it may be said
that the system was at no time perfectly followed, for,
even when the words were distinguished, there was
always a tendency to separate them inaccurately.

The first lines of the main divisions of the text, as for
example the several books of the Bible, were often
written in red for distinction.

In order to save space, and to get as much as possible
into a line, or to avoid division of a word, the letters
were often written smaller towards the end of the line;
and in Latin MSS., with the same object, two or more
letters were linked or combined in a monogrammatic
form.

At first, in uncial Latin MSS., there was no enlarge-
ment of letters in any part of the text to mark the

---

[7] The later copies of this Psalter also maintain the same
arrangement.

[8] A Psalter in four parallel columns (the Greek and the three
Latin versions), A.D. 1105, is in the Bibl. Nationale, MS. Lat.
2195. See *Pal. Soc.* i. 156.

F

beginnings of sections or chapters; yet, in some of the earliest examples, the first letter of the page, without regard to its position in relation to the text, is made larger than the rest.

Rubrics and titles and colophons (that is, titles, etc., written at the ends of books) were at first written in the same characters as the text; afterwards it was found convenient, as a distinction, to employ different characters. Thus in later uncial Latin MSS. titles might be in capitals or rustic capitals; in minuscule MSS. they might be written in capitals or uncials. The convenience of having the title at the beginning of a MS., instead of only in colophon-form at the end, was soon recognized; but the use of the colophon still continued, the designation of a work being frequently recorded in both title and colophon down to the latest period.

Running titles or head-lines appear in even some of the earliest MSS., in the same characters as the text, but of smaller size.

In the division of words at the end of a line, it was the ancient practice to break off with a complete syllable. In Greek, however, in the case of compound words, the last consonant of the prefix was carried on to the next syllable, if this was a vowel or began with a vowel, as κα-τεί-δον; and the same method was observed with a preposition and the following word, as κα-τε-μοῦ. With such a system in vogue it is not surprising to find it extended occasionally to other cases, as ταῦ-τοόχ. In simple words the sigma was not uncommonly carried on to a following consonant, as μέγι-στος.

In Latin MSS., while the observance of the true syllabic division was maintained according to ancient usage, and, when two consonants came together, they were properly assigned to their several syllables, as *dic-tus*, *prop-ter*, *ig-navus*, *pris-cus*, *hos-pes*, *hos-tis*, yet in some ancient texts the first consonant is drawn over to the second, as *di-ctus*, *ho-stis*, etc., in accordance with the Greek practice noticed above; and in some MSS. we

find the older style altered to suit the later, as in the
Fulda MS. of the Gospels, corrected in the sixth
century by Victor of Capua,[1] and the Harley Gospels of
about the year 600.[2]

The coupling stroke or hyphen, to indicate connection
of the two parts of the divided word, appears to have
been unknown in the early centuries. A point per-
forms this duty in early instances. In the eleventh
century the hyphen at the end of the line shows itself
on a few occasions; in the twelfth century it becomes
more systematic, and is also repeated at the beginning
of the next line.

Punctuation.—Greek.

The earliest form in which a system of punctuation
appears is that found in ancient inscriptions, wherein
the several words are divided from one another by
single, double, or treble dots or points. This, however,
is not punctuation in the sense in which we use the term
—the system whereby sentences are marked out, and
the sense of the text is made clear.

The ancient practice of writing literary texts continuously, without distinction of words, was not, indeed,
quite universal; for the astronomical treatise known as
the Ἐνδόξου τεχνη, earlier than 154 B.C., at Paris, is an
instance to the contrary. But it was certainly by far
the more ordinary method, and in the uncial vellum
MSS. of the earlier middle ages it may be said to have
been the only method that was followed. In the documents of ordinary life the distinction of words was, from
early times, more frequently, though still only partially,
observed. When the minuscule writing came into use
as the literary hand, separation of the words from one
another gradually followed; but never was this system
fully perfected. For example, prepositions were still
attached to the following words, and there was always

[1] Zangemeister and Wattenbach, *Exempla Codd. Lat.*, tab.
xxxiv.
[2] Brit. Mus. *Cat. Anc. MSS.*, pt. ii, p. 14.

a tendency to detach a final letter, and to attach it to the next following word.

The inconvenience which we experience in reading a continuously written text could not have been so greatly felt by the scholars of the old Greek world; otherwise separation of words, and a perfect system of punctuation, would have been established long before was actually the case. Still the distinction of paragraphs was found a necessity at an ancient period. Hence arose the dividing stroke, the παράγραφος, known, at all events, as early as Aristotle's time, separating paragraphs by being inserted between them at the beginnings of lines; but, it should be remembered, the stroke really belonged to the concluding paragraph, and marked its termination, and did not form an initial sign for the new paragraph which followed. The paragraph-mark was not, however, uniformly the horizontal stroke; the wedge > (διπλῆ), the mark which is also often found at the end of a work, 7 (κορωνίς), and similar forms were employed. This system of distinguishing paragraphs appears in use in the early papyri, and analogously the dividing stroke marks off the speeches of the different characters in the surviving papyrus fragments of the tragedians, as, for example, in the very ancient remains of the *Antiope* of Euripides.

But to write every paragraph distinct by itself would have entailed a certain loss of space. If the last line were short, there would remain a vacant space after it, unoccupied by writing. In the earliest specimens therefore we find this space occupied by the first words of the next paragraph, a slight break being left to mark its commencement, thus :—

ΕϹΟΜΕΘΑ   ΟΥΓΑΡΔΗ
ΠΟΥΟΛΥΜΠΙΑΔΙΜΕΝ

The next step was to draw back the first letter of the first full line of the new paragraph, and leave it slightly projecting into the margin; and then lastly to enlarge it.

The letter made thus prominent being a sufficient indication of the commencement of the new paragraph, the stroke or wedge between the lines was no longer necessary and ordinarily disappeared. Thus the two lines given above would, in this last stage of development, be written thus :—

ϹΟΜΕΘΑ   ΟΥΓΑΡΔΗ
ΠΟΥΟΛΥΜΠΙΑΔΙΜΕΝ

Of course, if the paragraph commenced at the beginning of a line, the large letter took its natural place as the initial; but, arranged as above, any letter, even one in the middle of a word, might be enlarged.

This system is found in action in the Codex Alexandrinus, attributed to the 5th century, and continued to be practised throughout the middle ages. But it should be noted that, although rendered unnecessary by the introduction of the large initial, the paragraph mark also appears in this MS., but generally in anomalous positions, particularly above the initial letters of the different books —an indication that the scribes of the day had already begun to forget the meaning and proper use of the mark.

We next have to consider punctuation by points. As already stated, these were used in ancient inscriptions. The earliest instance of their employment in a Greek MS. occurs in the very ancient fragment known as the Artemisia papyrus, at Vienna, wherein the double point (:) occasionally closes a sentence. Again, in the fragments of the *Phædo* of Plato, found at Gurob, the same double point appears as a mark of punctuation; and it may also be here added that a short horizontal stroke or dash also serves the purpose of separating the different speeches in the same fragments. The double point also, in addition to the παράγραφος, occasionally marks the close of the paragraphs in the Paris papyrus 49, a letter of about 160 B.C. But such isolated instances merely show that there was a knowledge of the value of such marks of punctuation, which, however, in practice were not systematically employed.

A more regular system was developed in the schools of Alexandria, its invention being ascribed to Aristophanes of Byzantium (260 B.C.). This was the use of the full point with certain values in certain positions (θέσεις) : the high point (στιγμὴ τελεία), equivalent to a full stop; the point on the line (ὑποστιγμή), a shorter pause, equivalent to our semicolon; and the point in a middle position (στιγμὴ μέση), an ordinary pause, equivalent to our comma. In the Codex Alexandrinus the middle and high points are pretty generally used. But the middle point eventually disappeared; and about the ninth century the comma was introduced. It also became a common practice to mark the conclusion of a paragraph or chapter with a more emphatic sign, such as two or more dots with or without a horizontal dash, :, :-, .·.. The mark of interrogation also first appears about the 8th or 9th century.

Punctuation.—Latin.

The punctuation of Latin MSS. followed in some respects the systems of the Greeks. In the poem on the Battle of Actium, found at Herculaneum, points are used to mark off the words, a practice borrowed from inscriptions; and in the early MSS. of Virgil in the Vatican Library points are found employed for the same purpose, although they appear to be due to a second, but still early, hand. From the Latin grammarians we know that they adopted the Greek system of punctuation by points (θέσεις, *posituræ*), to which they gave the titles of "distinctio finalis," "subdistinctio," and "distinctio media"; but in practice we find that the scribes used the points without consistently adhering to their meaning.

In some of the more ancient MSS. marks of punctuation are entirely wanting, only a short space being left blank in the line to indicate the conclusion of a passage or paragraph, as in Greek MSS., but without the accompanying dividing line (παράγραφος) or the enlarged letter at the beginning of the first full line, which the Greek scribes employed. Yet the paragraph mark was used to separate paragraphs or divisions of the text (as, for example, in the poem on the Battle of Actium) when the new paragraph began a line; and its eventual conversion from a mere sign of separation between two paragraphs into a sign belonging to the head of the new paragraph was a natural development. Our modern ¶ is directly derived from the simple ancient form Γ.

In early uncial MSS. it is not uncommon to find the point, more often in the middle position, used as an ordinary stop; and at the end of a paragraph or chapter, a colon, or colon and dash, or a number of points, occasionally indicate a final stop. In the seventh century the high point is used with the force of a comma, the semicolon with its modern value, and a point and virgule, ·7, or other combinations of points, as a full stop. In the Carlovingian period and the next centuries we have the inverted semicolon, holding a position between our comma and semicolon, and the comma itself. The origin of the former of these is uncertain. It appears first with some regularity in MSS. of the eighth century; but it is noticeable that a mark which resembles it occurs in the Actium poem, being there formed by the addition of an oblique stroke to an ordinary point. Along with these later signs also appears the mark of interrogation in common use.

Breathings and Accents and Other Signs.—Greek.

Breathings and accents, like the Greek system of punctuation by points noticed above, are also attributed to Aristophanes of Byzantium, as part of the δέκα προσῳδίαι, of which he is called the inventor.

The rough (Ͱ) and the smooth (˧) breathings (πνεύματα) at first represented the left and the right half of the letter H, which itself was originally the aspirate. They

were soon worn down to ∟ and ⌐, in which shapes they
are found in early MSS.; and eventually these square
forms became the rounded ‹ and ›, the period at which
they definitely arrived at this last stage being the 12th
century. Only occasionally are marks of breathing found
in the more ancient MSS., and then it is generally the
rough breathing that is distinguished.

The accents (τόνοι) are: the grave ˋ (βαρεῖα), or
ordinary tone; the acute ´ (ὀξεῖα), marking a rise in
the voice; and the circumflex ˆ (ὀξυβαρεῖα or περισπω-
μένη), combining the other two, and indicating a rise
and fall or slide of the voice. Originally, in theory, all
syllables which were not marked with the acute accent
or circumflex received the grave accent, as Θὲὸδὼρὸς;
and several examples of this actually occur in the Harris
Homer. In the same MS., and occasionally in the
Bankes Homer, we also see instances of the indication
of normally oxytone words (in which the acute accent
falls on the last syllable) by placing a grave accent on
the penultimate, as ἐλὼν. In later MSS. a double accent
marks emphatically μὲν and δὲ.

Breathings and accents were not systematically applied
to Greek texts before the seventh century.

The rest of the ten signs attributed to Aristophanes
of Byzantium, to assist in the correct reading of texts,
are as follows:—

The χρόνοι, or marks to distinguish a long (¯) and a
short (˘) syllable, instances of their employment occurring in the Harris Homer and in some other early documents on papyrus.

The διαστολή or ὑποδιαστολή, a virgule or comma inserted between words where the distinction might be
ambiguous, as εστι, νους, not εστιν, ους.

The hyphen (ὑφέν), a curve or line drawn under the
letters to indicate connection, as, for example, to indicate
compound words. In the Harris Homer the hyphen,
in the form of a long straight line, is used for this
purpose.

The apostrophe (ἀπόστροφος), which, besides marking
elision, was used for other purposes, and whose form

varied from a curve to a straight accent or even a mere dot. It was very generally placed in early MSS. after a foreign name, or a name not having a Greek termination, as, for example, 'Αβρααμ', and after a word ending in a hard consonant, as κ, χ, ξ, ψ, and also in ρ. When a double consonant occurred in the middle of a word, an apostrophe was placed above the first or between the two letters. In a papyrus of A.D. 542 (*Pal. Soc.* ii. 123), a dot represents the apostrophe in this position; and in a MS. of the 8th or 9th century (*Pal. Soc.* ii. 126), a double apostrophe is employed. The apostrophe is also used to distinguish two concurrent vowels, as ιματια'αυτων. In some instances it is even placed between two different consonants, as *e.g.* αριθ'μος, in the Vienna MS. of Dioscorides.

In addition to the marks and signs already noticed, there are some others which occur in Greek MSS.

Marks of diæresis, placed over ι and υ when at the beginning of a word or when they do not form a diphthong with a foregoing vowel, occur in papyri, being either a single or double dot or short stroke, or, in some instances, a short accent; in later MSS. the form is usually a double dot.

Quotations are indicated by marks in the margin, the most common being the arrow-head, > or <, and the cross, horizontal stroke, or waved stroke being also used. More rarely, quoted passages are indented, that is, written within the marginal line of the text.

To distinguish words consisting of a single letter, a short acute accent or similar mark is found in use, as, in the Codex Alexandrinus, to mark η in its various meanings as a word. Apparently from ignorance or confusion the scribes of this MS. even placed a mark on η when merely a letter in a word. The article ὁ is found similarly distinguished in a papyrus of A.D. 595 (*Pal. Soc.* ii. 124).

To fill small spaces left vacant at the end of a line, an arrow-head or tick was employed; as, for example, in the papyrus of Hyperides (*Lycophron*), and in the Codex Sinaiticus.

Arbitrary signs, or signs composed of dots or strokes, are used as reference marks to marginal scholia, or to indicate insertion of omitted words or passages. In the papyrus of Hyperides (*Lycophron*) the place for insertion of an omitted line is marked, and has the word *ἄνω*, while the line itself, written in the margin above, has *κάτω*. In the papyrus of Aristotle on the Constitution of Athens, a letter or word inserted between the lines has sometimes a dot on each side.

In the same manner various signs are employed to indicate transposition, such as numerical letters, or (as in the papyrus of Aristotle) slanting strokes and dots (/·) placed above the words.

To distinguish words or other combinations of letters from the rest of the text, a line was drawn above them; thus the grammatical forms in the papyrus attributed to Tryphon, in the British Museum, and the reference letters in the Oxford Euclid of A.D. 888 are so marked.

Besides actually striking out a letter or word or passage with a pen-stroke, the ancient scribes indicated erasure by including the word or passage between inverted commas or brackets or dots, one at the beginning and one at the end; sometimes by accents above, as *e.g.* τῶν (to erase the ν), τά and ταυτά (to cover the whole word), as seen in the Codex Alexandrinus; sometimes by a line above, as καῑ; sometimes by a dot above, rarely below, each letter.

Accents and other Signs.—Latin.

Accents were seldom used by Latin scribes. Occasionally they mark a monosyllable word, as the exclamation *ó*, or a preposition, as *á*; and sometimes they are employed to emphasize a syllable.

As in Greek MSS., quotations are indicated by marks in the margin or by indentation; and arbitrary signs are used to mark the place of insertion of omissions. Common reference marks are *hd hs = hic deest, hoc supra* or *hic scribas*, etc. Transposition of words might be indicated in various ways, as by letters or numbers,

and very commonly by oblique strokes above the line,
as *mea mater = mater mea.*

Finally, for correction, the simple method of striking
out with the pen and interlining or adding in the margin was followed, as well as that of marking words or
letters for deletion with dots above or below them.

Besides the above, other marks and signs are found in
both Greek and Latin MSS., such as the private marks
of correctors or readers. There are also critical symbols,
such as the diple and the asterisk employed by Aristarchus in the texts of Homer, and the obelus and
asterisk used by St. Jerome to distinguish certain passages in versions of the Latin Psalter. But the consideration of these is beyond the scope of the present
work.

Palimpsests.

A palimpsest MS. is one from which the first writing
has been rubbed off in order to make the leaves ready to
receive fresh writing. Sometimes this process was repeated, and the leaves finally received a third text, the
MS. being in such a case doubly palimpsest. This
method of obtaining writing material was practised in
early times. The term "palimpsest" is used by Catullus,[1] apparently with reference to papyrus; also by
Cicero in a passage[2] wherein he is evidently speaking of
waxen tablets; and by Plutarch, who narrates[3] that
Plato compared Dionysius to a βιβλίον παλιμψηστον, his
tyrannical nature, δυσεκπλυτος, showing through like the
imperfectly erased writing of a palimpsest MS., that is,
a papyrus roll from which the first writing had been
washed. The word, however, indicating, as it does, the
action of scraping or rubbing, could originally have only
been strictly applied to material strong enough to bear
such treatment, as vellum or waxen tablets. Papyrus
could only be washed, not scraped or rubbed, and the

---

[1] *Carm.* xxii. 5. [2] *Ad Fam.* vii. 18.
[3] *Cum princip. philosoph.*, ad fin.

application of the term to a twice-written papyrus or waxen tablet or vellum MS. indifferently, proves that the term had become so current as to have passed beyond its strict meaning.

If the first writing were thoroughly removed from the surface of vellum, none of it, of course, could ever be recovered. But, as a matter of fact, it appears to have been often very imperfectly effaced ; and even if, to all appearance, the vellum was restored to its original condition of an unwritten surface, yet slight traces of the text might remain which chemical re-agents, or even the action of the atmosphere, might again intensify and make legible. Thus many capital and uncial texts have been recovered from palimpsest MSS. Of modern chemical re-agents used in the restoration of such texts the most harmless is probably hydro-sulphuret of ammonia.

Great destruction of vellum MSS. of the early centuries of our era must have followed the fall of the Roman empire. Political and social changes would interfere with the market, and writing material would become scarce and might be supplied from MSS. which had become useless and were considered idle encumbrances of the shelves. In the case of Greek MSS., so great was their consumption that a synodal decree of the year 691 forbade the destruction of MSS. of the Scriptures or of the fathers, imperfect or injured volumes excepted. It has been remarked that no entire work has in any instance been found in the original text of a palimpsest, but that portions of different MSS. were taken to make up a volume for a second text.

The most valuable Latin texts are found in the volumes which were re-written from the seventh to the ninth centuries. In many instances the works of classical writers have been obliterated to make room for patristic literature or grammatical works. On the other hand, there are instances of classical texts having been written over Biblical MSS. ; but these are of late date.

In the great Syriac collection of MSS. which were

obtained from the monastery in the Nitrian Desert of Egypt and are now in the British Museum, many important texts have been recovered. A volume containing a work of Severus of Antioch, of the beginning of the 9th century, is written on palimpsest leaves taken from MSS. of the Iliad of Homer and the Gospel of St. Luke of the 6th century (*Cat. Anc. MSS.* i. pls. 9, 10) and of the Elements of Euclid of the 7th or 8th century. Another volume of the same collection is doubly palimpsest, a Syriac text of St. Chrysostom, of the 9th or 10th century, covering a Latin grammatical work of the 6th century, which again has displaced the annals of the Latin historian Licinianus of the 5th century (*Cat. Anc. MSS.* ii. pls. 1, 2). At Paris is the Codex Ephraemi, containing portions of the Old and New Testaments in Greek, of the 5th century, which are rewritten with works of Ephraem Syrus in a hand of the 12th century; and some fragments of the *Phaeton* of Euripides are found in the Codex Claromontanus. At the Vatican are portions of the *De Republica* of Cicero, of the 4th century, under the work of St. Augustine on the Psalms of the 7th century; and an Arian fragment of the 5th century. At Verona is the famous palimpsest which contains the MS. of Gaius of the 5th century, as well as the Fasti Consulares of A.D. 486. At Milan are the fragments of Plautus, in rustic capitals of the 4th or 5th century, covered by a Biblical text of the 9th century. Facsimiles of many of these MSS. are given by Zangemeister and Wattenbach in their *Exempla Codicum Latinorum.*

CHAPTER VI.

THE Greeks and Romans measured the contents of their MSS. by lines. In poetry the unit was of course the verse; in prose works an artificial unit had to be found, for no two scribes would naturally write lines of the same length. It has been calculated that this unit was a standard line of fifteen or sixteen syllables, or thirty-four to thirty-eight letters, that is, an average Homeric line, called by the earlier writers ἔπος, afterwards στίχος.

Records of the measurements of prose works are found in two forms: in references to the extent of the works of particular authors made by later writers, and in the entries of the actual figures in MSS. These latter entries may actually give the extent of the MSS. in which they are found; but more frequently they transmit the measurements of the archetypes. The quotations found in Greek writers are fairly numerous, and were no doubt mainly derived from the catalogues of libraries, where details of this nature were collected. Such a catalogue was contained in the famous πίνακες of the Alexandrian libraries published by Callimachus about the middle of the third century B.C. The earliest instances of the entry of the actual number of lines occur in papyri. A fragment of Euripides,[1] of a period earlier than the year 161 B.C., has at the end the words CTIXOI MΔ. In the Herculanean papyri are found such entries as ΦΙΛΟΔΗΜΟΥ ΠΕΡΙ ΡΗΤΟΡΙΚΗC XXXX ΗΗ (= 4200 lines), or ΕΠΙΚΟΥΡΟΥ ΠΕΡΙ ΦΥCΕΩC

---

[1] *Un papyrus inédit de la Bibl. de M. A. Firmin-Didot*, Paris, 1879.

ΓΕ. ΑΡΙΘ. XXXHH (= 3200 lines), which, however,
are probably traditional numbers copied from earlier
examples. In addition to the number of lines we sometimes find a record of the number of columns or
σέλιδες. Among the mediæval MSS. which have stichometrical memoranda, a copy of the *Halieutica* of
Oppian, of the 15th century, at Madrid, contains a
statement of the number of leaves (φύλλα) as well as
lines in the several books, not of this particular MS.,
but of its archetype. In like manner the Laurentian Sophocles of the 11th century has similar
memoranda of the length of the several plays. The
Laurentian MS. of Herodotus, of the 10th century,
and the Paris MS. of Demosthenes, of the same period,
afford data of the same kind. In certain of these more
recent MSS., as well as in the early papyri, the ancient
system of Greek numeration is employed—a proof of
the antiquity of this method of calculating the length of
written works; but, on the other hand, the later system
of alphabetical numeration is followed in some of the
Herculanean rolls.

The practice of stichometry can actually be traced
back to nearly a century before the time of Callimachus, who has been sometimes credited with its invention. Theopompus, as quoted by Photius,[2] boasts that
he had written 20,000 ἔπη in rhetorical speeches, and
150,000 in historical books. When we thus find a
writer of the fourth century B.C. measuring his works in
terms which are clearly intelligible and need no explanation for those to whom he addresses himself, we
can understand that even at that early period the
system must have been long established by common
usage.

While stichometrical data can be gathered in fairly
large numbers from Greek literature, those which are
to be found relating to Latin authors are comparatively
few; but, such as they are, they show that the Latin

[2] *Bibliotheca*, cod. 176, § 120. See also Isocrates, *Panathen*.
136.

versus corresponded closely with the Greek ἔπος or στίχος.[3]

Besides the system of stichometry just explained, and to which, on account of its dealing with the full measurement of literary works, the title of " total stichometry " has been applied, there was also another system in practice which has been named " partial stichometry." This was the numbering of lines or verses at convenient intervals, which, in the first place, served the same purpose of literary reference as our modern system of numbering the verses of the Bible or the lines of a play or poem. Instances of such partial stichometry indeed are not very numerous among existing MSS.; but they are sufficient to show that the system was recognized. Thus, in the Bankes Homer, the verses are numbered in the margin by hundreds, and the same practice is followed in other papyri of Homer (*Classical Texts from Papyri in the Brit. Mus.*); so likewise in the Ambrosian Pentateuch of the 5th century, at Milan, the Book of Deuteronomy is numbered at every hundredth στίχος. Euthalius, a deacon of Alexandria of the fifth century, also announces that he marked the στίχοι of the Pauline Epistles by fifties. And in the Codex Urbinas of Isocrates, and in the Clarke Plato of A.D. 888, at Oxford, indications of partial stichometry have been traced.

The most practical use of such systems of stichometry was no doubt a commercial one. By counting the number of lines, the payment of the scribes could be exactly calculated and the market price of MSS. arranged. When once a standard copy had been written and the number of στίχοι registered, subsequent copies could be made in any form at the pleasure of the scribe, who need only enter the ascertained number of lines at the end of his work. Thus, in practice, we find papyri and early vellum MSS. written in narrow columns, the lines

[3] See a notice printed by Mommsen in *Hermes*, xxi. 142, *Zur Lateinischen Stichometrie*, of a MS. at Cheltenham which affords evidence of the computation, about A.D. 359, of the length of the works of Cyprian by the standard of a Virgilian line.

of which by no means correspond in length with the regulation στίχοι, but which were more easily read without tiring the eye. The edict of Diocletian, *De pretiis rerum venalium,* of A.D. 301, settled the tariff for scribes by the hundred lines ; and a survival of the ancient method of calculating such remuneration has been found in the practice at Bologna and other Italian universities, in the middle ages, of paying by the *pecia* of sixteen columns, each of sixty-two lines with thirty-two letters to the line. An analogous practice in our own day is seen in the copyist's charge by the folio of either seventy-two or one hundred words.

We have hitherto considered στίχοι as lines of measurement or space-lines. But the same term was also applied to the lines or short periods into which certain texts were divided in order to facilitate reading : in other words, sense-lines. The works which would naturally more than others call for such an arrangement would be those which were read in public : the speeches of orators, or the sacred books of the Bible used for Church lessons. We have evidence of an early and regular division of the orations of Demosthenes and Cicero into short periods : the *cola* and *commata* to which St. Jerome refers in his preface to Isaiah.[4] Manuscripts of the works of the Latin orator are still in existence, the text of which is written in this form, one of them being a MS. of the *Tusculans* and the *De Senectute* attributed to the 9th century, at Paris ; and it is evident from certain passages in the writings of early rhetoricians that they were familiar with this system in the orations of Demosthenes.

Suidas explains a *colon* as a στίχος forming a complete clause ; Joannes Siculus lays down that a clause of less

---

[4] "Nemo cum Prophetas versibus viderit esse descriptos metro eos æstimet apud Hebræos ligari, et aliquid simile habere de Psalmis vel operibus Salomonis : sed quod in Demosthene et Tullio solet fieri, ut per cola scribuntur et commata, qui utique prosa et non versibus conscripserunt, nos quoque, utilitati legentium providentes, interpretationem novam novo scribendi genere distinximus."

G

than eight syllables is a *comma*, and that one of from
eight to seventeen syllables is a *colon*. In the place cited
above, St. Jerome tells us that he has, for convenience in
reading, followed the system of the MSS. of Demosthenes and Cicero, and arranged his translation in this
"new style of writing." But he had already found the
same system followed in the Psalms and poetical books
of the Old Testament—just where one would look for the
first experiment of casting the text in sense-lines. Hence
the title βιβλοι στιχηρεις or στιχηραι which was applied to
them. The system was gradually extended to the other
books of the Bible, the term στιχος being now used
altogether to mean a sense-line, although the ancient
stichometrical measurements of the text into space-
lines were still recorded at the ends of the books.
Euthalius is credited with having written at least the
Acts and Epistles in this stichometrical sense-arrange-
ment; although it seems more probable that he only
revised the work of predecessors, also accurately measuring the space-lines and numbering them as noticed
above. As might be expected, one arrangement of
the text of the Bible in rhythmical sentences or lines
of sense would not be consistently followed by all editors
and scribes; and hence we find variations in the length
of lines and sentences in the different extant Biblical
MSS.

TACHYGRAPHY.

Greek.

The Greeks appear to have had a system of shorthand
at a very early date. A fragment of an inscription found
recently on the Acropolis at Athens has been shown by
Gomperz[1] to be a portion of an explanation of a kind of
shorthand, composed of arbitrary signs, as old as the fourth
century B.C. A passage in Diogenes Laertius was for-

---

[1] *Ueber ein bisher unbekanntes griech. Schrift-system aus der
Mitte des vierten vorchristlichen Jahrhunderts*, Wien, 1884.
See also P. Mitzschke, *Eine griech. Kurzschrift aus dem vierten
Jahrhundert*, in the *Archiv für Stenographie*, No. 454.

merly interpreted to imply that Xenophon wrote shorthand notes (ὑποσημειωσάμενος) of the lectures of Socrates ; but a similar expression elsewhere, which will not bear this meaning, has caused this idea to be abandoned. The first undoubted mention of a Greek shorthand writer occurs in a passage in Galen (περὶ τῶν ἰδίων βιβλίων γράφη), wherein he refers to a copy made by one who could write swiftly in signs, διὰ σημείων εἰς τάχος γράφειν ; but there is no very ancient specimen of Greek tachygraphy in existence. The occurrence, however, in papyri of certain symbols as marks of contraction or to repre- sent entire words, and particularly the comparatively large number of them found in the papyrus of Aristotle's work on the Constitution of Athens, written about A.D. 100, goes to prove that the value of such symbols was commonly understood at that period, and indicates the existence of a perfected system of shorthand writing. A waxen book of several tablets, acquired not long since by the British Museum (Add. MS. 33,270), and assigned to the 3rd century, is inscribed with characters which are surmised to be in Greek shorthand, the only words written in ordinary letters being in that lan- guage. A system of shorthand was practised by the early Christians for taking down sermons and the pro- ceedings of synods.

But we must descend to the tenth century before we meet with Greek tachygraphic MSS. which have been deciphered. The first is the Paris MS. of Hermogenes, which contains some marginal notes in mixed ordinary and tachygraphical characters, of which Montfaucon[6] gives an account with a table of forms. Next, there is a series of MSS. which owe their origin to the monastery of Grotta Ferrata, viz. the Add. MS. 18,231 of the British Museum, written in the year 972, and others of the same period (*Pal. Soc.* ii. pl. 28, 85, 86), which are full of partially tachygraphic texts and scholia, and also contain passages in shorthand pure and simple. And lastly there is the Vatican MS. 1809, a volume of which forty-seven pages

---

[6] *Palæogr. Græc.* p. 351.

are covered with tachygraphic writing of the eleventh century, which have been made the subject of special study by Dr. Gitlbauer for the Vienna Academy. Some shorthand passages which occur in a fourteenth century MS., and a passage from a fifteenth century MS. in the Vatican, have recently been published.[7]

The shorthand system of these later examples is syllabic, the signs, it is thought, being formed from uncials; and it has been concluded that it represents, if not a new creation of the ninth or tenth century, at least a modification and not a continuation of the older system —in a word, that two systems of Greek shorthand have existed. For it is found that the forms of contraction and abbreviation in Greek MSS. of the middle ages are derived from two sources, most of them springing from an ancient system, but others clearly being contributed by the later system of shorthand.

Latin.

According to Suetonius,[8] the first introduction of shorthand signs, *notæ*, in Rome was due to Ennius; but more generally the name of Cicero's freedman, Tiro, is associated with the invention, the signs being commonly named *notæ Tironianæ*. Seneca is said to have collected the various *notæ* known at his time, to the number of 5000. Shorthand appears to have been taught in schools under the empire; and the emperor Titus himself is said to have been expert in writing it. There seems to have been, as it is natural there should have been, a connection between Greek and Latin tachygraphy, certain symbols being the same in both.

Down to the ninth century the notes appear to have been in common use. In the Frankish empire they are found in the signatures and subscriptions of charters. They were also used by revisers and annotators of MSS.

---

[7] T. W. Allen, *Fourteenth Century Tachygraphy*, in the *Journal of Hellenic Studies*, xi. 286; Desrousseaux, *Sur quelques Manuscrits d'Italie*, in the *Mélanges* of the Ecole Française de Rome, 1886, p. 544.

[8] "Vulgares notas Ennius primus mille et centum invenit."

The scholia and glosses in a MS. of Virgil, at Berne, of the latter half of the 9th century (*Pal. Soc.* ii. pl. 12) are partially written in these signs; but about this period they passed out of ordinary use. And yet there appears to have been an attempt made to check their total extinction; for there are still in existence MSS. of the Psalter, of the ninth or tenth century, in shorthand, which, it has been suggested, were written for practice. And the survival of Tironian lexicons, or collections of the signs, copied at this time, seems to point to an effort to keep them in the recollection of men. Professional scribes and notaries continued to use them in subscriptions to charters down to the eleventh century.

CRYPTOGRAPHY.

The various methods which at different periods have been adopted for the purpose of concealing the meaning of what is written, either by an elaborate system of secret signs or "cyphers," or by a simpler and less artificial system, such as the substitution of other letters for the true letters required by the sense, only incidentally come within the scope of a work on Palæography. The cypher-system, like short-hand, has a special department of its own. It is only the modified practice of substituting letters and other common signs which need for a moment detain us, as it is followed occasionally in mediæval MSS. This simple system, as might be naturally inferred, appears to be of some antiquity. Julius Cæsar and Augustus, according to Suetonius, both had their own private methods of disguise, by substitution of consonants for vowels. In the middle ages consonants for vowels, or vowels for consonants, or other exchange of letters occur; sometimes we have the substitution of Greek letters or of numerals or other signs. But the surviving instances are not very numerous and generally appear in colophons for the purpose of disguising a name or year of date, at the caprice of the writer.

CHAPTER VII.

ABBREVIATIONS AND CONTRACTIONS.

Greek.

ABBREVIATIONS and contractions[1] play an important part in Palæography. Two reasons in particular dispose men to curtail written words: (1) the desire to avoid the labour of writing over and over again words of frequent recurrence, which can as easily be understood in an abbreviated as in an extended form; and (2) the necessity of saving space.

From the earliest times there must have been a constant striving among individuals to relieve the toil of writing by shortening words. The author would soon construct a system of contraction of his own, and, especially if he were writing on a subject into which technical words would largely enter, his system would be adopted by other writers in the same field. In law deeds, in public and private accounts, in the various memoranda of the transactions of daily life, common and oft-repeated words must have been always subject to curtailment—at first at the caprice of individuals, but gradually on recognized systems intelligible to all.

The simplest form of abbreviation is that in which a single letter (or at most, two or three letters) represents a word. Thus, there is the ancient Greek system of indicating numerals by the first letter, as $\Pi = \pi \acute{\epsilon} \nu \tau \epsilon$, $\Delta = \delta \acute{\epsilon} \kappa a$, H (aspirate) $= \acute{\epsilon} \kappa a \tau \acute{o} \nu$, and so on. On ancient coins, where available space was limited, we find the names of Greek cities indicated by the first two or three

---

[1] I use the word "abbreviation" for the shortening of a word by suppressing its termination; "contraction" for the shortening of a word by omitting letters from the body.

letters. Certain ordinary words also occur in inscriptions in shortened forms. The Roman usage of employing single letters to represent titles of rank is familiar to us from inscriptions, and has been handed down in the works of classical authors; the S.P.Q.R. of the great Republic will occur to the recollection of everyone. Such abbreviations by constant usage became a part of the written language.

The fullest development to which a system of abbreviation can attain is, of course, a perfected shorthand; but this is far too artificial for the ordinary business of life. Something between simple single-letter signs and complex tachygraphical symbols is required, and hence we find in the middle ages a good working system developed by Greek and Latin writers, which combined the advantages of both kinds of abbreviation. The letter system was extended, and certain tachygraphical symbols were taken over as representatives of entire words in common use or as convenient signs for prefixes and terminations.[2]

In tracing, then, the history of Greek and Latin abbreviations and contractions, as far as it can be ascertained from existing documents, we must be prepared to find in the systems of each certain elements which are of great antiquity. When we see in the case of mediæval minuscule Greek MSS. considerable differences in the system there in use from that which appears in uncial

[2] The art of reading contracted writing can necessarily only be acquired by those who have a knowledge of the languages in which the MSS. are written, and who will patiently persevere in their study. The beginner will find the first difficulty of mastering the elementary forms of contraction of the middle ages most easily overcome by transcribing passages *in extenso*. For Greek, MSS. in minuscule writing of the tenth, eleventh, and twelfth centuries; for Latin, charters of the thirteenth and fourteenth centuries, are the best subjects to begin with. As regards the latter, they are generally short, the contractions are numerous; but at the same time particular phrases and contractions continually recur. The student has thus the advantage of passing under his eye a great variety of handwriting and of comparing the forms which individual letters and contractions take in the several documents; while the recurrence of legal terms and phrases, which soon become familiar, gives him the key to correct reading.

MSS., we might be led to infer that it was a new invention; but a closer examination will prove that in its elements it is the same as that which was practised hundreds of years before, in the third century B.C. We may even carry our view still farther back. For, if in some of the earliest documents which have survived abbreviated forms are in existence, not made at random but following certain laws in their formation, we have sufficient ground for assuming that the practice of abbreviation was, even at that remote time, one of some antiquity, and that a long period must have passed for the development of a system intelligible to all readers. A still further, and even stronger, proof of the very ancient origin of this practice is afforded by the numerous symbols for particular words which are found in the earliest papyri.

There does not exist, however, sufficient material for the construction of a continuous history of Greek abbreviation between the two periods noted above, viz., the third century B.C. and the ninth century of our era, when the minuscule came into use as the literary hand. It will be therefore convenient, first of all, to consider the forms of abbreviation and contraction which are found in the uncial MSS. of the Scriptures and liturgies, which partially fill the gap of the vacant centuries. The earliest dates from the fourth century. In such MSS., which were, more than others, required for public reading, the rules followed are very simple, nor are the examples of abbreviation numerous. The omission of N at the end of a line is marked by a horizontal stroke, as O I K O−; a form common to all MSS. The middle of a word was omitted, the first and last letter (or at most one or two more) being given and surmounted by a horizontal stroke, as $\overline{\Theta C} = \Theta\epsilon\acute{o}s$. Words so contracted were confined generally to sacred names and titles and words of frequent occurrence, and their inflections. They are (besides $\overline{\Theta C}$) : $\overline{IC} = \text{'}I\eta\sigma o\hat{v}s$, $\overline{XC} = X\rho\iota\sigma\tau\acute{o}s$, $\overline{YC} = v\acute{\iota}\acute{o}s$, $\overline{KC} = \kappa\acute{v}\rho\iota o s$, $\overline{\Pi P}$ and $\overline{\Pi AP} = \pi\acute{a}\tau\eta\rho$, $\overline{MP} = \mu\acute{\eta}\tau\eta\rho$, $\overline{ANOC} = \check{a}\nu\theta\rho\omega\pi o s$, $\overline{OYNOC} = o\dot{v}\rho a\nu\acute{o}s$, $\overline{\Theta KOC} = \theta\epsilon o\tau\acute{o}\kappa o s$, $\overline{\Pi NA}$

πνεῦμα, $\overline{CHP}=σωτήρ$, $\overline{CTPOC}$ and $\overline{CPOC}=σταυρός$, $\overline{\Delta A\Delta}=Δαυίδ$, $\overline{IHΛ}$ and $\overline{ICΛ}='Ισραήλ$, $\overline{IHΛM}='Iηρου-σαλήμ$. There are also a few other words contracted, as $\mathsf{K}=καί$, ᛩ = μοῦ, ᛩ =μοι; and the verbal termination $\overline{T}=ται$. Occasionally a proper name appears abbreviated on a different system, as $\overline{I\omega}='Iωάννης$.

Leaving these sacred and liturgical contractions for the present, we turn to the papyri of the third and second centuries B.C., which have been recovered from the tombs of Egypt, and see that here the system of simple abbreviation, or curtailment at the end of a word, was followed. Either the word was indicated by its initial letter alone with an abbreviating dash, as ύ = υἱοί; or the letter which immediately preceded the omitted portion was written above the line, as a key to the reading, thus : $τε^λ=τέλος$; or two letters were so written, as $τ^{εκ}=τέκνα$, $ομ^{οι}=ὁμοίως$. It is true that examples of such abbreviation are comparatively rare, but there are quite enough to prove that the system was recognized.[3] Certain of these over-written letters, even at this early period, betray a tendency to degenerate into dashes,[4] and this natural degeneration becomes more intensified in course of time. Thus, in the second and third centuries after Christ, this dash system is found to be developed to a considerable degree.

The same method of curtailing the endings of words may be traced in the Herculanean rolls, which must be at least as early as the first century of our era, together with certain monogrammatic forms, as $\overline{π}=πρός$, $\chi=χρόνος$; and the scribes of the recently discovered papyrus of Aristotle's work on the Constitution of Athens, of

---

[3] See *Flinders Petrie Papyri*, ed. Mahaffy (Royal Irish Academy, *Cunningham Memoirs*), 1891; particularly No. xxiii.

[4] Dr. U. Wilcken, *Observationes ad hist. Ægypti prov. Rom.* p. 40), selects from the Paris Papyrus No. 5 (*Notices et Extraits des MSS.*, pl. xvi.), of the year 114 B.C., the following, among other, contractions, $τρ^ε = τρδ[πε ζαν]$, $πτολε\frown=πτολεμ[αίου]$, $ασκλη^η=άσκληπ[ιάδης]$. In these we have the cursive form of a ($\prec$), of μ ($\frown$), and of π ($^$), which we find in the most cursively written documents of the third century B.C.

about A.D. 100, employed a regular system of abbreviation for prepositions and other words.[5] In the papyri
of succeeding centuries the same system is found at
work.   To descend to a later period, the palimpsest fragments of the Iliad in uncial writing of the sixth century,
in the British Museum, have several words curtailed, an
s-shaped mark indicating the omitted endings.   More
numerous are the examples in the fragment, preserved
at Milan, of a mathematical treatise of the seventh century, also written in uncials.   In this MS., dealing with
a subject in which technical expressions constantly occur,
an opportunity for the full employment of abbreviations
presented itself, and, accordingly, not only the ordinary
abbreviated endings, but still more tachygraphical signs
are used.   From the analogy of later MSS. it may be
taken for certain that all technical works, intended as
they were rather for the student than for public reading,
were subject to unrestrained contraction from very early
times.   In the few remaining Greek documents on
papyrus of the seventh and eighth centuries, the same
system is employed.   Thus, when the flood of the literary
minuscule writing of the ninth century suddenly rises
and sweeps over the uncial, it naturally brings with it
the old system of abbreviation which was still existent
in the cursive hand from which that writing sprang.
The history of that system, as we have seen, can be
traced only imperfectly, from lack of material, and is, as
it were, screened by the intervening system of the
uncial biblical and liturgical MSS., which, by the fact of
their surviving in fair numbers, have thrust themselves
into more general notice.

  With the disuse of uncial writing, however, as the

---

  [5] They are: ꝫ = termination αι, ὰ = ἀνά, γ′ = γάρ, δ′ = δε, δ′ =
διά, \ = εἶναι, / = ἐστί, ⌐ = εἰσί, θ′ = θαι, κ′ = καί, κ = κατά, μ′ = μέν,
μ′ = μετά, ο′ = οὖν, π̄ = παρά, π′ = περί or περ, ς′ = σύν, τ′ = τήν, τ′ = τῆς,
τ′ = τῶν, υ′ = ὑπέρ, υ′ = ὑπό ; and also ✳ = χρόνος, and the unusual
ⳑ = αὐτήν. Many of these abbreviations are used for syllables as
well as for independent words. In addition, terminations are
occasionally abbreviated with the over-written letter as μα^χ =
μάχην

ordinary literary hand, the biblical system of contraction did not perish. The same scribes who had copied out the majuscule texts were now employed upon the new minuscule, and naturally introduced into the latter the contractions which they had been accustomed to write in the former. In minuscule writing, therefore, from the ninth century onwards, any form of contraction or abbreviation may be looked for. At first, however, they were, in general, very sparingly used in the calligraphic MSS. of the period, although, when necessary, the apparatus was ready at hand to be applied, as in the case of marginal and interlinear scholia, where contractions were always more freely used than in the text of a MS. The horizontal stroke which marked contracted words in the biblical uncial texts served the same purpose in minuscules; it also distinguished letters which were used as numerals or special signs. But the ordinary terminal abbreviations were marked by an oblique stroke drawn under the line, as in $a\delta'/=\dot{a}\delta\epsilon\lambda\phi\acute{o}\varsigma$, $\pi o\lambda'/=\pi\acute{o}\lambda\epsilon\mu o\varsigma$, although this stroke was also often dispensed with, and a mere flourish added to the over-written letter. This over-written letter was also subject to modifications. It was doubled occasionally to indicate a plural, as, $\pi a\iota^{\delta\delta}/=\pi a\acute{\iota}\delta\omega\nu$, $\sigma\tau\iota^{\chi\chi}=\sigma\tau\acute{\iota}\chi o\iota$. It was also in some instances the emphatic letter of the omitted portion of the word, as $\lambda\acute{\gamma}/=\lambda\acute{\epsilon}\gamma\epsilon\iota\nu$, $\kappa^{\tau}/=\kappa a\tau\acute{a}$. And the arrangement of letters was sometimes inverted, as $\lambda_\gamma=\lambda\acute{o}\gamma o\varsigma$, $\wp=\ddot{o}\sigma\iota o\varsigma$.

But with the new minuscule writing also appears a further development of contraction in the use of certain signs, mostly tachygraphical, which are employed either as component parts of words, or as entire, independent words. They are employed to some extent also in late uncial MSS. They generally are found as terminations, but in MSS of the early minuscule period they are also used in the middle or at the beginning of words. For the most part, they are placed above the level of the words to which they belong; in a few instances they are pendent or in the line of writing. At the later period, when the writing became more cursive, these tachygraphical signs were linked with the letters below them

in a flourish. They also, even at an early date, show a
disposition to combine with the accents, as in Ꙃ which
is the sign ς (ης) combined with a circumflex. This combination begins in the twelfth century.

We will now proceed to give these signs in the alphabetical order of their meanings, beginning with the
vowels. But it will assist the memory materially if it is
borne in mind that, as in Greek tachygraphic writing
one sign represented several syllables, different in spell-
ing but phonetically the same, so the signs which we
are now considering may be phonetically grouped. For
example, in the two groups : —

$$\wedge \ \eta\nu. \quad \wedge\wedge \ \epsilon\iota\nu. \quad \nearrow \ \iota\nu.$$
$$\varsigma \ \eta\varsigma. \quad \varsigma\varsigma \ \epsilon\iota\varsigma. \quad \overset{..}{\varsigma} \ \iota\varsigma.$$

we see a sign representing a particular syllable differentiated by being doubled or marked to represent its
homophones. The same system will be observed in
other instances.

a is early represented by the tachygraphical sign,
a horizontal stroke —.[6] It was written either above
or in line with the preceding letter, as $\bar{\tau}$ or τ-, but in the
latter position, to aid the eye, it received the addition
of two dots, as τ^+, or, coalescing, $\dot{\tau}$. But this sign $\div$
thus dotted also indicated τa, as the two dots (:) were
also the tachygraphical sign for τ. In course of time
the construction was forgotten, and $\div$ was taken to mean
simply *a*, and, last of all, the — dropped out, and the
two dots remained to represent the letter.

ϵ is frequently represented by a short waved stroke, as
in the word $\mu_\iota^\epsilon = \mu\epsilon\gamma a$, and in participial terminations, as
$\lambda\epsilon\gamma\acute{o}\mu_\iota^\iota = \lambda\epsilon\gamma\acute{o}\mu\epsilon\nu o\varsigma$. This sign resembling that for the
diphthong $a\iota$, the two may be identical, ϵ and $a\iota$ being
homophones.

η is also occasionally found in a similarly waved-
stroke form, nearly always written in the line, as $\acute{\epsilon}\pi\epsilon\iota\delta\grave{\iota}$,
$\tau\grave{\iota}\nu$.

ι is very rarely represented by two dots (a late usage),
as $\pi^{\epsilon\iota} = \pi\epsilon\rho\grave{\iota}$.

---

[6] This mark for *a* appears in abbreviations in papyri of the
beginning of the third century. Wilcken, *op. cit.*

ω appears in the tachygraphical form of a kind of circumflex, as $ἄν͠γε=ἄνωγε$.

αι. The abbreviated sign of this termination is, in its earliest forms, an oblique or angular or s-shaped stroke, as $κ₁\ κ\ κ₁$; later, ordinarily a waved stroke, as $κ_s$ (which was afterwards exaggerated into a flourish); sometimes ∨, as $ἡμέρ^ν=ἡμέραι$.

αις. The earlier sign was $ι$, as $στήλ^ι=στήλαις$; later ", as $ταύτ"=ταύταις$. This second form appears to be a doubling of the sign for εs, a phonetic equivalent.

αν. An angular L and rounded $ι$ are found in early MSS. Then a further development in the curve took place, and a 6-shaped sign comes into use. $ὅτ^ι=ὅταν$, $πάσ̌=πάσαν$, $π̂ι=πᾶν$, $γεννάδ^δ=γεννάδαν$.

αρ. The horizontal stroke —, for a, and a ring representing $ρ$, were combined as the sign $ᴐ$, as $μ̃ιυρεῖ=μαρτυρεῖ$. Or it was turned upwards, $ἀμ̃τιάν=ἀμαρτίαν$; or written in the line, as $μ₊ᴐτυς=μαρτυς$, with dots representing a.

ας. The constant sign was $ᴊ$, as $στίχ^σ=στίχας$; $χρήσ^σθαι=χρήσασθαι$.

αυ. From a combination of —, for a, and the upsilon, comes the sign $ᴠ$, as $θ͠μάζει=θαυμάζει$. A rare sign is $ℏ$, as $τοιήτη=τοιαύτη$.

ειν. At first was used a single sign ∧ (*i.e.* also the sign for ην, a phonetic equivalent), as $ἐπιμέν^=ἐπιμένειν$. Then this was doubled for distinction's sake ∧∧; afterwards one or both of the hooks are thrown off $//$, $//$; and finally the strokes are reduced in length $//$. $εἰπ͡ᴧ=εἰπεῖν$, $λειπ"=λείπειν$.

εις. The sign $ς$, which represents ης, was sometimes also used for εις; more generally it was doubled, as $τιθᴂ=τιθεὶς$. Another rare form is $Oʃ$ which appears to be the ordinary ligature of ε and ι with a cross stroke.

εν. An angle L, as $μ̃=μὲν$, which afterwards took a more rounded form, as $γέγοὺ=γέγονεν$, degenerating at a later period into L, or even into a looped flourish like a wide a. The tachygraphic sign $ᴜ$ is also occasionally found in use.

ερ. The oblique stroke, the tachygraphic sign for ε, combines with a loop, for ρ, and makes the sign *b*, as ὥσπ*ᵇ* = ὥσπερ, εἴπ𝖻=εἴπερ. More rarely a bar is used as ὑπⱦ = ὕπερ, ὥσπⱦ = ὥσπερ.

ες. The early sign was *ʃ*, as φάγοντʃ = φάγοντες. But two dots, representing tachygraphically the letter τ, being frequently added in the common termination τες, *ʃ̈*, a confusion between *ʒ̈* and *ʃ* was the result, and at last *ʒ̈* came to be used for ες, as λύοιτʒ̈ = λύοντες, and superseded the simple *ʃ*. The sign, thus changed, varies occasionally in form as, ᵌ Ꞌᴣ G.

ην. The angular form ∧, as τ᷄ ἀρχ̂ = τὴν ἀρχὴν, was sometimes curved, as τοιαυτ᷄ ⹀ τοιαύτην. Later it degenerated into ⋏, ⋏, as ἀρεⱦ = ἀρετὴν.

ηρ. A not common sign is ∾, as ἀ᷆ⱱ̑ = ἀνὴρ.

ης. A sign resembling ς, as ⱦ̇ = τῆς. This sign early combined with the circumflex as ⴳ. It is sometimes doubled.

ιν. The sign for ην was often used also for this termination. It was also differentiated by two dots, thus, τάξᷟ=τάξιν. It passed through the same stages of degeneration as its prototype.

ις. The sign for ης was also used for ις. It was also differentiated by two dots, thus, αὐτⱦ̈=αὖτις. The signs for ις and ης are sometimes confused.

οις. A horizontal stroke terminating in an angular or round hook, ⟶ ⟶; λόγ᷄ =λόγοις. In later MSS. the sign is subject to flourishing. In some instances the position is oblique, as τ∫̂ =τοῖς.

ον. The oblique stroke ⟍, as λόγ᷄=λόγον. The danger of confusion with the grave accent led to its being lengthened; but this eventually resulted in the lengthening of the accent also, as τ⁗=τὸν. In late MSS. the sign degenerates into a flourish, or waved line.

ος. The tachygraphical sign for ος is sometimes used, as λογ᷄=λόγος; sometimes the uncial c, as ἕκαστ𝖼= ἕκαστος.

ου. An early form √ appears in a few places, as ⱦⱦ᷄ =

τούτου; this is afterwards curved, as τ̂=τοῦ. The form Ⴤ, which is not uncommon, is a monogram of the two letters.

ουν. The *o* with a waved stroke beneath, as ποι̦ c̄= ποιοῦντος, ἤγ͜ϙ=ἤγουν.

ους. The sign ५, which is formed by combination of υ=ου and ς; as λόγ५=λόγους, ἵππ ५ = ἵππους. The double waved stroke ″ (as in εις) is also used : as χρον″= χρόνους; also single, as αὐτ′=αὐτούς.

ων. A sign resembling a circumflex ; in early MSS., of small size, as τούτ̂=τούτων ; afterwards, a sweeping flourish, as διαφο͡ρ͡=διαφορῶ.

ωρ. A not common sign ⸏ or ⸏, as ὕδ⸴=ὕδωρ, ῥήτ⸴= ῥήτωρ.

ως. A curving line ⸜, ᷄, as οὔτ⸴=οὔτως, ⸜͜περ= ὥσπερ. Later, the sign turns downwards, as καλ∫=καλῶς.

Certain prepositions and particles are represented by special signs, as—

ἀντί : Ɔ, a very rare sign.

ἀπο : ℓ⋁ and ⸱∨ ; a rare sign is ᒧ.

ἀρα : ⱴ.

διά : ⟁, or Δ with a waved pendant.

ἐπί : ∂̂, the ∂ being the cursive form of π.

ἵνα : ⸂.

κατά : ᐯᵀ, ∨⁺, ⸦.

πρός : Ƨ, ⸨.

ὑπέρ : ⅄, or Ⴤ.

ὑπό : ᵡ, U⋁.

παρά : π̣, also π⋇.

γάρ : ᶃ, or ᶃ, ⌐⁺, ⌐ᵟ ; that is, *gamma* crossed with an inverted ρ, or with a bar or flourish.

μέν : ⌐⸜.

δέ : ⸃, which becomes round ⸃. In course of time it was confused with the sign for ες (*j*); hence the scribes came to add dots.

ἤγουν : ηⰯ .

καί. From the tachygraphical form ५ (κε) came the sign ८, which went through various changes : ৮ ५ ३ ૩ ૭.

ὁμοῦ : ⁜, very rare.

ὅτι : ⁙. ૪ (the dots indicating the τ); also .ρ̇.

ὥσπερ : ૪.

The auxiliary ἐστί or ἐστίν was represented by the tachygraphic ·/. (ἐστί) or ⟋ (ἐστίν) ; but this distinction was not kept up. Later, from confusion with the sign for ιν (⟋), the position of the dots was altered, and the sign became ⟋̇, which afterwards passed into the flourished style, on the pattern of the signs for ην and ιν. A double ἐστί, ·//., was used for εἰσί; and in the same manner ⫽ or ⫽ =εἰσίν. And, perhaps on the same analogy, ∾ =εἶναι.[7] The future ἔσται is found in the forms ૭ , ८.

Certain signs were also used for technical words, as ξ = ἀριθμός, ξξ=ἀριθμοί ; ꙗ, ꙗ =ἴσος, ἴσοι ; ✕=ἐλάσσων. And, finally, there were certain symbols for certain words, as ⊙=κύκλος, ૮=ἡμέρα, ૧=νύξ, L=ἔτος, ૪ = ἄρουρα, ⊦, S, ৮=δραχμή, and others.

Latin.

Of Latin abbreviations the most ancient forms, as already stated, are those which consist of a single letter (nearly always the initial letter), representing the whole word. The most ordinary instances of such single-letter abbreviations, or *sigla*, are those which indicate proper names, or titles, or words of common occurrence, and which are familiar to us, not only in the inscriptions on coins and monuments, but also in the texts of classical writers ; being generally distinguished from other letters or words by the full point which is placed after them. The same system was followed in the middle ages and survives at the present day.

But the representation of words by single letters could only be carried out to a certain limited extent. Obviously the same letter must do duty for many words

---

[7] In Pap. cxxxvii., in the British Museum, probably of the 2nd century, these forms are used : ╱ = ἐστί, ╲ = εἶναι, ╲╲ = εἰσί; and û for the feminine cases of the participle, οὖσα, οὔσης, etc.

and confusion be the consequence. Hence arises a
farther extension of the system: the use of special
marks, or of two or more letters. The Romans wrote
M'.=Manius, to distinguish that name from M.=Marcus ;
Cn.=Gnæus, to prevent confusion with C.=Gaius. These
simple methods of abbreviation led on to others, the
development of which can be traced in the early legal
MSS., such as the Gaius of Verona, or the waxen
tablets, and particularly in the "Notarum Laterculi" or
"Notæ Juris"—the lists of abbreviations used in the
Roman law-books.[8] In these documents, as regards
single-letter abbreviations, we find not only such forms
as A.=*aut,* C.=*causa,* D.=*divus,* E.=*est,* and so on,
any of which might occur independently in a sentence,
but also whole phrases, as, C. D. E. R. N. E.=*cujus de
ea re notio est,* or A. T. M. D. O.=*aio te mihi dare
oportere,* showing to what an extent this elementary
system could be employed in books of a technical
nature. Indeed, in technical works, single-letter
phrases continued to be used in MSS. down to the
invention of printing. But the inconvenience of such
abbreviations is seen in such double meanings as A.=*aut*
or *annus,* C.=*causa* or *circa,* D.=*divus* or *dedit,* F.=
fecit or *familia* or *fides.* Yet the sense of the context
might be depended upon for giving the correct inter-
pretation, and confusion was also, in some instances,
obviated by the addition of a distinguishing mark, such
as a horizontal stroke placed above the letter or an apostrophe or similar sign placed after it, as N̄=*non,* N'=*nec.*
The representation of words by two or more of their letters
is seen in such abbreviations as IT̄=*item,* ACT.=*actum,*
AN̄=*ante,* ED.=*edictum,* IMP̄=*imperator,* COM.=
comes, EŌ=*eorum,* CUĪ=*cujus,* FŪ=*fuit,* in which the
first letters of each word are written ; or in such contractions as EX̄P=*exemplum,* OM̄B=*omnibus,* MMT̄=
momentum, BR̄=*bonorum,* HD̄=*heredem,* where the
salient letters are expressed, in some instances with a

[8] See in Keil, *Grammatici Latini,* iv. 265, the *Notarum Laterculi,* ed. Mommsen.

H

view to indicating the inflections. From this latter method was developed the more systematic syllabic system, in which the leading letters of the syllables were expressed, as E$\overline{\text{G}}$=*ergo,* H$\overline{\text{R}}$=*heres,* Q$\overline{\text{D}}$=*quidem,* Q$\overline{\text{B}}$=*quibus,* Q$\overline{\text{R}}$=*quare,* S$\overline{\text{T}}$=*satis,* M$\overline{\text{T}}$=*mentem,* T$\overline{\text{M}}$=*tamen,* S$\overline{\text{N}}$=*sine,* B$\overline{\text{N}}$=*bene,* D$\overline{\text{D}}$=*deinde,* and the like.

But still there remained the need of indicating inflections and terminations more exactly than by this simple process. This want was supplied in the first place by the adoption of certain of the Tironian symbols —others of those shorthand signs being at the same time used for certain prepositions or prefixes—and also by smaller over-written letters, as $\overset{o}{\text{Q}}$=*quo,* $\overset{m}{\text{V}}$=*verum,* $\overset{c}{\text{H}}$=*hunc,* $\overset{c}{\text{T}}$=*tunc.* This over-writing was not, however, confined to the indication of terminations : it was also adopted for general use to mark leading letters, as in $\overset{i}{\text{S}}$=*sint,* $\overset{o}{\text{N}}$=*noster,* $\overset{o}{\text{S}}$=*sors,* and others. As will presently be seen, it holds an important place in the scheme of later mediæval contraction.

The principles of the different methods sketched out above held good also throughout the later middle ages ; but of the simple letter-forms only a certain number survived. They were too arbitrary to be continued in general use, and more exact and convenient combinations and signs took their place. Even where they still survived in form their original meaning was sometimes superseded ; *e.g.* the early syllabic contraction T$\overline{\text{M}}$= *tamen* under the later system becomes *tantum.* The period of transition from the old to the new system lies in the course of the eighth and ninth centuries, at the time when the Carlovingian schools were effecting their great reform in the handwriting of Europe, and had the authority to enforce the adoption of settled forms. By the eleventh century the later system had grown to full development. It reached its culminating point in the thirteenth century, the period when contraction was more excessively used than at any other ; but after that date marks and symbols are less rigidly formed and gradually degenerate into hasty dashes and flourishes.

Having thus traced the general construction of Latin abbreviation and contraction, we may now briefly notice the various signs and marks which are employed for this purpose in the MSS. of the middle ages.

Abbreviated Latin words may be ranged in two classes: (1) Those in which the ending is suppressed, as fec̄=*fecit*; (2) Those in which letters are omitted from the middle, or from the middle and end, of the word, as cā=*causa*, ōīō=*omnino*, p̄rb=*presbyter*. To the first class the French have given the title "abbré-viations par suspension"; we call them simply "abbre-viations," and include among them those early forms, noticed above, which are composed of one, two, or more of the first letters of a word, and the numerous examples, particularly verbs, which, more especially in the ninth and tenth centuries, simply threw away the last syllable. The words in the second class are "contractions," being contracted by the omission of medial, or medial and final, letters.

Marks or signs of abbreviation or contraction are either general or special. General signs are those which indicate the suppression of one or more letters without giving a direct clue to what such letters may be. Special signs indicate the suppression of particular letters. Among the latter must be also included over-written letters which, in some instances, have in course of time changed their forms and have worn down into mere symbols.

The earliest and simplest mark of abbreviation is the full point, usually placed on a level with the middle of the letter or letters of the abbreviated word as A˙=*aut*, FF˙=*fratres*, or—to give the commonest, and often the only, abbreviations in early majuscule MSS.—B˙=(ter-mination) *bus*, Q˙=*que*. In place of the full point, a colon or semicolon was next employed, as in B: B; Q: Q;, and the latter, becoming the favourite form, grew, by rapid writing, into a 3-shaped sign, which appears from the eleventh century onwards as b3=*bus*, q3=*que*.

From its frequent recurrence in the latter common word it even came to represent the *q* as well as *ue*, in composition, as at3=*atque*, ne3=*neque*. But it was not confined to the representation of terminal *us* and *ue;* it also appears for termination *et*, as in deb3=*debet*, p̵l3= *placet*, s3=*set* (*i.e. sed*): a survival of which is seen in the z in our common abbreviation viz.=*videlicet*. At a later period it also represented final m, as in na3=*nam*, ite3=*item*, ide3=*idem*.

The same 3-shaped sign likewise is found sometimes as the sign for *est* in composition, as in inter3=*interest*. But here it has a different derivation, being a cursive rendering of the symbol ÷=*est*.

The horizontal stroke is the most general mark both of abbreviation and contraction, and in both uses it may indicate the omission of many letters. We have seen it in use in the "Notæ Juris." It is usually either a straight or a waved line. In early carefully-written MSS. it is ornamentally formed with hooks at the ends ⌐⌐. In the case of charters, it is sometimes fancifully shaped, as an oblique crotchet, or as a loop or knot. In its simplest use as a mark of abbreviation it is found in majuscule MSS. at the end (rarely in the body) of a line to indicate omission of final M or N. It was placed above the line, at first to the right, as AUTE¯=*autem;* and in some instances a point was added to distinguish omission of M from omission of N, as ENI⁻̇=*enim*, NO¯=*non*. Afterwards the simple stroke was placed above the last letter, as ENĪ, NŌ.

Analogous to the horizontal stroke is the oblique stroke, which takes the place of the horizontal chiefly in words in which the tall minuscule letters b and l occur, as ap̵li=*apostoli*, m̵lto=*multo*, lib̵e=*libere*, proc̵l=*procul*.

Of the same class is the waved vertical stroke (sometimes in the form of a curve rising from the preceding letter), often used to signify the omission of *er* or *re;* as b̍niter=*breviter*, c̍tus=*certus*.

Less frequent, because it dropped out of general use, is the final oblique stroke, also found in the earlier abbreviations, usually for terminations *us, ur, um* (after *r*), as an╪ = *anus*, amam╪ = *amamus*, amat╪ = *amatur*, re⅄ = *rerum*. Of these, the last termination *rum* continued to be represented in this way, especially in words in the genitive plural.[9]

Another general sign of early use was the round curve or comma above the line, which, as late as the ninth century, continued to represent the terminations *ur, os, us.* In later MSS. the curve alone was retained to indicate the termination *us* (sometimes *os*), and so became a special sign (see below).

A long drooping stroke attached to the end of a word is often found as a general sign to indicate the omission of any termination. It is, however, specially used for termination *is.* In the fourteenth century it develops into a loop, as dictℓ = *dictis.*

A sign nearly resembling an inverted *c* or the numeral 9, Tironian in its origin, usually signifies the syllable *con* or *com*, also more rarely *cun* or *cum*, as 9do = *condo*, 9munis = *communis*, cir9scriptus = *circumscriptus*, 9cti = *cuncti*.[10] It always stands in the line of writing. A similar sign (to which reference has already been made), above the line, represents the termination *us*, as bon⁹ = *bonus;* also more rarely *os*, as n = *nos*, p⁹t = *post.* In the last word it is sometimes used for the whole termination *ost*, as p⁹.

A sign somewhat resembling the numeral 2 placed obliquely ⅔, also derived from a Tironian note, is written for the termination *ur*, as amat⅔ = *amatur.* It is also placed horizontally, as fert² = *fertur.* Being commonly employed in the case of verbs, it also sometimes stands for the whole termination *tur*, as ama².

The letter p having a curve drawn through the down stroke, ℘, is to be read *pro.* In Visigothic MSS., however, it signifies *per*, very rarely *pro*, which is usually in such MSS. written in full. P crossed with a horizontal bar,

---

A curious result of the use of this sign is seen in the second name for Salisbury, "Sarum." The Latin Sarisburia in abbreviated form was written Sar╪, and came to be read *Sarum.*

[10] The letter c surmounted by a horizontal line also represents *con.*

p, is *per*, also *par, por*, as p̶tem=*partem*, optet,=*oportet*.
The same letter with a horizontal or waved oblique
stroke or curve placed above it (when not at the end of
a word) becomes *pre*, as p̄sertim=*presertim*, p'bet=
prebet.

The following conventional signs, mostly derived
from Tironian notes, are also used with more or less
frequency :—

Ƙ=*autem*, ϶=*ejus*, = =*esse*, ⸫=*est* (which degenerates into a ʒ-shaped sign: see above), p̄=*per*, 7=*et*
7̄=*etiam*, ℕ (later ⊢⊢ and ·⊢⊢· and thence ·n·)=*enim*,
·i·=*id est*, ł=*vel*, ⊖=*obiit, obitus*, v̇ and u̇=*ut*.

In this place may also be noticed the Latin contracted
form of our Lord's name. The name of Jesus Christ
was always written in Greek letters by mediæval scribes,
and in contracted form it appeared in majuscule MSS.
thus : **IHC XPC**, in Greek uncials. When these words
had to be written in minuscule letters, the scribes treated
them as purely Latin words written in Latin letters,
and transcribed them ih̄c (or ih̄s) xp̄c. Hence arose the
idea that the form Ihesus was the correct one, and by
false analogy the letter h was introduced into other
proper names, as Iherusalem, Iheronimus. Similarly
the terminating letter c, for s, was carried over by
scribes to other words, as ep̄c=*episcopus*, sp̄c=*spiritus*,
tp̄c=*tempus*.

Most ordinarily, over-written letters are vowels, to
which the letter r has to be supplied to solve the reading, as gᵃtia=*gratia*, cᵃta=*carta*, tᵉs=*tres*, uᵉba=*verba*,
pⁱor=*prior*, uⁱtus=*virtus*, agᵒs=*agros*, cᵒpus=*corpus*,
pᵘdens=*prudens*, tᵘris=*turris*. The more usual contractions of this character are those in which the r pre-
cedes the vowel. Other letters may also be understood,
as in qᵃ=*qua*, boᵃ=*bona*, qⁱbus=*quibus*, mⁱ=*mihi*, mᵒ=
modo. The letter a when over-written frequently takes
the open form (u) which degenerates into a mere zigzag
horizontal line or flattened u (∿).

When consonants are over-written the number of
letters to be supplied is quite uncertain : a single vowel
is omitted in such words as nᶜ=*nec*, hᶜ=*hic*; several

letters are understood in such a contraction as p^t=*potest.* The over-written consonant is usually the last letter of the word.[1]

In some instances two or more letters are over-written as hu^{jot}=*hujusmodi,* incorp^{les}=*incorporales ;* but such full forms are seldom wanted.

By metathesis, the contractions of certain common words, in which the letter g is prominent, take a special form, as g^i and g^r=*igitur,* g^a=*erga,* g^o=*ergo.*

The amount of contraction in a MS. depended to a considerable extent upon the character of the text. As has been already observed, technical books were more contracted than works of general literature. In MSS. written in majuscule letters, and particularly in biblical and liturgical codices, which were specially required for public reading, the contractions are very few: the omission of final M or N, Q·=*que,* B·=*bus,* Q$\overline{\text{M}}$ or Q$\overline{\text{N}}$M=*quoniam,* D$\overline{\text{S}}$=*Deus* and its inflections, D$\overline{\text{M}}$S or D$\overline{\text{N}}$S=*Dominus* and its inflections, the name of our Lord (see above), S$\overline{\text{C}}$S=*sanctus,* S$\overline{\text{P}}$S=*spiritus,* and a few other common words. With the introduction of minuscule writing for the book-hand, and when MSS. were employed for private use, there was more scope for this convenient system of saving labour and space; but in works intended for popular use there was seldom an excess of contraction or the employment of arbitrary forms such as to render the reading of the text difficult. When once the elements and principles of the system are understood, and the eye has been fairly practised, no ordinary MS. will present difficulties to the reader. As regards texts written in the vernacular languages of those countries of Europe which have adopted the Roman alphabet, it will be found that contractions are more rarely used in them than in MSS. written in Latin. A system suited to the inflections and

---

[1] With regard to over-written s, it may be noted that in Visigothic writing a sign resembling that letter is used in the word q$^\bullet$ *que,* which however is derived from the cursive form of over-written u.

terminations of this language could not be well adapted to other languages so different in their structure.

Numerals.

In Greek MSS. we find two systems of expressing numbers by signs, both being taken from the alphabet. It appears to have been the older practice to use the initial letter of the name of the number for its symbol, as ΤΤ for 5, Δ for 10, H (aspirate) for 100, X for 1000, M for 10,000. This has been called the Herodian system, after the name of the grammarian who described it. It is found in use in the papyri, especially in the stychometrical memoranda of the numbers of the lines contained in them; and such notes are also found transmitted to vellum MSS. of the middle ages.

The other system was to take the first nine letters of the alphabet for the units, and the rest for the tens and hundreds, disused letters being still retained for numeration, viz., F, *digamma*, for 6, which in its early form appears as ϛ or ς, and afterwards, in the middle ages, becomes ϙ, like the combined σ and τ or *stigma*; ϙ, *koppa*, for 90; and a symbol derived from the old letter *san*, which appears in papyri [2] as T or Τ, and at later periods as ϡ which, from its partial resemblance to *pi*, was called *sampi* (=*san*+*pi*), for 900. This system was in full use in the third century B.C.

The practice of numbering the successive books of a work, as *e.g.* the twenty-four books of the Iliad, by the successive letters of the alphabet, is hardly a system of numeration in the proper sense of the word. In certain cases, we find it convenient to make use of our alphabet in a somewhat similar way, to mark a series.

The numerals were usually distinguished from the letters of the text by a horizontal stroke: thus $\bar{a}$. To

---

[2] See *e.g. Cat. of Greek Papyri in the Brit. Mus.*, pp. 47, 5ᷱ.

indicate thousands a stroke was added to the left of the numeral: thus $\mathcal{T}=3000$; which at a later period was detached, thus $\mathcal{T}$. Dots were sometimes added to indicate tens of thousands, as $\ddot{a}$, $\cdot\dot{\mathrm{A}}\cdot$, $\cdot\dot{\mathrm{B}}\cdot$. Special symbols were sometimes used for fractions, sometimes an accent or a line above the numeral indicated the fraction: as $\cup$ or $\mathcal{C}=\frac{1}{2}$, $\acute{\gamma}=\frac{1}{3}$, $\cup\acute{\gamma}=\frac{1}{2}+\frac{1}{3}=\frac{5}{6}$, $\gamma^{\circ}=\frac{2}{3}$, $\delta'=\frac{1}{4}$, etc. The o which appears for the numerator in $\frac{2}{3}$ is derived from the cursive form of β, and is found in other combinations in papyri. The δ for $\frac{1}{4}$ also appears in form of a Roman d; and $\frac{3}{4}$ is represented by a variant of it, $\epsilon\!\!\!\downarrow$. The symbols $-$, $=$, $\digamma$, $\digamma$, $\digamma$, stand for obols, from one to five.

The Roman system of numerals was used throughout the middle ages (and, indeed, it lasts to our own day), and was not displaced by the introduction of the Arabic system, although the latter, from its convenience, was widely adopted. The Roman system was continued as the more official, and money accounts were calculated in its numerals.

This is not the place to discuss the origin of the Roman numerals; it is sufficient to say that the system was not an alphabetical one, for, although C (100) has been said to be the first letter of *centum* and M (1000) the first letter of *mille*, both these signs had a different derivation, and by a natural process only took the forms of the letters which they resembled most nearly.[3]

To distinguish the numerals from the letters of the text they were placed between points: thus $\cdot$XL$\cdot$. Besides the ordinary method of indicating thousands by repetitions of M, units with horizontal strokes above were also employed for the purpose: thus, $\cdot\bar{\mathrm{I}}\cdot$, $\cdot\bar{\mathrm{II}}\cdot$, $\cdot\bar{\mathrm{III}}\cdot$, etc. Certain special signs occur in some MSS.: as the Visigothic $\mathcal{T}=1000$, and $\mathcal{X}=40$, and the not very uncommon sign $\mathsf{G}=6$ which has been derived from the Greek symbol, but which may be only a combination of

See Zangemeister, *Entstehung der römischen Zahlzeichen*, in the *Sitzb. der k. Preussischen Akademie*, 1887.

U (V) and I. A cross stroke traversing a numeral sometimes indicates reduction by half a unit, as ii$+$= 2½, $\times$=9½, x$\times$=19½.

Arabic numerals first appear in European MSS. in the twelfth century, their early use being general in mathematical works; by the fourteenth century they had become universal. They have not much changed in form since their first introduction, the greatest difference from the modern shapes being seen in $\wp$=4, and ५=5.

CHAPTER VIII.

GREEK PALÆOGRAPHY.

Papyri.

THE first discovery of Greek papyri in Egypt took place in the year 1778, when fifty rolls were found in the neighbourhood of Memphis. Unfortunately, all but one were carelessly destroyed; the survivor was presented to Cardinal Stefano Borgia, under whose auspices it was published in 1788, *Charta papyracea Musei Borgiani Velitrii*, by Schow. It is of the year 191 after Christ. This find was followed early in the present century by the discovery of a collection, enclosed, according to the story of the Arabs who found it, in a single vessel, on the site of the Serapeum or temple of Serapis at Memphis. The finders divided the hoard among themselves, and hence the collection found its way piecemeal into different libraries of western Europe. Paris secured the largest number, which have been published, with an atlas of facsimiles, in the *Notices et Extraits des Manuscrits de la Bibliothèque Impériale*, etc., vol. xviii., 1865. A certain number fell to the share of the British Museum, and will be published in the *Catalogue of Greek Papyri in the British Museum.* Some are in the Vatican, and others are at Leyden.

The larger number of the documents thus brought to light have perpetuated a little domestic romance, and have preserved the memory of two poor twin sisters and the wrongs they endured in the second century B.C. Thaues and Thaus were the daughters of a native of Memphis, who in an unhappy hour married a woman named Nephoris. Deserted by her, and maltreated by her paramour, he fled away and died; and the twins were forthwith turned out of doors. But a friend was at hand. Among the recluses of the temple of Serapis was one Ptolemy, son of Glaucias, a Macedonian by birth, whose father had settled in the nome of Heracleopolis, and who had entered on his life of seclusion in the year 173 B.C. As an old friend of their father, he now came forward and obtained for the two girls a place in the temple. Their duties, upon which they entered in the year 165 B.C., included the offering of libations to the gods, a service which entitled them to certain allowances of oil and bread. All went well for a brief six months, but then the supplies began to fall into arrears. The poor twins tried in vain to get their rights, and their appeals to the subordinate officials, who had probably diverted the allowances to their own use, were disregarded. Again the good Ptolemy came to the rescue and took the matter in hand; and very pertinaceously did he pursue the claims. Petition after petition issued from his ready pen. Appeals to the governor; appeals to the king; reference to one official was referred again to another, who in his turn, passed it on to a third; reports were returned, duly docketed, and pigeon-holed; again they were called for, and the game was carried on in a way which would do credit to the government offices of the most civilized nation. But Ptolemy was not to be beaten. We know that he at length succeeded in getting for the twins payment of a large portion of arrears, and at the moment when the documents cease he is still left fighting. That his efforts were eventually crowned with a full success we cannot doubt; and thus ends the story of the twins.

These documents, then, and certain others including other petitions and documents of the persistent Ptolemy, form the bulk of the collection which was found on the site of the Serapeum at Memphis. Its palæographical value cannot be too highly estimated. Here, thanks chiefly to the ready pen of an obscure recluse, a fairly numerous series of documents bearing dates in the second century B.C. has descended to us. If the sands of Egypt had preserved a collection of such trivial intrinsic importance, probably from the accident of its being buried in the tomb of the man who had written so many of its documents, what might not be looked for if the last resting-place of a scholar were found? The expectations that papyri inscribed with the works of Greek classical authors, and written in Egypt or imported thither during the reigns of the Ptolemies or in the Roman period, would sooner or later come to light gradually began to be realized.

Several papyri containing books, or fragments of books, of Homer's Iliad have been recovered. The most ancient appears to be the one (the "Harris Homer") containing a large portion of Book xviii., which was found in 1849–1850 by Mr. A. C. Harris, in the Crocodile Pit at Ma'abdeh, in the Fayoum, and is now in the British Museum (*Cat. Anc. MSS.*, i. pl. 1; *Pal. Soc.* ii. pl. 64). It is probably of the 1st century B.C. Of later date is the "Bankes Homer," containing the greater part of Book xxiv., which was bought at Elephantine by the traveller William Bankes, and is also in the British Museum (*Cat. Anc. MSS.*, i. pl. 6; *Pal. Soc.* ii. pl. 153). A third important MS. of Homer, which has also lately found its way into the national collection (Brit. Mus., Papyrus cxxvi.), is the papyrus in form of a book, inscribed on the front of each leaf with the Iliad, from line 101 of Book ii. to line 40 of Book iv., the longest portion of the poem that has hitherto been found on papyrus. It was discovered in the same Crocodile Pit as the Harris Homer, and also belonged to Mr. Harris. It is not, however, of early date, being probably as late as the 4th century; but it has a special interest from the existence, on the back of three of the leaves, of a portion of a treatise on Greek grammar, which gives an outline of various parts of speech, and which bears in its title the name of Tryphon, a grammarian who flourished in the latter half of the first century B.C. The treatise, however, is probably only an abstract of the work of that writer. Besides these comparatively perfect Homeric papyri, there are others of a more fragmentary character:

as the British Museum papyrus cxxviii., containing considerable portions of the Iliad, Books xxiii. and xxiv., and the fragments in the Louvre of Books vi., xiii., and xviii. (*Not. et Extr.*, pl. xii., xlix.), all of an early period; of later date, papyri cxxvii. and cxxxvi. in the British Museum, containing portions of Books iii., iv., v., vi., and xviii. Lastly there are the fragments of Book ii. in large characters, perhaps as late as the fifth or sixth century, found by Mr. Flinders Petrie at Hawara, and presented to the Bodleian Library (*Hawara, etc.*, ed. Petrie, 1889, pl. xxiii.).

An important addition has been made to classical literature by the recovery of several of the orations of the Athenian orator Hyperides. The papyrus containing his orations for Lycophron and Euxenippus is in unusually good condition and measures eleven feet in length. It may be of the 1st century B.C. Other portions of the same roll contain fragments of his oration against Demosthenes (see editions of Professor Babington, 1850, 1853; *Cat. Anc. MSS.*, i. pl. 2, 3; *Pal. Soc.*, i. pl. 126). A fourth work of the same author is the funeral oration which he delivered over the Athenian general Leosthenes and his comrades, who fell in the Lamian war in 323 B.C. (ed. Babington, 1858). The date of this text was formerly placed in the 1st or 2nd century B.C.; a horoscope of a person born in A D. 95 being inscribed on the other side of the papyrus. But it has now been proved that the oration is on the *verso* side of the papyrus (*i.e.* the side on which the fibres run vertically), and therefore was written subsequently to the horoscope; and, further, the faults in orthography and the rough character of the writing have led to the conclusion that it is a student's exercise. All the papyri of Hyperides just enumerated are in the British Museum, and in a collection of documents recently acquired by the trustees there has also been found the concluding portion of an oration, which is believed to belong to the speech against Philippides, in writing earlier than the Christian era. The Museum of the Louvre has also purchased lately an important papyrus of the period of the Ptolemies, in which is a work which is identified as an oration of Hyperides against Athenogenes (*Revue Egyptologique*, 1892). When it is borne in mind that none of the works of this orator was known to have survived until the reappearance of these long-buried papyrus rolls, the significance of the recovery of a lost author and the promise which was thus held out of possibly greater prizes have accustomed the world to be ever on the look-out for the " semper aliquid novi " from Africa.

The large collection of papyrus documents and fragments which a few years ago passed into the possession of the Archduke Rainer attracted considerable attention. Slowly, and with the expenditure of much patience and skill, they are being deciphered and published. But sifted, as they chiefly are, from the sand and light soil of the Fayoum, the rags and tatters of ancient dust-bins, they could not be expected to yield any text of considerable extent. A fragment of Thucydides has come to light (*Wiener Studien*, vii. 1885), and other such pieces may yet be found. But they would rank only with such discoveries as that of the fragment of the writings of the poet Alcman, now in the Louvre (*Not. et Extr.*, pl. l.), whetting the appetite it is true, but adding very little to the stock of Greek literature. The Rainer collection is, however, of very great palæographical importance. It covers a wide period, and illustrates in particular the writing of the early centuries of our era, of which we have hitherto had but scanty examples.

But the most important recent discovery that has been made, as far as palæography is concerned, is that of Mr. Flinders Petrie at the village of Gurob in the Fayoum. Here he found that the cartonnage coffins which he obtained from the necropolis were composed of papyri pasted together in layers, fortunately not in all instances too effectively. The result of careful separation has been that a large number of documents dated in the third century B.C. have been recovered. These, together with a few of the same century which are scattered in different libraries of Europe, and whose early date had not in some instances been hitherto recognized, are the most ancient specimens of Greek writing (as distinguished from sculptured inscriptions) in existence above ground.[1] Besides miscellaneous documents, there are not inconsiderable remains of registers of wills, entered up from time to time, and thus presenting us with a variety of different handwritings as practised under the early Ptolemies. Still more interesting in a literary aspect are the fragments of the *Phædo* of Plato, and of the lost play, the *Antiope,* of Euripides, which have happily been gleaned from the Gurob mummy-cases. The tragedians had already been represented by the finding some years ago of a fragment of papyrus, on which were written some lines supposed to come from the *Temenides* of Euripides, and others from the *Medæa* (H. Weil, *Un papyrus inédit de la Bibl. de M. A. Firmin-Didot,* 1879); and the date of the writing is at least as old as the year 161 B.C. But by the recovery of the classical fragments at Gurob, we are brought within almost measurable distance of the authors. Indeed, this copy of the *Phædo,* written, as there is good reason to believe, within a hundred years of the death of Plato, can hardly differ in appearance, in a very material degree, from the copies which were published in his lifetime. The only other extant document that can be compared, as regards style of writing, with these fragments, is the papyrus at Vienna, inscribed with an invocation of a certain Artemisia, which has been ascribed to the 4th century, and may with certainty be placed as early as the first half of the 3rd century B.C. It will be noticed below.

These discoveries, of such inestimable value for the history both of Greek palæography and of Greek literature, had been scarcely announced, when the world was astonished by the appearance of a copy, written about the end of the first or beginning of the second century,

---

[1] A selection of these papyri has been recently published in the *Cunningham Memoirs* of the Royal Irish Academy (*On the Flinders Petrie Papyri,* by Rev. J. P. Mahaffy, 1891).

of Aristotle's treatise on the Constitution of Athens, the Πολιτεία τῶν 'Αθηναίων, a work which had vanished from sight more than a thousand years ago. The papyrus containing this valuable text came into possession of the British Museum in the course of the year 1890. Like the Funeral Oration of Hyperides, the work is written on the back of a disused document, the account-roll of a farm bailiff in the district of Hermopolis in Egypt, rendered in the reign of Vespasian, A.D. 78-79. Four hands were employed in the transcription, the first of which is probably that of the scholar who desired the copy for his own use; for a text written so roughly, and that, too, on the back of a waste papyrus, would have had no sale in the market. This recovery of a lost classic of such traditional fame has cast into the shade all previous finds of this nature, however important many of them have been; and there is every reason to hope that the more systematic and careful exploration of Egypt in our days may achieve still greater results. By the side of the work of Aristotle, other papyri which have lately passed into the British Museum, containing fragments of works of Demosthenes, of the 2nd or 1st century B.C., and of Isocrates of the 1st century after Christ, may appear insignificant; but the acquisition of a papyrus of fair length, restoring to us some of the lost poems of the iambographer Herodas, who flourished in the first century B.C., is one more welcome addition to the long lost Greek literature which is again emerging into light.[2]

Outside of Egypt, Herculaneum is the only place in which Greek papyri have been found. Here, in a house which was excavated in the year 1752, a number of charred rolls were discovered, which were at first taken for pieces of charcoal, many being destroyed before

---

[2] Aristotle's Πολιτεία has been published, together with an autotype facsimile of the papyrus; and the poems of Herodas, with collations of other papyri, are printed in *Classical Texts from Papyri in the British Museum*, 1891: both works edited by F. G. Kenyon for the Trustees of the British Museum. A facsimile of the papyrus of Herodas has also been issued.

their real nature was recognized. Almost immediately attempts were made to unroll them; and with more or less success the work has been carried on, at intervals, down to the present day. The process is a difficult one; the hardened crust, into which the outer portion of the rolls has been converted by the action of the heated ashes which buried the devoted city, must be removed before the inner and less injured layers can be reached, and so fragile are these that the most skilful and patient handling is required to separate them without irreparably injuring the remains. Copies of the texts recovered have been engraved and published in the series of volumes, the *Herculanensia Volumina*, printed at Naples.

In the year 1800, the Prince of Wales, afterwards George the Fourth, undertook the expense of unrolling and copying the papyri; but the work was interrupted by the French invasion of 1806. The tracings and copper-plates which had been prepared by his agent were presented by the Prince to the University of Oxford in 1810, together with a few unopened rolls, part of a number which had been given to him by the Neapolitan Government. Four of the rest and the unrolled fragments of a fifth were subsequently presented by the Queen to the British Museum in 1865. In 1824 and 1825 two volumes of lithographs of some of the Oxford facsimiles were published; and recently, in 1885, others have been given in the *Fragmenta Herculanensia* of Mr. Walter Scott.

But none of the facsimiles in these publications can be considered sufficient for palæographical study, and unfortunately the blackened condition of the rolls is such that little can be done by the agency of photography. Two autotype plates copied from some of the original fragments, will be found in the facsimiles of the Palæographical Society (i. pl. 151, 152).

Of the rolls which have been opened, a large proportion are found to contain works of the Epicurean Philodemus, while others are the writings of Epicurus and the leading members of his school. From the fact that several of Philodemus's works are in duplicate,

it has been suggested that the principal part of the
collection was formed by Philodemus himself, and that the
house in which it was found was that of L. Calpur-
nius Piso Cæsoninus, the patron of the philosopher and
the father-in-law of Julius Cæsar. However this may be,
the date of the destruction of Herculaneum, A.D. 79,
forms a posterior limit for the age of the papyri.
Roughly, then, their period may be fixed at the end
of the first century B.C. or the beginning of the first
century of the Christian era.

The Antiquity of Greek Writing.

The most important lesson which we, as palæographers,
learn from these ancient papyri is, that throughout all
periods, as far back as we can reach, we have side by
side two classes of Greek writing : the Literary or Book-
hand, in which works of literature were usually (but
not always) written, and the Cursive hand of every-day
life ; that, however remote the date of these documents,
we find in them evidence that then all sorts and conditions of men wrote as fluently as we do now ; that the
scribe of those days could produce as finely written
texts as the scribe of later times ; and that the educated
or professional man could note down records of daily
business with as much facility as any of their de-
scendants. And if we find these evidences of a wide-
spread knowledge of Greek writing so far back as the
third century B.C., and writing, too, of a kind which
bears on its face the stamp of matured development,
the question naturally arises, to what remote period are
we to assign the first stage of Greek writing, not in a
primitive condition, but so far developed as to be a
practical means of intercourse. There has hitherto
rather been a tendency to regard the earliest existing
Greek inscriptions as the first painful efforts of unskilled
hands. But it is far more natural to suppose that,
almost simultaneously with the adoption of an alphabet,
the keen-witted Greek trader must have profited by
the example of Egyptian and Phœnician and have
soon learnt how to express himself in writing. It is

impossible at least to doubt that the Greek mercenaries who were able to cut so skilfully not only their names but also longer inscriptions on the statue of Abu Simbel some 600 years B.C., were perfectly able to write fluently with the pen.

But without speculating further on this subject, we may rest content with the fact that in the papyri of the third century B.C. we have styles of writing so confirmed in their character that we have no difficulty in forming an approximate idea of the character of the writing of the best classical period of Greece. Indeed, judging by the comparatively slow changes which passed over Greek writing in the hundred years from the third to the second century B.C., we probably have before us, in our oldest specimens, both literary and cursive, styles not very different from those of a hundred years earlier.

Divisions of Greek Palæography.

It will here be convenient to state the plan adopted in the following sketch of the progress of Greek writing.

The courses of the two styles of writing, which have already been referred to as the Literary hand or Book-hand and the Cursive hand, will be kept distinct for the earlier centuries, previous to the adoption of the minuscule as a literary hand in the ninth century. Again, a general distinction will be observed between MSS. written on papyrus (as well as examples on pottery or wax) and MSS. written on vellum. The examples of the book-hand on papyrus will first be considered; next, the cursive writing on the same material. Then the history of the uncial hand on vellum will be traced; and, lastly, the long series of mediæval minuscule MSS., coming down to the sixteenth century, will be examined.

It will be observed that cursive writing is here only specially dealt with under the early period. Although the cursive writing of the day was moulded into a settled style to serve as a book-hand in the ninth century, it naturally still continued in use as a current hand in the ordinary affairs of life; and, if sufficient independent

material had survived, this current hand would have
formed a separate division of the subject. But no such
material exists. We have no great collections of Greek
charters and documents cursively written, such as we
have in Latin. We must therefore look for the traces
of the progress of the Greek cursive hand in the more
hastily written minuscule literary MSS. of successive
centuries.

The different terms which are used to describe various
styles of letters may here be explained. In both Greek
and Latin palæography, large letters are called "majus-
cules"; small letters, "minuscules." Of large letters
there are two kinds: Capitals, or large letters, formed,
as in inscriptions, chiefly by strokes meeting at angles
and avoiding curves, except where the actual forms of
the letters absolutely require them, angular characters
being more easily cut with the tool on hard substances
such as stone or metal; and Uncials, a modification of
capitals, in which curves are freely introduced as being
more readily inscribed with the pen on soft material
such as papyrus. For example, the fifth letter is E as
a capital, and Є as an uncial. The term "uncial" first
appears in St. Jerome's Preface to the Book of Job, and
is there applied to Latin letters, "uncialibus, ut vulgo
aiunt, litteris," but the derivation of the word is not
decided; we know, however, that it refers to the alphabet
of curved forms.

In early Greek papyri, as well as in early vellum MSS.,
the ordinary character in use is the uncial. As will be
presently seen, in some of the very earliest specimens
on papyrus certain of the letters still retain the capital
forms of inscriptions. These instances, however, are
rare. At the earliest period of Greek writing of which
we have knowledge the uncial character was, no doubt,
quite developed.

Minuscule, or small, letters are derived from majus-
cules; but, although in early cursive specimens we find
at once certain forms from which the later minuscules
directly grew, a full minuscule alphabet was only slowly
developed.

CHAPTER IX.

The Literary or Book-Hand in Papyri.

OUR first division of Greek writing is the Literary or
Book-hand in papyri. It is not, however, to be understood that all surviving literary remains are written in
this hand; for there are exceptions, certain works having
been copied out, apparently, by scholars for their own
use, or at least by persons not writing for the book
trade, in less formal hands which we must class as
cursive. There is, indeed, in the case of the early papyri,
some difficulty in drawing the line of division between
the literary hand and the cursive hand, certain documents being written with sufficient care to give them a
claim to be separated from the cursives and yet with
not enough formality to be included under the book-
hand. On the other hand, there are one or two instances
of the formal literary hand being used for ordinary
documents. We would define the literary hand to be
that which professional scribes would employ in writing
books for the market; and in the following review of
this division, only such MSS. are noticed as are thus
formally written, together with one or two (not literary)
documents in which this class of hand is adopted.

The earliest surviving specimens of Greek writing of
the book-hand are contained in the papyrus fragment
in the Imperial Library at Vienna, which is inscribed
with an invocation of a certain Artemisia against the
father of her child, and in the fragments of the *Phædo*

of Plato and the *Antiope* of Euripides, recently discovered at Gurob.[1]

The invocation of Artemisia [2] may be placed at least as early as the first half of the third century B.C. This ascription is supported by the similarity of the hand-writing of the other fragments mentioned above, which there is every reason to believe are nearly of the same period. The writing approaches the epigraphic style, the letters standing quite distinct and unconnected, and some of them showing transitional forms.

PAPYRUS OF ARTEMISIA—3RD CENTURY B.C.

(ω δεσποτο σεραπι καθε[οι]— | η δαμασιος θυγατηρ κα[τα]— | και της θηκης ει μεν ου[ν]— | [ως]περ μεν ουν αδικα εμε— | μη τυχειν εκ παιδων θ[ηκης]— | καταβοιης ενθυτα κε[ιμενης]—)

It will be observed that the cross-stroke of the **A** is horizontal, the bottom of **B** pointed, the top horizontal of **E** extended; **Θ** and **O** are small; the cross-stroke

---

[1] See above, p. 112.

[2] First described by Petrettini, *Papiri Greco-Egizi del I. R. Museo di Corte* (1826), p. 4, who gives a very rough facsimile; afterwards by Blass in *Philologus*, xli. 746, and in Müller's *Handbuch der klassischen Alterthums-Wissenschaft* (1886), i. 280; and again by Wessely in *Eilfter Jahresbericht über das Franz-Joseph-Gymnasium in Wien* (1885), p. 4. A facsimile is given in *Pal. Soc.* ii. pl. 141.

of **T** generally extends more to the left than to the right; and the shapes of **C** and **ω** are transitional, that of the former between the angular and curved forms, and that of the latter between the epigraphic Ω and the **ω** of MSS. In this papyrus the double point (:) is also used as a mark of punctuation, as found in inscriptions.

As already stated, the fragmentary papyrus of the *Phædo* of Plato may be placed in the first half of the 3rd century B.C., for it was found in company with official and other documents which are actually dated in the reigns of the second and third Ptolemies; and these would naturally have been regarded as of a more common and ephemeral character than a literary work of a great writer, and would have been thrown aside in an earlier period of existence.

THE "PHÆDO" OF PLATO.—3RD CENTURY B.C.

(—[αισθη]σεων πειθουσα δε εκ τουτωμ³ | [με]ν αναχωρειν οσομ³ μη αναγκη | χρησ[θ]αι αυτην δ εις εαυτην συλ | λεγεσθαι και αθροιζεσθαι παρακε | λευεσ[θ]αι πιστευειν δε μηδενι αλλωι)

This beautiful MS. of Plato would no doubt have been treasured by its original owner for many years, if not for a lifetime, and it can only have been by some accident that it was at length used up as waste material. The small portion of the *Antiope* of Euripides which has met with the same fate and has descended

---

³ Final ν is changed into μ before a following μ.

to us in the same way must be nearly of the same date. But the writing of the latter is not quite so good, and though there may be little to choose between the two MSS., yet preference may be given to the MS. of Plato. The text of the latter is written in narrow columns of twenty-two lines, which are from 2½ to 3 inches in length. The width of the papyrus appears to have been about 8½ inches. The facsimile represents a few of the most perfect lines of one of the fragments.

The writing is a very beautiful uncial hand, minute and exact, the chief general characteristic being the great breadth, almost flatness, of many of the letters (*e.g.* Γ, Ζ, Η, Μ, Π, Ω), as compared with their height. That this is a characteristic of the period, and not a personal usage of the writer of the MS., is proved by its prominence in other documents of the third century B.C. As in the Artemisia papyrus, in certain forms the writing departs from the recognized curves of the uncial, and approaches more nearly to the rectangles of lapidary inscriptions. This is seen in the Α, and in many instances of Ε, in which the upper horizontal stroke is not only perfectly straight, but also of disproportionate length. Certain letters are distinguished by their small size, as Θ (which also often has only the dot in the centre instead of the transverse bar), Ο, C, and Ω. The head of the iota is in many instances thickened a little, and sometimes it is slightly hooked on the right. This peculiarity appears to mark the letter in early periods, the hook or thickening being removed to the left side of the head in later times.

The next papyrus from which we shall select a specimen of the literary or book-hand is the fragment of a dialectical treatise, now at Paris, which was written earlier than the year 160 B.C., as proved by the existence on the back of it of memoranda of that year (*Not. et Extr.*, pl. xi., no. 2). There remain fourteen narrow columns of the work, written in slightly sloping uncial letters, not to compare in elegance with the writing of the Plato fragments just noticed, but very simply formed and evidently written by a professional scribe. In this

MS. is noticeable the tendency of the columns to work
downwards to the left, as is seen in other papyri of an
early period : that is, the marginal line of writing is not
perpendicular, but each successive line begins a little
more to the left than the one above it, with the result
that the last line of a column may begin as much as an
inch outside the true perpendicular drawn from the
commencement of the first line.

DIALECTICAL TREATISE.—BEFORE 160 B.C.

(ναι ου αλκμαν ο ποιητης | ουτως απεφαινετο ου | κ ης
ανηρ αγροικος ουδε | σκαιος ει ουτως απο | φαινοιτ αν τις
δευτ εμ | πεδος ειμι ουδ αστοισι | προσηνης ου ανακρε—)

Where the letters are so simple, there is no special
remark to be made about them individually, except in
regard to the alpha, in which the left down-stroke and
the cross-stroke are made together without lifting the
pen, their point of junction being sometimes looped.
This form of the letter is seen also, with a more decidedly
developed loop, in the fragments of Demosthenes and
Hyperides, on papyrus, in the British Museum, which
may be of the 2nd or 1st century B.C., and in some
of the Herculanean papyri. It will be noticed in the
facsimile that the paragraphs of the text are marked off
by the insertion of marginal strokes between the lines,
according to the ancient system.

The papyrus containing the orations of Hyperides for

Lycophron and Euxenippus is probably of the 1st century B.C. The writing, of a round type, is remarkably regular and elegant (see facsimile, ed. Babington ; *Cat. Anc. MSS.*, pls. 2, 3 ; *Pal. Soc.* i. pl. 126).

ORATION OF HYPERIDES FOR LYCOPHRON.—1ST CENT. B.C.

(—δι ταφηναι εαν ουν | κελευητε ω ανδρες | δικασται καλω τινα | βοηθησοντα ανα | βηθι μοι θεοφιλε | και συνειπε ο τι εχεις | κελευουσιν οι δικα | σται ‖ απολογια υπερ | λυκοφρονος)

Here, as in the previous example, the columns of writing trend away to the left. The facsimile represents the last few lines of the oration for Lycophron, and again affords an instance of the ancient system of punctuation, and also of the slight degree of ornamentation in which a scribe of that period would allow himself to indulge, namely, the flourish which is drawn in the margin after the last words, and the light touches of the pen which decorate the colophon or title of the speech.

The writing of the Harris Homer is of quite a different cast from that which has just been examined. The letters have more squareness and are more rigid; they are very delicately formed, and have all the simplicity characteristic of age. This papyrus, containing portions of Book xviii. of the Iliad, may be placed without hesitation as early as the 1st century B.C.

HARRIS HOMER.—1ST CENTURY B.C.

(καλα τα μεν πηληι θεοι δοσαν αγλαα δω[ρα]
ηματι τωι οτε σε βροτου ανερος εμβαλον ε[υνηι]
ως οφελες σύ μεν αυθι μετ αθανατης αλι[ησιν]
ναιειν πηλευς δε θνητων αγαγεσθαι α[κοιτιν]
νυν δ ινα και συ πενθος ενι φρεσι μυριον[ειη])

The papyrus is so much discoloured that there is great difficulty in obtaining a good reproduction by photography; but the plate given in the facsimiles of the Palæographical Society (ii. 64) is fairly successful. The text has been considerably corrected and accented by a later hand. For the sake of clearness these additions have been omitted in our facsimile.

To follow chronological order, we now give a specimen from one of the Herculanean rolls.

PHILODEMUS.—ABOUT A.D. 1.

(τως ουχ επι τοις μετα την τελευτην | οταν δε τις ευ γε
βεβιωικως ηι και | φιλοις αξιοις εαυτου κεχρημενος υ | πο
δε τυχης η πονηριας ανθρωπων | κεκωλυμενον τυχειν ουδ
ελαχισ | τηι συνεξεται λυπη το μηδ εσεσθαι | προς εαυτον
λογιζομενος ωι γαρ ε | πιγινεται το λυπηρον ουκ εσκεν
αλ—)

It is reproduced from one of the published copper-
plates, in default of more satisfactory facsimiles, as explained above; and represents a few lines from Philodemus
περὶ θανάτου. The date may be about the beginning of
the Christian era. The writing is neat and regular, and
the letters are simple in form.

All the MSS. from which the above facsimiles have
been selected may be said to represent the book-hand
as generally written on papyrus, as distinguished from
the uncial writing which is found in the early vellum
MSS. None of our specimens could be pointed to as the
immediate parent of this latter hand, although no one would
dispute that there is a relationship. The forms of individual letters may be very similar, both in the papyrus
hand and in the vellum hand, and yet, if we were to place
two such MSS. as the Lycophron of Hyperides and the
Codex Vaticanus side by side, we should not venture to
derive the writing of the latter directly from that of the
more ancient MS. But here a most valuable document,
lately discovered, comes to our assistance in the task of
determining the parentage of the later uncial hand.
This is a fragmentary papyrus containing a deed concern-
ing property in Arsinoë in the Fayoum, which bears the
date of the seventh year of the Emperor Domitian, A.D. 88.
The writing is not in the cursive character that one looks
for in legal documents, but is a formal style, in which a
likeness to the uncial of the early vellum MSS. is at once
most obvious. In the first century, then, there was in
use a set form of writing from which that uncial hand
was evidently derived by direct descent. And it may be
concluded with fair certainty that this style of writing
must have been in existence for a considerable period of
time; for here we find it common enough to be employed

by an ordinary clerk.[4] The fortunate accident of its
having been thus used in a dated document has provided
us with the means of settling the periods of other important MSS.

ΟΛΕΜΑΙΔΙΕΥΕΡΓΕΤΙΔΙΤΟΥΔ
ΚΑΙΠΤΟΥΤΟΥΓΥΝΗΙ ΔΙΟΔΩ
ΠΕΘΕWCWCΕΤWN ΤΡΙΔΚΟΝ
ΓΡΑΦΗΝΑΠΟΤΗCΠΡΟΓΕΓΡΑ

CONVEYANCE.—A.D. 88.

(—[ππ]ολεμαιδι ευεργετιδι του α— | και η τουτου γυνηι
διοδω[ρα]— | πεθεως ως ετων τριακον[τα]— | γραφην απο
της προγεγρα[μενης]—)

It is to be noticed that the writer of this document does
not keep strictly to the formal uncial letters. As if more
accustomed to write a cursive hand, he mingles certain
cursive letters in his text : side by side with the round **Є**,
there stands in one or two places the cursive (*not* shown
in the facsimile), in which the cross-stroke is only indicated by the finishing curve ; and, more frequently, the
cursive upsilon is employed as well as the regular letter.
Among the other letters, may be remarked the tendency
to make the main stroke of the alpha rather upright,
which eventually leads to a distinctive form of the letter,
as seen fully developed in the palimpsest MS. of the
Gospel of St. Matthew at Dublin (Codex Z) ; in some of
the titles of the Codex Alexandrinus ; and above all in
the Codex Marchalianus of the Vatican[5]—this being in
fact the Coptic form of the letter.

It is also remarkable that in one or two places the

---

[4] We have proof that uncial writing was used as the copy-hand
for writing lessons in schools, such copies being found on early
waxen tablets (see above, p. 23).

[5] Lately reproduced in facsimile, with a commentary by
A. Ceriani, Rome, 1890.

writer has employed large letters at the beginning of
the clauses into which he breaks up the text. This
practice foreshadows the use of large initial letters,
which it has been customary to consider as rather a
mark of advance in the early vellum Greek MSS.

The Bankes Homer, from which our next facsimile is
chosen, is the best preserved papyrus of the Iliad that
has yet been found, being nearly eight feet in length and
containing sixteen columns of text; and the material
being still fairly white and the writing quite legible.

BANKES HOMER.—2ND CENTURY.

(ποι[ητης].—ως εφατ' ουδε τις αυτοθ' ενι πτόλ[εἰ λιπετ' ανηρ]
ουδε γυνη· παντας γαρ αάσχετον[ἱκετο πενθος·]
αγχὸυ δε ξύνβληντο πυλᾶων νε[κρον αγοντι·]
πρωται τόν γ άλοχός τε φιλη και [πότνια μητηρ]
τιλλέσθην επ αμαξαν εὔτροχο[ν αἴξασαι]
ἁπτόμεναι κεφαλης· κλαιων δ'[αμφισταθ'ὁμιλος])

This MS., which, with the data obtained from the
preceding document, may now be assigned with more
certainty than before to the 2nd century, shows a
further development of the uncial hand of vellum MSS.,
which is here reduced to the exact forms of letters which
were to remain essentially unchanged for many centuries.
It may be noticed that the horizontal strokes of Є and Θ
are placed rather low, and even vary in position: one of
those indications of carelessness or decline from a higher
standard which is generally looked for in a hand which
is beginning to fall into desuetude. Judging from the
analogy of later periods, and from the fact that the late
Hawara papyrus of Homer is also written in the same

cast of uncial writing, one is tempted to suggest that, in producing choice copies of a work of such universal popularity and veneration as the Iliad, a traditional style of writing may have been maintained, just as in the middle ages the sacred texts and liturgies still continued to be written in a form of handwriting which had generally passed out of use. If this view is correct, we may find in it an explanation of the adoption of the uncial character (the form of writing which before all others had been consecrated to the texts of Homer) for important copies of the sacred text of Scripture.

One or two points of interest in the Bankes Homer, apart from the actual handwriting, may be mentioned. The lines are marked off in hundreds by numerical letters inserted in the margins; and the speeches of the different persons are indicated by their names, and the narrative portions by a contracted form of the word ποιητής, as shown in the facsimile. With very rare exceptions, corrections, accents and breathings and other marks are by a later hand.

As an example of a rougher style of uncial writing of about the third century, a few lines from the recently found papyrus of the iambographer Herodas are selected (Brit. Mus., Papyrus cxxxv.).

HERODAS.—3RD CENTURY.

(δουληστι δουλης δω ταν ωθριη θλιβει
αλλ ημερη τε κηπι μεζον ωθιται
αυτη συ μινον η θυρη γαρ ωικται
κᾶνεῖθ ο παστος ουχ ορηις φιλη κυννοι
οι εργα κὸινην ταυτ ερις αθηναιην)

There is no attempt at calligraphy in this MS., which is probably a cheap copy made for the market by a scribe who was neither very expert nor accurate.

About the same period or a little later, we meet with specimens of sloping uncial writing on papyrus, in which the letters are laterally compressed, derived no doubt from the round style and developed as a quicker method of copying. It is remarked that the round uncial of vellum MSS. develops exactly in the same way a style of sloping writing at a later period. An early and elegant example is given by Wilcken, *Tafeln zur ältern griech. Palæographie*, 1891, taf. iii.; and another is found in the papyrus of the Iliad, Books ii.—iv. (Brit. Mus. Papyrus cxxvi.), which is probably of the 4th century.

HOMER.—4TH CENTURY.

(ες πεδιον προχέοντο σκαμάνδ[ριον]—
σμερδαλεον κοναβιζε ποδων—
έσταν δ' εν λιμῶνι σκαμανδ[ριω]—
μυριοι οσσα τε φυλλα και ἄνθεα—
ηΰτε μυιαων αδιναων εθνε[α]—
αι τε κατα σταθμον ποιμνηιον—)

Accents are occasionally used; and in the left margin is seen a paragraph mark formed by a couple of oblique strokes.

CHAPTER X.

Cursive Writing in Papyri, etc.

WE now leave the Book-hand and turn to the examination of Cursive Greek writing as found in papyri, ostraka, tablets, etc. For this branch of palæography there is comparatively larger material, which is being increased every day by the numerous fragments which are rapidly making their way from Egypt into European libraries. But yet, while in the aggregate the material is abundant, there are certain periods, notably the first century B.C., which are but scantily represented.

For the earliest specimens of cursive Greek writing, as for the principal early examples of the book-hand, we turn to the fragments discovered by Mr. Petrie at Gurob in the Fayoum. As already stated, the coffin-makers, in order to form the cartonnage of mummy-cases, made use of much cursively written material, documents of all kinds, and more particularly of a register or registers of wills entered up periodically by different scribes, and therefore affording the most valuable evidences of the handwriting of the third century B.C. The oldest fragment as yet discovered among these remains is assigned to the year 268 B.C. The hands vary from the most cursive scrawls to what may be termed the careful official hand. But throughout them all a most striking feature is the strength and facility of the writing, besides in many cases its boldness and breadth. The general characteristic of the letters, more especially in the clerical or official hands of the registers, is great width or flatness, which is very apparent in such letters as Δ, M, N, Π, Ѡ. In other documents this is less

apparent, and the writing does not seem far removed in
style from that of the next century. Some independent
pieces, such as correspondence, are written in very
cursive characters which have a peculiar ragged appearance and are often difficult to read.

These documents, however, are not the only specimens
of cursive writing of the third century B.C. within our
reach. A few scattered pieces have already for many
years been stored in the various museums of Europe,
but the antiquity of some of them has not been recognized,
and they have been thought to belong to the period of
the Roman occupation of Egypt. At Leyden there is a
papyrus (Pap. Q), containing a receipt of the 26th
year of Ptolemy Philadelphus, 260 B.C. At Berlin,
Paris, and London there are three wooden tablets
inscribed with deeds relating to a loan of the 30th and
31st years of the same king, about 254 B.C. Among
the papyri of the British Museum, three, formerly
ascribed to a later date, are now more correctly placed
in the third century, viz., a petition for redress of
grievances (Pap. cvi.) of the 25th year, apparently, of
Ptolemy Euergetes I., B.C. 223; and two others (l. and
li.A) without dates. The Paris collection also contains
a long money account for public works (*Not. et Extr.* xviii.
2, pl. xliv.) of the same century, which has been in-
correctly assigned to the Roman period. A facsimile of
a letter of introduction, evidently of this time, is given
by Passalacqua.[1] Egger describes a papyrus at Athens,[2]
and various Greek endorsements and dockets on Demotic
papyri are noticed by Revillout.[3] Ostraka or potsherds
also have been found with inscriptions of this period.

Of cursive writing of the second century B.C. we
have abundant material in the great collections of
London, Paris, Leyden, etc., referred to above (p. 107);
of the first century B.C. very little has yet been found,

---

[1] *Catalogue Raisonné des Antiquités découvertes en Egypte*, Paris,
1826. Also described in *Notices et Extraits des MSS.* xviii., p. 399.
[2] *Journal des Savants*, 1873, pp. 30, 97.
[3] *Chrestomathie Démotique*, 1880, pp. 241, 277; *Revue Egypt.* ii.
114.

except in ostraka; of the first century of our era, several papyri have recently come to light, and there are numerous ostraka; and of the later centuries there are abundant specimens at Vienna and Berlin, and an ever increasing number in Paris and London and other places, the searches in the Fayoum continually adding to the stock.

Greek cursive writing, as found in papyri, has been divided (Wilcken, *Tafeln*, 1890) into three groups: the Ptolemaic, the Roman, and the Byzantine. Roughly, the Ptolemaic comprises documents down to about the end of the first century B.C.; the Roman, those of the first three centuries of the Christian era; and the Byzantine, those of later date.

The character of Ptolemaic writing, as seen in papyri of the third and second centuries B.C. is unmistakeable.

For the first century B.C. there is not material to enable us to form a judgment; but it must have been a period of marked transition, if we may judge from the great difference between the writing of the first century of our era and that of the second century B.C. And the documents of the later centuries, of the Byzantine period, show as much distinctiveness of character, when compared with those of the Roman period of the early centuries after Christ.

Our first example of cursive writing of the third century B.C. is taken from one of the entries in the registers of wills found at Gurob, being the will of Demetrius, the son of Deinon, dated in the year 237 B.C. (Mahaffy, *Petrie Papyri*, pl. xiv.).

This is a remarkably fine hand, to which the fac-simile hardly does justice, and may be classed as a good example of the official writing of the time, penned by a skilful and experienced registrar. While not as cursive as many other specimens of the period, and while the letters are in general deliberately formed and are not much connected with one another, there are certain characters which appear in the most cursive shapes, side by side with their more formal representations.

WILL OF DEMETRIUS.—237 B.C.

([βασι]λευοντος πτολεμαιου του ππ— | [αδε]λφων ετους ι
εφ ιερεως απολλωνιδου— | θεων αδελφων και θεων ενεργε-
τ[ων]— | [φιλαδελ]φου μενεκρατειας της φιλαμ[μονος]— |
[κρ]οκοδιλων πολει του αρσινοιτου ν[ομου]— | δημητριος
δεινωνος χρηστηρι[ος]—)

In the third line, in the word και, we have the cursive
angle-shaped *alpha*, that letter being elsewhere more
normally formed ; and in the termination ων, there is a
tendency to flatten out the *omega* into a mere line after
the initial curve, and to write the *nu* in a crooked
stroke.

We next take a section from a document of the 13th
year of Ptolemy Philopator, 211 or 210 B.C., recording
the payment of a tax at Thebes (*Pal. Soc.* ii. pl. 143).

TAX-RECEIPT.—211 OR 210 B.C.

(ετους ιγ τυβι δ πεπτωκεν επι το— | τελωνιον του εγκυ-
κλιου εφ ου ερ[μοκλης]— | βασιλει παρα θοτευτος του

ψεμμιν[ιος]— | [πε]τεχωνσις αθανιωνος το γινομενο[ν] |
εγκυκλιου προσοδον αρουρων ενδεκ[α]— | εν πεστενεμενωφε
του παθυριτ[ου]—)

In this specimen of the elegant cursive, which is not
easy to read, we have the angle-shaped *alpha* consistently
employed, and very cursive combinations of the terminations ων and αυ, besides instances of the more rapidly
written forms of *eta, lambda,* and *pi.* How very cursive
this style of writing might become is seen in the two
last words of the facsimile.

As a contrast to the two carefully written examples
which have just been given, our third specimen of the
writing of the third century B.C. is selected from a
rough letter of a steward addressed to his employer
(Mahaffy, *Petrie Papyri,* pl. xxix.).

LETTER OF A STEWARD.—3RD CENTURY B.C.

(εχει δυνις γ εχρησαμην | δε και παρα δυνεως αρτα | βας δ
κριθοπυρων αυτου | επαγγελομενου και φιλοτιμου | οντος
γινωσκε δε και οτι | υδωρ εκαστος των ορων την | αμπελον
φυτευομενην προτερον [4])

[4] As the letter has more than a palæographical interest, Professor Mahaffy's translation is quoted : ". . . to Sosiphanes, greet-
ing. I give much thanks to the gods if you are well. Lonikos
also is well. The whole vineyard has been planted, viz., 300
stocks, and the climbing vines attended to. But the olive-yard
has yielded six measures, of which Dynis has got three. Also I
have borrowed from Dynis four artabæ of bearded wheat, which

The style of writing is similar to that of the Leyden papyrus Q., which was written in the 26th year of Ptolemy Philadelphus, B.C. 260 ; and our letter may well be as early as the middle of the century. It will be seen that the letters are not linked together, but that they are hastily and roughly formed. The writer, though not a good penman, was evidently so far skilled that he could write rapidly and with ease; and the document may be regarded as a sample of the rough business hand of the period. Among the individual letters, the thoroughly cursive forms of *eta, lambda, nu, tau, upsilon,* and *omega,* are to be distinguished. The letter *iota,* with the thickening on the right-hand side of the top of the letter, which has already been referred to as a mark of antiquity, and the very small size of *theta* and *omikron,* may also be noticed.

The more carefully written documents of the second century B.C., do not differ so much from those of the same style of the preceding century as might have been expected. As far, however, as an opinion can be formed from extant remains, it appears that the practice of linking together the letters, particularly by slight horizontal strokes attached to their tops, becomes more prevalent. This is seen to best advantage in some of the elegantly written papyri of this period, the links imparting a certain grace and finish to the line of writing.

The first example is taken from an official circular or instruction on the mode of collecting the taxes, written probably in the year 170 B.C. (*Not. et Extr.,* pl. xl., no. 62).

Here we have a very fine official hand, to be compared with that of the will of Demetrius, of 237 B.C., given above, of which it may claim to be an almost direct descendant. In this writing there is a greater tendency than in that of the earlier period to break up the letters,

he offered, was pressing to lend. Know also that each of the watchers says that the planted vines want water first, and that they have none. We are making conduits and watering. The third of the first month (?). Good-bye."

that is, to form their several limbs by distinct strokes. Thus we see the *tau* often distinctly formed in two portions, the first consisting of the left half of the horizontal and the vertical, and the second of the right half of the horizontal. The *upsilon* is also made on the same plan.

TREASURY CIRCULAR.—B.C. 170 (?).

([κατ αποσ]ταλησεται μετα φυλακης | —[γ]εγραμμενων γνω-
μης | —[υπ]αρξει εις την εγληψιν)

The system of linking referred to above is here very noticeable, such letters as partially consist of horizontal strokes naturally adapting themselves to the practice, while others not so formed are supplied with links, as in the case of *eta* and *nu*.

LETTER ON EGYPTIAN CONTRACTS.—B.C. 146.

(—[πε]ποηνται οικονομιαν και τα | [ονοματ]α αυτων πατρο-
θεν ενтασσειν | —[γραφ]ειν ημας εντεταχεναι εις | [χρημα
τισ]μον δηλωσαντες τον τε)

A more cursively written specimen of this time is found in a letter of a certain Paniscus regarding the execution of Egyptian contracts, ascribed to the year 146 B.C. (*Not. et Extr.*, pl. xliii., no. 65 *bis*).

Here we have a full cursive alphabet in use, with numerous examples of rapid combinations of letters, as *αι, αν, ων, εν, ειν,* and a tendency to write in curves without lifting the pen, as exemplified by the gamma-shaped *tau,* and the *epsilon* with the cross-stroke run on in continuation of the lower curve.

The great papyrus at Paris, known as the Casati contract, referring to a sale of property at Thebes, is written in a rather closely-packed hand, of which a specimen is here given. The date of the document is 114 B.C. (*Not. et Extr.*, pl. xiii., no. 5).

CASATI CONTRACT.—B.C. 114.

(αυτωι μερος εβδομον ης γειτονες— | ωικοδομημενον πηχεως τριτον— | και εν πμουνεμουννει απ οικιας— | μενεους λιβος οικια ζμαυρ[εους])

It will be observed that the letters are not altogether so cursive as those of the last specimen, and that the general appearance of the writing is more compact, although continuous. This effect is chiefly produced by the linking of the letters, both in the natural manner and by the employment of added links after such letters as *eta, iota, nu, pi,* and *upsilon.*

It is curious that hitherto scarcely any dated Greek writing of the first century B.C. has come to light. But, judging by the documents of the beginning of the first century of our era, the progress made in the development of cursive writing in the previous hundred years must have been very considerable. For example, if we examine such a document as that given in facsimile in *Wiener Studien,* iv. (1882), p. 175, of A.D. 8, the advance made in the cursive character of several letters is very apparent (see Table of Letters).

We now give a specimen from a receipt, found in the Fayoum, for rent paid in kind in the 8th year of Tiberius, A.D. 20. (*Pal. Soc.* ii. pl. 144).

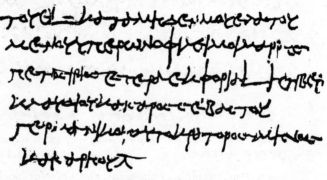

RECEIPT.—A.D. 20.

(του θ ετους κατα μηδεν μου ελατου | μενου υπερ ων οφιλει μοι μαρρης | πετοσιριος ετερα εκφορια ετους η τιβερι[ου] | κλαυδιου καισαρος σεβαστου | γερμανικου αυτοκρατορος μηνος | καισαρηου λ̄)

The handwriting is rough and irregular, and there is a general slackness in the formation of the letters which marks the late period of the writing, as compared with the cursive specimens which have already been examined. The prevailing use of the *epsilon* having its cross-stroke drawn, without lifting the pen, in continuation of the upper curve of the letter should be remarked, as this form now becomes very common.

The papyrus on the back of which the recently discovered text of Aristotle's work on the Constitution of Athens was transcribed, was first used, as already stated, to receive the farm accounts of land in the district of Hermopolis in Egypt, in the reign of Vespasian, A.D. 78-79. The following facsimile represents a portion of one of the headings (*Cat. Gk. Papyri in Brit. Mus.*).

FARM ACCOUNT.—A.D. 78-79.

(ετους ενδεκατου αυτοκ[ρατορος]— | ουεσπασιανου σεβαστου μ[ηνος]— | δαπαναι του μηνος χοιαχ— | το δι αυτου επιμαχου εμου δ[ιδυμου])

This is a good example of the light and graceful hand in which many of the tax rolls and other accounts are found to be written. Among individual letters, attention should be drawn to the much-curved *sigma* with its head bent down, a form which, though found occasionally, particularly at the end of a word or line, in earlier papyri, now comes into more general use.

The first of the cursive hands employed upon the Constitution of Athens is next represented. The date is probably not much later than that of the farm account, and may reasonably be placed about A.D. 100.

ARISTOTLE, CONSTITUTION OF ATHENS.—ABOUT A.D. 100.

(προς τους εξεταζειν τα γενη βουλομ[εν]ους επε[ιτα]— |
πεντηκοντα εξ εκαστ[ης] φυλης τοτε δ ησαν εκα[τον]— |
[συμ]βαινηι μεριζειν προς (corr. κ[ατα]) τας προϋπαρχουσας
τριτ[τυς]— | αναμισγεσθ[αι] το πληθο[ς] διενειμε δ[ε]
κ[αι] τ[ην] χωραν κ[ατα]— | δ[ε]κα δ[ε] τ[ης] μεσογειο[υ]
κ[αι] ταυτας επονομασας τριττ[υς]— | παντ[ων] τ[ων]
τοπων κ[αι] δημοτας εποιησεν αλλη[λων]— | προσαγορευ-
οντες εξελεγχωσιν τους νεοπολι[τας])

The hand is cramped and employs many abbreviations
(see above, p. 90). The prevalent use of the *epsilon*
referred to under the facsimile of the receipt of A.D. 20,
and the occurrence of a peculiar form of *eta*, somewhat
resembling *upsilon* (see *e.g.* l. 2, πεντηκοντα), should
be noticed. This form probably came first into use in
the first century B.C., as it is quite established at the
beginning of our era.

DEED OF SALE.—A.D. 154.

(μητρος ταναπωλις τω[ν]— | [μ]ερει και του μετηλλα-
χοτος— | [τ]ο υπαρχον αυτω μερος ημ[ισου]— | ερμωνος
ακολουθως τη)

Our next example, of the middle of the second century, is taken from a deed of sale, from Elephantine, of the 17th year of Antoninus Pius, A.D. 154 (*Not. et Extr.,* pl. xxi., no. 17).

Here there is a considerable advance on the writing of the previous century, the letters being carelessly formed and misshapen, but still without any marked exaggeration.

The following is a facsimile from a fragmentary papyrus of official documents of the reign of Alexander Severus, A.D. 233 (*Not. et Extr.,* pl. xlvi., no. 69 *e*).

OFFICIAL DEED.—A.D. 233

(—στρατηγος υπο νυκτα— | —τω γυμνασιω αμα αυρ[ηλιω] — | —[ε]στεψεν εις γυμνασιαρ[χον]— | —ελαιαν αρπαη-σιος ιερ—)

Being an official hand, the writing is more regular than the last specimen, the vertical position of the strokes lending it an archaic appearance, with which however the loose formation of certain letters is inconsistent.

The cursive writing of the Byzantine period is generally distinguished by its loose and flourished style, in which . we see the development of the long strokes of certain of the minuscule letters of mediæval writing, as the ordinary delta (δ), the h-shaped *eta,* and the long *lambda* drawn below the line. The following three specimens must suffice to illustrate the writing of this period.

(1) A section from an act of manumission of A.D. 355 (Young, *Hieroglyphics*, pl. 46).

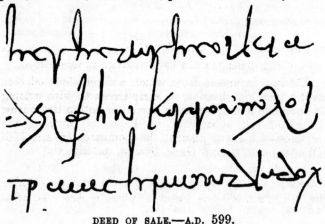

MANUMISSION.—A.D. 355.

([π]ροειπον και νεμεσθε— | —πειθεσθαι εμε την ελευ[θε-
ρουντα]— | —[ελευθε]ρουμενοις καθως π— | —[ειτ]ε επι
ετεροις εκγονοις— | —ακωλυτον εσται της δου[λειας])

(2) Portions of a few lines of a deed of sale at Panopolis, A.D. 599 (*Not. et Extr.*, pl. xlviii., no. 21 *ter*).

DEED OF SALE.—A.D. 599.

(—ης της αυτης οικια[ς] | —[α]δελφην κατα το υπολοι
[πον] | —[πα]τρωας ημων διαδοχ[ης])

(3) Another example from a similar deed of sale of
A.D. 616 (*Not. et Extr.,* pl. xxiv., no. 21).

DEED OF SALE.—A.D. 616.

(εξης υπογραφοντος— | καταγραφην καθ απλ[ην]— | ταυτη
τη εννομω πρ[ασι]— | δια παντος—)

Reference to the Table of Letters will convey some
idea of the variety of the handwritings of this period.

The last document from which a facsimile is selected
to illustrate the division of early Greek Cursive writing
is the fragmentary papyrus, inscribed with a letter from
the Emperor, apparently to Pepin le Bref, on the
occasion of his war against the Lombards in A.D. 756[5]
(Wattenbach, *Script. Græc. Specim.,* pl. xiv.-xv.).

[5] In a notice of this document in the *Revue Archéologique,*
tom. xix., 1892, Monsieur Omont is inclined to date it as late as
A.D. 839.

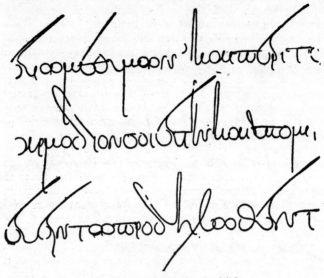

IMPERIAL LETTER.—A.D. 756.

(—εστω μεθ υμων' και περι το[υ]— | —αρμοδιον σοι εστιν
και υπομ— | —[ειρην]ευειν τω προδηλωθεντ[ι]—)

In this specimen of the writing of the Imperial
Chancery, most carefully written, we have the prototype
of the minuscule literary hand of the ninth century.
Making allowance for the flourishes. permissible in a
cursive hand of this style, the letters are almost identical.
A fragment of similar writing is in the British Museum
(Pap. xxxii.).

A glance at the accompanying Table of Alphabets,
selected from documents written more or less cursively
on papyrus and dating from about B.C. 260 to A.D. 756,
will satisfy us of the danger of assuming that some
particular form of a letter belongs to a fixed period.
The not infrequent recurrence of old forms at later
times forbids us to set up such criteria. On the other

hand, the birth and growth of particular forms can be usually traced, and the use of some such form may assist us in placing an anterior limit to the date of the document in which it is found. Thus, the occurrence of the open c-shaped *epsilon* might confirm an opinion that the document was not earlier than the first century B.C., the time when the letter, probably, took that shape ; but, at the same time, the occurrence of the old simple form would be no criterion of age, as that form keeps reappearing in all times. So, too, the down-curved sigma appears in MSS. which may be assigned to the first century B.C. ; yet the old form continued in common use for centuries later. The character of the writing, however, distinctly changes with the lapse of time ; and, though particular letters may be archaic in shapes, the true age of the text, judged by its general appearance, can usually be fixed with fair accuracy. The natural tendency to slackness and flourishing as time advances is sufficiently apparent to the eye as it passes along the lines of letters in the Table ; still more so if it passes over a series of documents, in which the juxta-position of the letters and the links which join them into words are so many aids to forming a judgment.

Viewed as representative of three periods, Ptolemaic, Roman, and Byzantine, the series of letters are fairly distinguishable and capable of being grouped. The first three columns, of the Ptolemaic period, stand quite apart in their simple forms from those of the Roman period which begins with the fourth column ; and this distinction is made more striking by the absence of anything to represent the first century B.C. The columns of the Roman period blend more gradually into those of the Byzantine period ; but taken in their entirety the flourished alphabets of the late centuries afford a sufficient contrast to the less untrammelled columns of the middle, Roman, period.

Certain letters are seen to change in form in a com-paratively slight degree during the nine hundred years covered by the Table, exclusive of the last column ; some are letters which are not very frequently used,

L

others are such as do not very readily run on to following letters. How far the natural tendency of a cursive writer to link together his letters could affect their shapes is seen in even some of the earliest forms. For example, the occasional horizontal position of the last limb of *alpha* or *lambda* was due to its connection with a following letter in the upper level of the line of writing; and the opening of the lower right-hand angle of *delta* and the lifting of the right-hand stroke into a more or less elevated position was owing to the same cause. To the same tendency are due the artificial links which appear attached so early to such letters as *eta, kappa, nu, pi*; and in the case of *tau* this linking may have decided the ulterior shape of the letter (as a cursive), having the cross-bar extending also to the right above the vertical, as in its normal form, instead of being kept only to the left, as seen in the earliest examples in the Table.

How soon certain letters in their most cursive forms might become so alike that they might be mistaken for each other is illustrated by the pretty close resemblance between the curved early forms of *lambda, mu,* and *pi*; and, again, there is very little difference between the ordinary *gamma* and the *lambda* with horizontal final stroke. Such similarities naturally increased as the letters assumed more flexible shapes in the Roman period. The *v*-shaped cursive *beta* and the *v*-shaped cursive *kappa* are nearly identical; and the u-shaped forms of the same letters are very similar. *Nu* and *pi* likewise bear a close resemblance in more than one of their forms; and the γ-shaped *tau* and the long *upsilon* are not unlike.

We may examine the course of change of some of the letters in detail:—

The capital form of *alpha* written quickly falls naturally into the uncial shape, in which the cross-bar is connected by a continuous stroke of the pen with the base of the first limb. To throw away the final limb and leave the letter as a mere acute angle was a natural step for the quick writer to take; and perhaps there is no better example to prove the very great age of cursive Greek writing than this form of the letter which is found in the earliest documents of the Table.

The history of *beta* is the history of a struggle between a capital form and a cursive form. Throughout the whole course of the nine hundred years from B.C. 260 to A.D. 633, the two forms stand side by side. The variations of the cursive form are interesting; at first it slurred the bows of the capital by a downward action of the pen, the letter being thus n-shaped, closed at the top and generally open at the base : in the Roman period the action of the pen was reversed, and the letter became u-shaped, open above and closed at the base.

In *delta* we see quite early a tendency to lengthen the apex in a line ; but it was only in the Byzantine period that it took the exaggerated form, at first resembling a Roman d, from which was finally evolved the minuscule letter which we write to the present day.

That *epsilon*, the letter more frequently used than any other in the Greek alphabet, should have been liable to many changes is only to be expected. In the Table the most radical alteration of its shape from the formal semicircle with the cross-bar, to the *c*-shape in which the cross-bar survives only as a link-stroke, is seen under the first century ; and this is the period when this latter form evidently became most prevalent, although it no doubt existed earlier.

From the first, *eta*, in its cursive form, had already assumed the shape of a truncated Roman h, the main limb of which was extended in the Byzantine period to the full height of that letter, to which it bears an exact resemblance in the last columns of the Table. The curious shape which it is frequently found to assume in the first century, like the numeral 7 or, rather, the Hebrew ٦, appears, as far as we can judge from existing documents, to have been restricted to about that period.

The shifting of the bent head of *iota* from the right to the left in the course of time has already been noticed.

In *kappa* we have again, as in the case of *beta*, a continued struggle between the capital and the cursive forms, both holding their ground to the end.

The flat and wide-spread forms of *mu* in the Ptolemaic period are very distinctive. The letter appears in the Roman period to have kept very much to its normal capital shape, and only at a later time to have developed its first limb into the long stroke with which it always provided as a minuscule.

The early cursive form of *nu*, of the Ptolemaic period, in which the last limb is thrown high up above the line, did not hold its ground against the square forms, the resemblance of which to certain forms of *pi* has already been referred to. The variety of shapes of both these letters is remarkable.

It might perhaps have been expected that *sigma* would have developed the late round minuscule σ sooner than it did. One sees an approach to it in certain forms of the first century. The down-curving letter of that period might have led directly to it; and it is remarkable that the normal C-shape should have lasted to so late a period as the common form of the letter.

With regard to the closing letters of the alphabet, which appear to have been less subject to variation than most of those which precede them, little need be said. It may be noticed how early the main-stroke of *phi* was drawn outside the loop; and that, in its earliest stage, *omega* was generally in the form of an unfinished *w*, wanting the final curve, or even not far removed from the epigraphic Ω.

CHAPTER XI.

Uncial Writing in Vellum MSS.

WE have seen the Uncial Book-hand in papyri, and have had in the facsimiles of a conveyance of A.D. 88 (p. 126) and of the Bankes Homer (p. 127) specimens of the round hand which is the direct prototype of the writing on vellum which we are now about to examine.

The first thing to strike the eye in the earliest examples of vellum uncial MSS. is the great beauty and firmness of the characters. The general result of the progress of any form of writing through a number of centuries is decadence and not improvement. But in the case of the uncial writing of the early codices there is improvement and not decadence. This is to be attributed to the change of material, the firm and smooth surface of vellum giving the scribe greater scope for displaying his skill as a calligrapher. In other words, there appears to have been a period of renaissance with the general introduction of vellum as the ordinary writing material.

The earliest examples of vellum uncial Greek MSS., which have survived practically entire, are the three great codices of the Bible: the Codex Vaticanus, the Codex Sinaiticus, and the Codex Alexandrinus. The Vaticanus is to all appearance the most ancient and may be ascribed to the 4th century. It is written in triple columns, without enlarged initial letters to mark paragraphs or even the beginnings of the several books. The writing in its original state was beautifully regular and fine; but, unfortunately, the whole of the text has been touched over, in darker ink, by a hand of perhaps the 10th century, only rejected letters or words being allowed to remain intact.

ΓΡΑΠΤωΝΛΕΓωΝ ΤΑ
ΔΕΛΕΓΕΙΟΒΑϹΙΛΕΥϹπερ
ϹωΝΚΥΡΟϹΕΜΕΛΝΕΔει
ΞΕΝΒΑϹΙΛΕΛΤΗϹΟΙΚΥ
ΜΕΝΗϹΟΚΥΡΙΟϹΤΟΥιϲ
ΡΑΗΛΚϹΟΥΨΙϹΤΟϹΚΑΙ
ΕϹΗΜΗΝΕΝΜΟΙΟΙΚΟ
ΛΟΜΗϹΑΙΑΥΤωΟΙΚΟΝ

CODEX VATICANUS.—4TH CENTURY.

(γραπτῶν λεγων· τα | δε λεγει ο βασιλεὺς περ | σῶν
κῦρος· ἐμὲ ἀνέδει | ξεν βασιλέα τῆς οἰκου | μένης ὁ κύριος
τοῦ ἰσ | ραὴλ κ[ύριο]ς ὁ ὑψιστος· καὶ | ἐσήμηνέν μοι οἰκο |
δομῆσαι αὐτῶ οἰκον)

The accents and marks of punctuation are additions
probably by the hand which retouched the writing.

The Codex Sinaiticus, Tischendorf's great discovery,
is probably somewhat younger than the Vatican MS.
and may be placed early in the 5th century.

ΤωΒΑϹΙΛΕΙΤΟΙΙΡΑ
ΓΜΑΚΑΙΕΠΟΙΗϹΕ
ΟΥΓωϹ
ΚΛΙΑΝΘΡωΠΟϹΗΝ
ΙΟΥΔΑΙΟϹΕΝϹΟΥ
ϹΟΙϹΤΗΠΟΛΕΙΚΑΙ
ΟΝΟΜΑΑΥΤωΜΑΡ
ΔΟΧΛΙΟϹΟΤΟΥΙΛΙ
ΡΟΥΤΟΥϹΕΜΕΕΙΟΥ

CODEX SINAITICUS.—EARLY 5TH CENTURY.

(τω βασιλει το πρα | γμα και εποιησε[ν] | ουτως : | και
ανθρωπος ην | ιουδαιος εν σου | σοις τη πολει και | ονομα
αυτω μαρ | δοχαιος ο του ϊαει | ρου· του σεμεειου.)

It is written with four columns in a page, the open book thus presenting eight columns in sequence, and, as has been suggested, recalling the line of columns on a papyrus roll. Like the Vatican MS., it is devoid of enlarged letters; but the initial letter of a line beginning a sentence is usually placed slightly in the margin, as will be seen in the facsimile.

The chief characteristic of the letters is squareness, the width being generally equal to the height. The shapes are simple, and horizontal strokes are fine.

With the Codex Alexandrinus there is a decided advance. The division of the Gospels into Ammonian sections and the presence of the references to the Eusebian canons are indications of a later age than that of its two predecessors. The MS. may have been written before the middle of the 5th century. There can be little doubt of the country of its origin being Egypt, for, besides the fact of its having belonged to the Patriarchal Chamber of Alexandria, it also contains in its titles certain forms of the letters **A** and **M** which are distinctly Egyptian.[1] It was sent as a present to King Charles the First by Cyril Lucar, Patriarch of Constantinople.

CODEX ALEXANDRINUS.—5TH CENTURY.

(θ[εο]ν σου και αυτω μονω λατ|ρευ| | σεις· και ηγαγεν αυτον | εις ϊ[ηρουσα]λημ· και εστησεν αυτον | επι τα πτερυγιον του ιερου | και ειπεν αυτω ει υ[ιο]ς ει του [θεου] | βαλε σεαυτον εντευθεν κ[ατω·] | γεγραπται γαρ οτι τοις αγγελ[οις] | αυτου εντελcιτε περι σου τ—)

[1] See p. 154.

In this specimen we see instances of contracted words. The MS. has enlarged letters to mark the beginnings of paragraphs ; the initial standing in the margin at the beginning of the first *full* line, whether that be the first line of the paragraph, or whether the paragraph begin, as shown in the facsimile, in the middle of the preceding line after a blank space.

The writing of the Codex Alexandrinus is more carefully finished than that of the Codex Sinaiticus. The letters are rather wide; horizontal strokes are very fine ; and there is a general tendency to thicken or club the extremities of certain letters, as Γ, T, Є, and C.

Other uncial MSS. which have been ascribed to the fifth century and a little later are : the Homer of the Ambrosian Library at Milan, interesting for its illustrations, which were copied probably from earlier originals and have . transmitted the characteristics of classical art (*Pal. Soc.* i. pls. 39, 40, 50, 51); the palimpsest MS. of the Bible, known as the Codex Ephraemi, at Paris (ed. Tischendorf, 1845) ; the Octateuch, whose extant leaves are divided between Paris, Leyden, and St. Petersburg; the Genesis of the Cottonian Library, once, probably, one of the most beautifully illustrated MSS. of its period, but now reduced by fire to blackened and defaced fragments (*Cat. Anc. MSS.* i. pl. 8); the Dio Cassius of the Vatican (Silvestre, pl. 60) ; and the Paris Pentateuch (*Ib.* pl. 61). A facsimile of an ancient fragment of Euripides at Berlin, which is certainly of a respectable age and which has even been ascribed to the 4th century, will be found in Wilcken's *Tafeln zür älteren griech. Palæographie*, pl. iv.

Uncial writing of the sixth century shows an advance on the delicate style of the fifth century in the comparatively heavy forms of its letters. Horizontal strokes are lengthened, and are generally finished off with heavy points or finials. The Dioscorides of Vienna (*Pal. Soc.* i. pl. 177), written early in the century for Juliana Anicia, daughter of Flavius Anicius Olybrius, Emperor of the West in 472, is a most valuable MS. for the palæographer, as it is the earliest example of uncial writing on vellum

to which an approximate date can be given. It is also
of great interest for the history of art, as, in addition to
the coloured drawings of plants, reptiles, insects, etc.,
which illustrate the text, it contains six full-page designs,
one of them being the portrait of the royal Juliana herself.

ΦΥΛΛΕΧΕΙΚΑΡΟΙΑΒΑCΙΛΙ
ΧΛωΡΑωCΚΡΑΜΒΗC·ΤΟΔC
ωCΤΤΕΡΤΤΡΙωΝ·ΚΑΥΛΟΓ
ΤΡΙΤΤΗΧΗ·ΤΤΑΡΑΦΥΑΔΑCΑ
ΚΕΦΑΛΛΙΟΜΟΙΛΙΜΗΚωΝ

DIOSCORIDES.—EARLY 6TH CENTURY.

(Φυλλα εχει καροια βασιλι[κη]— | χλωρα ως βραμ'βης·
το δε— | ωσπερ πριων· καυλον— | τριπηχη· παραφυαδας
α[πο]— | κεφαλαι ομοιαι μηκων[ι]—)

This is a specimen of careful writing, suitable to a
sumptuous book prepared for a lady of high rank. The
letters exhibit a contrast of thick and fine strokes; the
curve of both **Є** and **C** is thickened at both extremities;
the base of **Δ** extends right and left and has heavy dots
at the ends; the cross-strokes of **Π** and **T** are treated in
the same way. In the second line will be noticed an
instance, in the word βραμβης, of the use of the
apostrophe to separate two consonants,[2] a common
practice in this MS.

Other MSS. of this period are: the palimpsest Homer
in the British Museum (*Cat. Anc. MSS.* i. pl. 9; *Pal.
Soc.* ii. pl. 3), generally named, after its editor, the
Cureton Homer, and the palimpsest fragments of St.
Luke's Gospel (*Cat. Anc. MSS.* pl. 10), which together
with it were re-used by a later Syrian scribe; the frag-

[2] See p. 73.

ments of the Pauline Epistles from Mount Athos, some of which are in Paris and some in Moscow (Silvestre, pls. 63, 64; Sabas, pl. A); the Gospels written on purple vellum in silver and gold, and now scattered between London (Cotton MS., Titus C. xv.), Rome, Vienna, and Patmos, the place of its origin; the fragments of the Eusebian Canons, written on gilt vellum and sumptuously ornamented, in the British Museum (*Cat. Anc. MSS.*, i. pl. 11); the Coislin Octateuch (Silvestre, pl. 65); the Vienna Genesis, with illustrations of very great interest (*Pal. Soc.* i. pl. 178); the Rossano Gospels written in silver on purple vellum and also having a remarkable series of illustrations (ed. Gebhardt and Harnack, 1880); and the Dublin palimpsest fragments of St. Matthew's Gospel and of Isaiah (ed. T. K. Abbott, *Par Palimpsestorum Dublin.*), the handwriting of the former using the Egyptian forms of A and M, strongly marked (*Δ, Ш*).

There are also two bilingual Græco-Latin MSS. which are assigned to the sixth century, viz., the Codex Bezæ of the New Testament at Cambridge (*Pal. Soc.* i. pls. 14, 15), and the Codex Claromontanus of the Pauline Epistles at Paris (*Pal. Soc.* i. pls. 63, 64). But these were almost certainly written in France or, at all events, in Western Europe, and rather belong to the domain of Latin palæography, as the Greek letters are to some extent modelled on the Latin forms. The Greek portions of the great Laurentian codex of the Pandects at Florence (Wattenbach, *Script. Graec. Specim.*, tab. 7) should also be noticed as of this period.

The decadence of the round uncial hand in the successive centuries may be seen in the second Vienna Dioscorides (*Pal. Soc.* ii. pl. 45), which is thought to be of the early part of the 7th century, and in the Vatican MS. of Pope Gregory's Dialogues (*Pal. Soc.* ii. pl. 81), which was written, probably at Rome, in the year 800. But in these later centuries Greek uncial MSS. were more usually written in another style.

Soon after the year 600, a variety of the round uncia came into ordinary use—a change similar to that which

has been noticed as taking place in the uncial writing
on papyrus. The circular letters Є, Θ, O, C become
oval, and the letters generally are laterally compressed
and appear narrow in proportion to their height. The
writing also slopes to the right, and accentuation begins
to be applied systematically. At first the character of
the writing was light and elegant, but as time went on
it gradually became heavier and more artificial. A few
scattered Greek notes are found written in this style in
Syriac MSS. which bear actual dates in the seventh
century (Gardthausen, *Griech. Palæog.*, table 1 of
alphabets); and there are a few palimpsest fragments of
Euclid and of Gospel Lectionaries among the Syriac
MSS. of the British Museum, of the seventh and eighth
centuries; but there is no entire MS. in sloping uncials
bearing a date earlier than the ninth century.

As an early specimen we select a few lines from the
facsimile (Wattenbach, *Script. Gr. Specim.*, tab. 8) of
the fragment of a mathematical treatise from Bobio,
now in the Ambrosian Library at Milan, which is assigned
to the 7th century.

MATHEMATICAL TREATISE.—7TH CENTURY.

(τοιουτ[ων] ζητησεων οικεια και— | ως εφην τω δικαιως
αν κληθ[εντι]— | υιω προσηκουσα. | Πρωτ[ον] μ[εν]
γ[αρ] παντ[ος] στερεου σχημ[ατος]— | προς τι μετεωρον
ευχερεστερ[ον]— | χανικ[ης] ολκης οποταν εκ τ[ου] κεντ
[ρου])

It will be seen that in this MS., intended for students'
use and dealing with a secular subject, abbreviations are
fairly numerous.

In a more compact style, and rather heavier, is the Venetian codex of the Old Testament (Wattenbach, *Script. Gr. Specim.*, tab. 9), which is of the 8th or 9th century. Descriptive titles are written in round uncials, evidently in imitative style and devoid of the grace and ease of a natural hand, as will be seen from the facsimile.

OLD TESTAMENT.—8TH OR 9TH CENTURY.

καὶ μήτρα συλλήμψεως αἰωνίας ἵνα | τί τοῦτο ἐξῆλθον ἐκ μήτρας· τοῦ [βλέ], | πειν κόπους καὶ πόνους· καὶ διετέλ[εσαν] | ἐν αἰσχύνῃ αἱ ἡμέραι μου :— | † Ὁ λόγος ὁ γενόμενος πρὸς ἱερεμί[αν] | παρὰ κ[υριο]υ. ὅτε ἀπέστειλεν πρὸς αὐτὸν | ὁ βασιλεὺς σεδεκιας· τὸν πάσχωρ᾽ υ[ἱὸν])

At length, in the middle of the ninth century, we have a MS. with a date: a Psalter of the year 862, belonging to Bishop Uspensky (Wattenbach, *Script. Gr. Specim.*, tab. 10).

USPENSKY PSALTER.—A.D. 862.

(Ἐν ονοματι τῆς ἀγιας ἀ | χράντου καὶ ζωαρχικῆ[ς] | τριαδος,
π[ατ]ρ[ο]ς καὶ υ[ιο]υ καὶ | ἀγίου πν[ευματο]ς· ἐγράφη
καὶ | ἐτελειώθη τὸ παρὸν ψαλ | τήριον· κελεύσει τοῦ
ἀ | γίου καὶ μακαρίου π[ατ]ρ[ο]ς)

In this specimen further progress is seen in the contrast of heavy and light strokes.

Other MSS. of this character are: a small volume of
hymns in the British Museum, Add. MS. 26113, of the
8th or 9th century (*Cat. Anc. MSS.* i. pl. 14; *Pal. Soc.*
ii. pl. 4); a copy of Gregory of Nazianzus, written
between 867 and 886 (Silvestre, pl. 71); the Bodleian
Genesis (Gk. Misc. 312), of the 9th century (*Pal. Soc.* ii.
pl. 26); a Dionysius Areopagita at Florence, also of the
9th century (Vitelli and Paoli, *Facsim. Paleogr.*, tav.
17); and a Lectionary in the Harleian collection, of the
end of the 9th or beginning of the 10th century (*Cat.
Anc. MSS.* i. pl. 17).

But by this time uncial writing had passed out of
ordinary use, and only survived, as a rule, for church-
books, in which the large character was convenient for
reading in public.

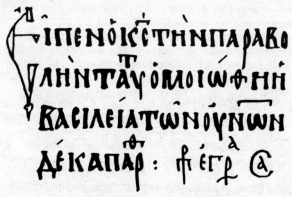

EVANGELISTARIUM.—A.D. 980.

('Εἶπεν ὁ κ[υριο]ς τὴν παραβο | λὴν ταυτ[ην] ὁμοιώθη ἡ |
βασιλεία τῶν οὐ[ρα]νων | δέκα παρθ[ενοις]: πρ[ο] ἐγρα[φη]
σα[ββατω])

In this capacity it underwent another change, the letters reverting from the sloping position to the upright position of the early uncial, and again, after a period, becoming rounder. This was evidently a mere calligraphic development, the style being better suited for handsome service books. Of this character are the Bodleian Gospels (Gk. Misc. 313) of the 10th century (*Pal. Soc.* ii. pl. 7); the Laurentian Evangelistarium of the 10th century (Vitelli and Paoli, *Facsim. Paleogr.*, tav. 7); the Harleian Evangelistarium (no. 5598), of the year 995 (*Pal. Soc.* i. pl. 26, 27); and the Zouche Evangelistarium, of 980 (*Pal. Soc.* i. pl. 154), from which a few lines are given above.

There are also a certain number of MSS. in which uncial writing appears to have been used for distinction, or contrast. Thus, in a MS. at Florence, of A.D. 886-911, containing Fasti Consulares and other matter arranged in tabulated form, the entries are made in a beautifully neat upright uncial (Vitelli and Paoli, *Facsim. Paleogr.*, tav. 13, 25, 31); so also in the Florentine Dionysius Areopagita of the 9th century, referred to above, while the text is in large slanting uncials, the commentary is in smaller upright uncials; and we have the Bodleian Psalter with catena (Gk. Misc. 5), of the year 950, in which the text of the Psalms is written in upright uncials, while the commentary is in minuscules (*Pal. Soc.* ii. 5; Gardthausen, *Gr. Palæogr.*, p. 159, tab. 2, col. 4.)

The use of small uncial writing for marginal commentaries and notes in minuscule MSS. is not uncommon during the earlier centuries after the establishment of the smaller style of writing as a book-hand. As a late instance of the uncial being used for the text, a page from a MS. of St. John Chrysostom, which is ascribed to the 11th century, will be found in Vitelli and Paoli, *Facsim. Paleogr.*, tav. 28. It appears to have lingered on till about the middle of the 12th century.

CHAPTER XII.

Minuscule Writing of the Middle Ages.

GREEK Minuscule MSS. of the middle ages have been divided into classes, as a convenient method of marking periods in a style of writing which, being used for the language of a limited area, and being subject to no exterior influence, underwent, like all isolated branches of writing, only a gradual change. These classes are :— (1) *codices vetustissimi*, the most ancient MSS. of the ninth century and to the middle of the tenth century; (2) *codices vetusti*, those which range from the middle of the tenth century to the middle of the thirteenth century; (3) *codices recentiores*, from the middle of the thirteenth century to the middle of the fifteenth century; (4) *codices novelli*, all MSS. of later date.

There are still some thousand dated Greek MSS. in existence, in the different libraries of Europe, which were written before the year 1500; a list is given by Gardthausen, *Griech. Palæogr.*, pp. 344, sqq. Of these almost all are written in minuscules. More than three hundred facsimiles, nearly all produced by photographic methods, and dating from the year 800 to 1593, have been published. Of the ninth century there are not a dozen dated MSS. extant; nine are represented in facsimile. Of the tenth century there are nearly fifty; and of these there are nearly forty facsimiles. Of the eleventh century, the number rises to nearly one hundred, and more than sixty are given in facsimile. It is curious that dated MSS. in the twelfth century are comparatively few—about seventy; twenty-five of which have been represented in facsimile. In the later centuries, of course, they become more numerous.

It has already been explained that the minuscule hand, which almost suddenly makes its appearance as a literary hand in the ninth century, was nothing more than the cursive writing of the day written with care. The trained scribes made the best use of the smooth vellum to exhibit in their work that contrast of fine and heavy strokes which has always been held to impart a beauty to handwriting. Under this careful treatment the sloping tendency of a current hand was resisted, and the writing in its new set form became upright.

There are, however, a few MSS. in existence which seem to prove that a calligraphic style, or reform, of the cursive hand, for literary purposes, was in partial use before the period of the literary minuscule of the ninth century.

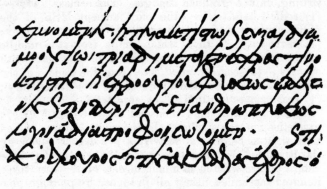

THEOLOGICAL WORKS.—8TH OR 9TH CENTURY.

(τεμνομενης· η τηι ακτιστω [και] συναιδιω[ι και ὁ] | μοουσιωι τριαδι μεταγενεστερας τινο[ς η] | κτισης ἠ ετεροουσιου φυσεως επεισ[αγομε] | νης [και] τον περι της ενανθρωπη-σεως [του κυριου] | λογον αδιαστροφον σωζομεν· [και] τι[μοθεος] | δε ὁ ελουρος ὁ τῆς αληθειας ἐχθρος—).

The writing of these MSS. slopes after the manner of a current hand, and yet the letters are formed with a

uniform precision which stamps it as a hand which had
been developed in some school of writing, which, however, to judge from the paucity of existing specimens,
probably had no very wide influence. A facsimile from
a MS. of this character, and ascribed to the 8th century,
is given by Gardthausen, *Beiträge zur Griech. Palaeographie,* 1877 ; and another from a liturgical roll at Mount
Sinai, of the 9th century, accompanies a paper by the
same writer, *Différences Provinciales de la Minuscule
Grecque,* in *Mélanges Graux,* 1884. A third MS., containing a collection of theological works, from which the
facsimile above is taken, is in the Vatican Library, and
is probably of the end of the 8th or beginning of the 9th
century (*Pal. Soc.* ii. pl. 126).

Many of the forms of letters in this writing which are
distinctly cursive, such as a looped *alpha,* the inverted
epsilon, the h-shaped *eta,* and the n-shaped *nu,* disappear
from, or are modified in, the more settled literary
minuscule hand.

But before examining in detail the progress of this
literary hand through the different periods or classes
which have been enumerated, its general course of
development may be traced in a few words.

In the cursive writing there was never an entire suppression of the original capital forms. For example, the
large **B, Δ, H, K, N,** and others are found side by side
with the more cursive forms of the same letters. It was,
therefore, only to be expected that, however rigorously
such capital forms might be excluded from the set
literary minuscule hand when it was written in its first
stage of exactness, they would by degrees creep in and
show themselves side by side with their purely minuscule
equivalents in literary works, just as they did in the
ordinary cursive writings of the period. This, in fact,
happened ; and the presence of capital forms in lesser or
greater numbers affords some criterion of the age of a MS.

Again, the degeneration of writing from the earliest
models of the ninth and tenth centuries to the hurried
styles of the fifteenth and sixteenth centuries is apparent
enough if we turn over a consecutive series of MSS. or

facsimiles. But this degeneration only became rapid, and, so to say, acquired its full impetus, in the later centuries. And certain classes, such as liturgical MSS., which custom had retained for special uses, were less tolerant of change, and served in some measure to retard the disuse of the formal hands of older times. In the earlier centuries breathings and accents are applied in a style in keeping with the exact writing of the text; the breathings are rectangular and the accents are short. Afterwards, the former being more rapidly written become curved; and the latter are dashed on with a bolder stroke. Their last stage is when they even blend with the letters which they mark.

The writing of the period of the *codices vetustissimi*, of the ninth century and to the middle of the tenth century, as far as is shown by surviving examples, is very pure and exact. The letters are most symmetrically formed; they are compact and upright, and have even a tendency to lean back to the left. Breathings are rectangular, in keeping with the careful and deliberate formation of the letters. In a word, the style being practically a new one for literary purposes, the scribes wrote it in their best form and kept strictly to the approved pattern.

The earliest dated example of this class is the copy of the Gospels belonging to Bishop Uspensky, written in the year 835. A facsimile, but not very satisfactory, appears in Gardthausen's *Beiträge* and in Wattenbach and von Velsen's *Exempla Codicum Graecorum*, tab. 1. Next comes the Oxford Euclid (D'Orville MS.), which belonged to Arethas, Archbishop of Cæsarea, and was written in 888.

The breadth of the letters will be noticed, as well as a certain squareness in the general character and the slight inclination to the left. Exact finish is best seen in such letters as *a* and δ, the final stroke of the former, when unconnected, being brought up to the top of the line, and the down-stroke of the latter being drawn right down to the base. The set forms into which the cursive

β, η, and κ are cast should also be noted. The ornamental effect of the writing is added to by the slight
turn or hook in which down-strokes terminate. Certain
of these characteristics remain in the minuscule writing of
succeeding centuries : others wear off and are lost as
time advances.

EUCLID.—A.D. 888.

(μεν εισι τα $\overline{ΛΞΓ}$ $\overline{ΡΦΖ}$ τρίγωνα. απεν[αντιον δε] | τα
$\overline{ΟΜΝ}$ $\overline{ΣΤΤ}$· ώστε κ[αι] τα στερεα παραλ[ληλεπίπεδα] |
τα ἀπο τῶν ειρημένων πρισμάτων [ἀναγραφομε] | να
ἰσοϋψη τυγχανοντα. προς ἀλληλά [εισιν ὡς αἱ] | βάσεις
κ[αι] τα ημιση· αρα εσται ὡς ἡ $\overline{ΛΞΓ}$ [βασις προς] | την
$\overline{ΡΦΖ}$ βασιν. ουτω τα ειρημένα πρ[ισματα προς] | αλληλα
ὅπερ ἔδει δεῖξαι :)

Our next facsimile, from a MS. at Paris (Omont,
Facsimilés, pl. 1), illustrates the same class of writing,
of rather larger type and more laterally compressed,
the uprightness of the character being thus more
evident.

M 2

LIVES OF SAINTS.—A.D. 890.

(—πιστάμην ὁποῖος ἦν· [καὶ] τού | των λεγομενων. ἐσύ-
ρισεν κα | τ αυτῆς ὁ δράκων παροξυν | θεὶς σφόδρα· ἡ
δὲ ἁγία δού | λη του θ[εο]ῦ τὸν στ[αυ]ρον ἐποίησεν | τῶ
μετόπω [καὶ] ἐν παντὶ τῶ σώ—)

A third specimen is taken from a very beautiful MS.
of St. Clement of Alexandria (Omont, *Facsimilés*, pl. 2).
written for Archbishop Arethas, abovementioned, in the
year 914.

ST. CLEMENT OF ALEXANDRIA.—A.D. 914.

(μενον ἐθνῶν· ἐπανελθόντα εἰς αἴγυπτον ἐπαγαγ[έσθαι
τεχνι] | τας ἱκανούς· τὸν οὖν ὄσιριν, τὸν προπάτορα
[τὸν αὐτοῦ] | δέδαλθῆναι ἐκέλευσεν αὐτὸς πολυτελῶ.

κ[ατασκευά] | ζει δὲ αὐτὸν βρύαξις ὁ δημιουργός· οὐχ ὁ
ἀθην[αῖος· ἄλλος] | δε τίς ὁμώνυμος, ἐκείνωι τῶι βρυάξιδι·
ὃς, ὕλη[ι])

And lastly of this period we give a few lines from a
MS. of Basil's commentary on Isaiah, of the year 942
(Omont, *Facsim.*, pl. 4), written in a rather larger character, but showing very little advance on the earlier
examples. Indeed, the writing of this first division of
the minuscule literary hand is subject to so little change
in its course, that it is extremely difficult to place the
undated MSS. in their proper order of time.

ST. BASIL.—A.D. 942.

(αἴσθησιν ἥξουσιν· ὅτι οἱ μὲ[ν κατὰ τὰ ἔθνη] | περιπα-
τοῦντες· ἐν σάλῳ εἰ[σὶ διὰ τὴν ἑαυ] | τῶν κακίαν· οἱ δὲ
τὸν νοῦν [ἑαυτῶν κεκα] | θαρμένον ἔχοντες· ὃς ὀνομά
[ζεται σιὼν· ἐπεὶ] | δὴ ἐκεῖθέν ἐστι τὸ σκοπευ[τήριον])

We now pass on to the *codices vetusti,* from the middle
of the tenth century to the middle of the thirteenth
century. But before surveying the more formal hands
of this period, a few words should be said regarding a
style of writing which is noteworthy, as certain important MSS. of classical literature, whose date it is of
interest to determine, are written in it.

It is not to be supposed that MSS. of the earlier
period of minuscule writing which has been discussed,
were only written by the most accomplished scribes and
in the best style. The working copies of students and

scholars were no doubt then as rough and cursive in comparison with the facsimiles given above as a modern scholar's own composition is in comparison with a printed text; and, except for choice copies, written for some special purpose, such, for example, as the Bodleian Plato of 895 (*Pal. Soc.* i. pl. 81 ; *Exempla,* tab. 3), or the Harley Lucian of the British Museum, of the beginning of the tenth century (*Cat. Anc. MSS.* i. pl. 18; *Pal. Soc.* ii. pl. 27), the extreme calligraphic style was not called for in books which were intended for private use. Hence a more fluent character of writing appears to have been practised as a book-hand for copies which would serve ordinary purposes: a good working hand, perfectly clear and well formed, more set and formal than a common cursive hand would be, but yet not finished off with precise care. In the tenth and eleventh centuries then, we find MSS. written in this style, and no doubt still earlier examples existed. We give facsimiles from two MSS., separated by an interval of nearly one hundred years: a Chrysostom of 954 and a St. Ephraem of 1049 (Omont, *Facsim.*, pls. 5, 21).

CHRYSOSTOM.—A.D. 954.

(καὶ ὁ μὲν ἐν ερημία τῶν | προστησωμένων ἦν· οὗτος | δὲ εἶχεν τοὺς ἐπιμελουμένους, | οἳ καὶ βαστάζοντες αὐτὸν | ἔφερον· καὶ τούτω μέν φησιν)

ST. EPHRAEM.—A.D. 1049.

(τοῦ κυρίου σου· μήποτε ὁ τὰ [ζιζάνια συμ] | μίξη τι
τῶν ἰδίων· ἔθος γὰρ. a[ὐτῷ ἐστι διὰ τοῦ] | ἀγαθοῦ τὸ κακὸν
κατεργάζεσθαι· [παρὰ κυρίου ζη] | τήσωμεν χάριν. ἵνα ἡμῖν
δω[ρήσηται γνῶσιν] | [καὶ] σύνεσιν τοῦ νήφειν ἐν πᾶσι·
[κάμινος δο] | κιμάζει ἀργύριον κ[αὶ] χρυσίον.)

In the older specimen the writing is rather stiffer
and not quite so fluent as in the other; and both are
good characteristic specimens of their respective centuries. The St. Ephraem is the work of a very experienced penman, who must have written with great
ease and rapidity, without in the least degenerating in
his style.

The four following facsimiles will give an idea of the
formal style of writing of the eleventh, twelfth, and
early thirteenth centuries; and from them it will be
seen how very gradual was the change in the actual
forms of the letters.

In the first, from a Chrysostom of 1003 (Omont,
Facsim., pl. 11), the exact regularity of the tenth
century is still remembered, but the writing is hardly
so graceful as in the earlier examples.

CHRYSOSTOM.—A.D. 1003.

(—ριστίαν ἀντι θυσίας. ἤ | νεγκε τῶ θ[ε]ω λέγων· εὔ | η
τὸ ὄνομα κ[υριο]υ εὐλογη | μένον· νῦν καὶ ἀεὶ· καὶ εἰς |
τοὺς αἰῶνας τῶν αἰώνω[ν])

The next is half a century later, from Saints' Lives
of the year 1055-6 (Omont, *Facsim.*, pl. 23). Here
there is a little more tendency to roundness and rather
less compactness.

LIVES OF SAINTS.—A.D. 1055-6.

(αὐτοῦ διοκλητιανοῦ | τὰ κατὰ ζῆλον | τοῦ ἀνδρὸς ἀγωνί |
σματα· ὃς τῆι ἀδο | κήτω φήμη κατα)

The third, a good characteristic specimen, from sermons of St. Theodore Studites, of 1136 (Omont, *Facsim.*, pl. 47), is more freely written; strokes are lengthened, marks of contraction and accents are more prominent, and breathings lose their old angular shape.

ST. THEODORE.—A.D. 1136.

(καὶ ποτίζειν καὶ οἷον δια | κόπτειν καὶ τέμνειν καὶ | ἀπο-καθαίρειν, ἵνα γέ | νησθε ἄμπελος εὐκλη | ματουσα, πολὺν φέ[ρουσα])

The fourth specimen is selected from a Lectionary of 1204 (Omont, *Facsim.*, pl. 51), in which the old style of hand is maintained, but betrays its more recent date by its irregular formation and exaggerated strokes.

LECTIONARY.—A.D. 1204.

(ἀποκριθεὶς δὲ ὁ πέ | τρος λέγει αὐτῶ | σὺ εἰ ὁ χ[ριστὸ]ς.
καὶ ἐπετί | μησεν αὐτοὺς ἵνα | μηδενὶ λέγωσιν πε—)

The marks above the line, in addition to the accents,
are to guide the intonation.

The two hundred years, from the middle of the
thirteenth century to the middle of the fifteenth century,
which are given to the *codices recentiores,* witness more
rapid changes than have been seen in the previous
periods. This was naturally to be expected with the
wider diffusion of learning and the consequent multiplication of copies of books of all kinds.

We will first examine the writing of the thirteenth
century, taking our first facsimile from a typical MS.
of the latter half of the century, written in the ordinary
formal style—a Chrysostom of 1273 (Omont, *Facsim.,*
pl. 60).

CHRYSOSTOM.—A.D. 1273.

(—τομὴν, [καὶ] ταύτη διὰ τοῦ στ[αυ]ροῦ τ[ῆς] | κατάρας
ἀπαλλάξας τῆς ἐπὶ | τῆ παραβάσει, οὐκ ἀφῆκε δια | πεσεῖν
τὴν ἐπαγγελίαν· ὅταν | Οὖν λέγη διάκονον περίτομ[ης] |
τοῦτο λέγη, ὅτι ἐλθὼν [καὶ] πάντα)

As a characteristic of the writing of this period, the
persistence of enlarged or stilted letters strikes the

eye. These forms are used sporadically in the preceding centuries, but not so commonly as to become a
feature as they do now.

Next is given a specimen from a MS. of Theophylactus on the Gospels, of 1255 (Omont, *Facsim.*, pl. 55),
a MS. not of so formal a type as the last, and therefore
bearing a more distinctive character of advance.

THEOPHYLACTUS.—A.D. 1255.

(θαύμ[α]τ[α]. οὔτε τὰ ἐπὶ τῶ τάφω μαρτυρούμενα— | τῶ
ἰδίω πάθει τῆ φιλαργυρία ὑπονοθεύ[ουσι]— | ἀσεβέστερον
φθέγξασθαι κ[αὶ] ἀνοητότ[ε]ρ[ον], ὅτι— | οὐ διὰ τ[ὸν] φόβον
ἀποκλεισθέντ[ες], κ[αὶ] μὴ τολ[μῶντες]— | πέθνησκον
ὕστερον δι᾽ αὐτὸν κηρύττοντ[ες] ὅ)

And here we turn aside from the more beaten track
to notice the small cursive hand of this period, which is
found occasionally in that class of MSS. to which reference has already been made as students' books. The
occurrence of a dated MS. written in this hand is of
great assistance, for the freedom with which it is
written rather influences the judgment to assign undated specimens to a later period than that to which
they really belong. It may be observed that, though
a good deal flourished, the innate character of the
writing is a certain stiffness and, if we may use the
term, a wiry aspect, which disappears in the later
cursive hands. The MS. which supplies the facsimile
is a commentary on Porphyry's Introduction to Aristotle,
of 1223 (Omont, *Facsim.*, pl. 52).

PORPHYRY.—A.D. 1223.

(τούτ[ων], ἐκεῖ εἰσὶν, [καὶ] αἱ ὑπόλοιπ[οι]. ὅπ[ο]υ [δὲ] μία
[ἐκλείπεται], | ἐκεῖ [καὶ] π[ᾶσ]αι ἐκλείπουσι. εἰρηκότ[ες]
τὰς κοινωνί[ας] [χωρή] | σωμ[εν] [καὶ] ἐπὶ τὰς δ[ια]φο[ράς].
δευτ[έρα] [δὲ] δ[ια]φορα αὐτ[ων] [ὑπέρχεται,] | ὁ τρόπο[ς]
τ[ῆς] κατηγορί[ας]. αἱ μ[ὲν] γ[ὰρ] ἐν τῷ τί [ἐστιν] κατηγο
[ροῦντες] | ὥσπερ τὸ γένος κ[αὶ] τὸ εἶδο[ς]· αἱ [δὲ] ἐν τῷ
ὁποῖον [τί ἐστιν] | ὥσπερ ἡ δ[ια]φο[ρὰ], [καὶ] τὸ ἴδιον,
κ[αὶ] τὸ συμβεβηκό[ς].)

To compare with this, a few lines follow from a MS.
written in the same style a hundred years later, the
History of Barlaam and Josaphat, of 1321 (Omont,
Facsim., pl. 78), the writing of which, it will be observed, is slacker.

BARLAAM AND JOSAPHAT.—A.D. 1321.

(φύσε[ως] ἡμ[ῶν], οὐδὲ ἐν τούτω τῶ μέρει ἀφῆ[κεν ἡμᾶς] |
ἀνιάτρευτα νοσ[εῖν]. ἀλλ᾽ ὡς πάνσοφος ἰα[τρὸς τῆ] | ὀλι-
σθῆρα ἡμ[ῶν] [καὶ] φιλαμαρτήμονι γνώμη, [συνέμιξε] | τὸ
φάρμακον τ[ῆς] μετανοί[ας]. κηρύξας ταύ[την εἰς] | ἄφεσ[ιν]
ἁμαρτιῶν. μετὰ γὰρ τὸ λαβ[εῖν] —)

To illustrate the writing of the fourteenth century,
we first select a Psalter of the year 1304 (Omont, *Facsim.*,
pl. 75), just one hundred years later than the formally-
written Lectionary of 1204, of which a facsimile is
given above.

PSALTER.—A.D. 1304.

(Διαμενεῖ εἰς τὸν [αἰῶνα ἐνώ] | πιον τοῦ θ[εο]ῦ: | Ἔλεος
καὶ ἀλήθει[αν αὐτοῦ τίς] | ἐκζητήσει: | Οὕτως ψαλῶ τῶ
ὀ[νοματί σου] | εἰς τοὺς αἰῶνα[ς] :)

The very conservative nature of the formal writing of
liturgical books could not be better illustrated than by
this large hand of the fourteenth century, which reverts
so distinctly to early models. But its artificial character
is at once apparent when it is compared in detail with

the more ancient writings of the tenth and eleventh
centuries which it imitates.

Next follow two specimens of a more general character,
in which the transition from the style of the middle
ages towards that of the modern school of writing is
very marked. The first is taken from a Manual of
Jurisprudence by Constantine Harmenopoulos, of 1351;
the second is from a MS. of Herodotus, of 1372 (Omont,
Facsim., pls. 85, 96).

In both of these specimens there will be observed
instances of the late practice of writing accents as if
integral parts of the letters.

CONSTANTINE HARMENOPOULOS.—A.D. 1351.

(τίθεται, καλεῖσθαι παρὰ τοῦ δικαστ[οῦ]— | ἑκάστης
κλήσεως, οὐκ ἔλαττον τριά[κοντα]— | διαστήματι περι-
κλειομένης· [καὶ] ἐα[ν]— | παραγένηται, ἢ ἐντολέα πέμψῃ,
δί[δοσθαι]— | ἑτέρου ἐνιαυτοῦ προθεσμία· ἧς ἐν[τὸς]—)

HERODOTUS.—A.D. 1372.

(τὴν ἀγγελίην, ὅτι οὐδὲν ποιήσομ[εν]— | ὑμέων προσε-
δέετο· πρίν ὢν παρεῖ[ναι]— | τὴν ἀττικήν, ἡμέας καιρός
ἐστι προβ[οηθῆσαι]— | βοιωτίην· οἱ μὲν, ταῦτα ὑποκριναμ
[ένων]— | ἀπαλλάσσοντο ἐς σπάρτην.)

In the fifteenth century the varieties of handwriting
become most numerous, and it is impossible to do more
than select a few specimens to illustrate the period.[1]
For the first half of the century two examples may
suffice, the first from a Polybius of 1416 (*Pal. Soc.* i.
pl. 134) ; and the other from a MS. of Simplicius upon
the Physics of Aristotle, written by John Argyropoulos
at Padua in 1441 (Omont, *Facsim. xv. et xvi. s.*, pl. 24),
in a style which recalls the cursive hand of the thirteenth
and fourteenth centuries represented above.

POLYBIUS.—A.D. 1416.

(—αν, φιλίνω μὲν πάντα δοχοῦσιν οἱ καρ | — καλῶς
ἀνδρωδῶς. οἱ δὲ ῥωμαῖοι, | —[το]ύτων ἐν μὲν οὖν τῶ λοιπῶ
βίω τὴν τοι | —[ἐκ β]άλλοι· καὶ γὰρ φιλόφιλον δεῖ εἶναι
τ[ὸν] | —[συμ]μισεῖν τοῖς φίλοις τοὺς ἐχθροὺς· καὶ | —τῆς
ἱστορί[ας] ἦθος ἀναλαμβάνη τις, ἐπι).

The frequent dotting of the *iota* in this MS. is peculiar.

---

[1] Monsieur Omont's *Fac-similés de Manuscrits Grecs des xv*
et xvi siècles*, 1887, contains an interesting series of specimens of
the writing of various Greek professional calligraphists of those
centuries, who settled in Italy and Western Europe under stress
of the Ottoman invasion and were employed as copyists by
patrons of literature, or as correctors for the press.

SIMPLICIUS.—A.D. 1441.

(—σαι τε [καὶ] βασανίσαι τῶν ᾽φυσικῶν | τὰς στοιχει-
ώδεις ἀρχὰς ἂν εὑρίσκει | πρώτας. δεικνὺς ἐκ τῶν ἐναντίων |
εἶναι τὰς γενήσεις· ὧν κοινότατον, | τό, τε εἶδος, [καὶ] ἡ
στέρησις. [καὶ] ἔτι, ἐκ | τοῦ τοῖς ἐναντίοις ὑποκειμένου. |
[καὶ] δὴ [καὶ] π[ερ]ὶ τῆς ὕλης, ὅτι τέ ἐστιν | ἀποδείξας,
[καὶ] ὅτι ὑποκείμενον τοῖς)

To illustrate the *codices novelli* of the fifteenth and
sixteenth centuries, first a few lines are taken from a
formally-written Menæum, or offices for saints' days, of
the year 1460 (*Pal. Soc.* i. pl. 233), the writing of which
recalls the style of the thirteenth century.

MENÆUM.—A.D. 1460.

(εἰδώλων θρησκίας ἐπὶ τὴν τῶν χριστιανῶν— | πρὸς σὲ
κοινωνίαν οὐ καταδέχομαι. ὁ δὲ τῷ— | μὴ δυνηθέντος
δὲ τοῦ π[ατ]ρ[ὸ]ς ἀπὸ τῆς εἰς χ[ριστὸ]ν πίστε[ως]— | τῷ
τῷ μνηστίρι καὶ ἐπάρχῳ εἰς τ[ὴν] κατὰ τοὺς κρατο[ῦντας]— |
ὁ δὲ τοῦ χιτῶνος γυμνώσας αὐτὴν καὶ νεύροις— | τῶν
καταξάνας. [καὶ] τῶν τριχῶν ἐκκρεμάσας)

The next example is from a carefully written copy of
the Odyssey, the work of the calligraphist John Rhosos,
of Crete, who was employed in Rome, Venice, Florence,
and other cities of Italy. It is dated in 1479 (*Pal. Soc.*
i. pl. 182).

HOMER.—A.D. 1479.

(῾Ως ἔφατ᾽οὐδ᾽ ἀπίθησε περίφρων εὐρύκλεια·
ἤνεγκεν δ᾽ ἄρα πῦρ καὶ θήιον, αὐτὰρ ὀδυσσεὺς
εὖ διεθείωσεν μέγαρον καὶ δῶμα καὶ αὐλ[ὴν].
γρῆυς δ᾽ αὐτ᾽ ἀπέβη διὰ δώματα κάλ᾽ ὀδυσῆος.
ἀγγελέουσα γυναιξὶ καὶ ὀτρυνέουσα νέεσθαι·
αἵ δ᾽ ἴσαν ἐκ μεγάροιο δάος μετὰ χερσὶν ἔχουσαι.)

Finally, to conclude this section of Greek Palæography,
the following five facsimiles represent some of the many
styles of the more or less cursive handwriting of the
century between 1497 and 1593:—

i. Pausanias, written at Milan, in 1497, by Peter
Hypsilas, of Ægina (Omont, *op. cit.*, pl. 44), in a good
and regular upright hand, compressed.

N

PAUSANIAS.—A.D. 1497.

(καταθέμ[εν]ος τάς τε βοῦς ταύτ[ας] [καὶ] ἀρχὴν τὴν
ἑαυτοῦ. πεποίηκε δέ— | ἀντήνορος τὰ πρῶτα τῶν ἔδνων·
ἑκατὸν βοῦς τῶν πενθερῶ— | τοὺς τότε χαίρειν μάλιστα
ἀν[θρώπ]ους. ἐνέμοντο δὲ ἐμοὶ δοκεῖν αἱ το— | ὑπόψαμμός
τε γ[άρ] ἐστιν ὡς ἐπίπαν ἡ τῶν πυλίων χώρα· [καὶ] πόαν— |
μαρτυρεῖ δὲ μοι [καὶ] ὅμηρος ἐν μνήμη νέστορος ἐπιλέγων
ἀεὶ— | τοῦ λιμένος δὲ ἡ σφακτηρία νῆσος προβέβλητ[αι]
καθάπερ)

ii. Ptolemy's *Almagest*, written at Mantua, in 1518,
by Michael Damascenos, of Crete (Omont, *op. cit.*, pl.
36), in a compact hand, not unlike that of the last
specimen, but a little more elaborate.

PTOLEMY.—A.D. 1518.

(καὶ παρὰ τὸν ἐπίκυκλον, ἐγκεκλιμένους ἐπὶ πάντων— |
πρὸς τὸ τοῦ δια μέσων ἐπίπεδον· κ[αὶ] τὸν ἐπίκυκλον
πρὸς— | ὡς ἔφαμ[εν] διὰ τοῦτο γινομένης ἀξιολόγου
παραλλαγ[ῆς]— | παρόδον. ἡ τὰς ἀποδείξεις τῶν ἀνωμαλιῶν
μέχρι γε— | [ὡς] ἐν τοῖς ἐφεξῆς στήσομ[εν]. ἔνεκ[εν] [δὲ] τοῦ
διὰ τῶν κ[α]τ[ὰ] μέρο[ς]— | αὐτῶν ὅταν ὅ τε τοῦ διευκρι-
νημένου μήκους, καὶ ὁ—)

iii. The Manual of Jurisprudence by Constantine
Harmenopoulos, written in Chios, in 1541, by Jacob
Diassorinos, of Rhodes (Omont, *op. cit.*, pl. 23), in the
loose straggling hand characteristic of the period.

CONSTANTINE HARMENOPOULOS.—A.D. 1541.

(—θελον ἐν αὐτῇ γράψαι, καὶ ὕστερον ἐνθυμ[ηθῇ ταῦτα] |
τότε γραφ[έτω] χαρτίον ἄλλο, διαλαμβάνον περὶ [ὦν
ἐπεκάθετο] | ἐν τῇ διαθήκ[η] εἰπεῖν. καὶ λέγ[ε]τ[αι] τοῦτο
κωδίκελλ[ος, ἤγουν μι] | κρὸν χαρτόπουλον, ἡ βιβλίδιον. ὡς
τοῦ μὲν)

iv. Ælian's *Tactics*, written at Paris, in 1564, by
Angelus Vegecius, of Crete (Omont, *op. cit.*, pl. 2), in
quite a modern style of hand, but compact.

ÆLIAN.—A.D. 1564.

(τῶν δὲ ἐν τοῖς ῥομβοειδέσι σχήμασι τ[ὴν] ἵππον συντα- |
ξάντ[ων], οἱ μὲν οὕτως ἔταξαν ὥστε τοὺς ἱππέας κ[αὶ]
στοιχ[εῖν] | κ[αὶ] ζυγεῖν. οἱ δὲ, στοιχεῖν μὲν, οὐκ ἔτι
δὲ ζυγεῖν. οἱ δὲ, | ζυγεῖν μὲν, οὐ στοιχεῖν δὲ. ἑκάστη δὲ τάξις
οὕτως ἔχει. | οἱ μὲν τοὺς ῥόμβους [καὶ] στοιχεῖν κ[αὶ] ζυγεῖν
βουληθέντες, ἔτα | ξαν τὸν μέγιστ[ον] τὸν ἐν τῇ ἴλῃ ζυγὸν
μέσ[ον] ἐξ ἀριθμοῦ)

v. The *Syntagma Canonum* of Matthew Blastares,
written at Rome, in 1593, by John Hagiomauros, of
Cyprus (Omont, *op. cit.*, pl. 31), in a loose hand of
modern type.

BLASTARES.—A.D. 1593.

(—δάφει γράφειν ἀπείρηκεν· οὐ μήν ἀλλὰ καὶ— |
διαγράφειν ἀνενδιάστως ἐπισκήπτει [καὶ] ἐξαλ— | συμπατ-
ούμ[εν]ον τοῖς βαδίζουσιν, ἐξυβρίζοιτο— | ἡμῶν νίκης
τρόπαιον· τὸ καὶ διανοίᾳ, αἰδοῖ— | —μ[εν]ον, καὶ λόγῳ
διαφερόντως θαυμαζόμ[εν]ον κα—)

Greek Writing in Western Europe.

Before closing the division of our work which relates
to Greek Palæography, a few MSS. may be quoted
which illustrate the course of Greek writing in Western
Europe. We refer, however, only to those MSS. which
are written in actual Greek letters or in imitative letters,
not to those in which Greek words or texts are inscribed
in ordinary Latin letters, of which there are not a few
examples.

Two celebrated MSS. of the 6th century containing
bilingual texts have already been referred to [2] as having
been written in Western Europe. The " Codex Bezæ,"
of the Gospels and Acts of the Apostles, at Cambridge,
and the " Codex Claromontanus," of the Epistles of St.
Paul, at Paris, are both written in Greek and Latin in
uncial letters. But in these MSS. the Greek text is in
letters which are of the ordinary type of Greek uncials
of the period. In a third example of a bilingual text,
the Harley MS. 5792 (*Cat. Anc. MSS.* pt. i. pl. 13;
Pal. Soc. ii. pl. 25), which contains a Græco-Latin
Glossary, written probably in France in the 7th century,
the Greek writing betrays its western origin very
palpably. Still more distinctly imitative is the Greek
text in the " Codex Augiensis," of Trinity College, Cambridge, in which the Epistles of St. Paul were written
in Latin minuscules and Greek bastard uncials, in the
latter part of the 9th century, at Reichenau in Bavaria
(*Pal. Soc.* i. pl. 127) ; in a Græco-Latin MS. of some of
the Psalms, in the Library of St. Nicholas of Cusa, of the
same character, written early in the 10th century (*Pal.*

[2] See p. 154.

Soc. i. pl. 128) ; and in the " Codex Sangallensis " and " Codex Boenerianus " of Dresden, which once formed one MS. and contain the Gospels in Latinized Greek letters of the 10th century, with an interlinear Latin version (*Pal. Soc.* i. pl. 179).

A few instances survive of the employment of Greek letters in Latin signatures and subscriptions to documents of the sixth and seventh centuries from Ravenna and Naples (Marini, *I Papiri Diplom.*, 90, 92, 121 ; *Cod. Diplom. Cavensis,* ii. no. 250 ; *Pal. Soc.* ii. 3) ; and the same practice appears to have been followed in France and Spain as late as the eleventh century.[3] But we may regard such a superfluous use of a foreign alphabet, at least in most instances, as a mere affectation of learning. In the ornamental pages of fanciful letters, also, which adorn early Anglo-Saxon and Franco-Saxon MSS., a Greek letter occasionally finds a place, serving, no doubt, to show off the erudition of the illuminator.[4]

[3] *Bibliothèque de l'Ecole des Chartes,* (2nd series) tom. i. p. 443; Delisle, *Mélanges de Paléographie,* p. 95.
[4] Delisle, *L'Evangéliaire de Saint-Vaast d'Arras.*

CHAPTER XIII.

WE now proceed to trace the history of Latin Palæography; and the scheme which will be followed in this division of our subject may first be briefly described.

Latin majuscule writing, in its two branches of (1) Square capitals and Rustic capitals, and (2) Uncials—the most ancient forms of the Latin literary script—naturally claims our first attention. Next, the modified forms of Uncial writing, viz., the mixed hands of uncial and minuscule letters, and the later developed Half-uncial writing, will be examined. We shall then have to pass in review the various styles of Roman Cursive writing, beginning with its earliest examples, and from this we shall proceed to follow the course of the Continental National Minuscule hands, which were directly derived from that source, down to the period of the reform of the Merovingian school in the reign of Charlemagne. The independent history of the early Irish and English schools forms a chapter apart. From the period of Charlemagne to the close of the fifteenth century, the vicissitudes of the literary handwritings of Western Europe will be described; and this portion of our work will be brought to a close with some account of the Cursive writing, and particularly of the English Charter-hands of that time.

Majuscule Writing.—Capitals.

Latin Majuscule writing, as found in early MSS., is divided into two branches: writing in Capitals, and writing in Uncials. Capitals, again, are of two kinds, Square Capitals and Rustic Capitals. The most ancient

Latin MSS. in existence are in Rustic Capitals; but there is no reason to presume that the rustic hand was employed in MSS. before the square hand, nay, rather, following the analogy of sculptured inscriptions, the preference as to age should be given to square letters.

Capital writing, in its two styles, copies the letterings of inscriptions which have been classed under the heads of "scriptura monumentalis" and "scriptura actuaria," as executed in the time of Augustus and successive emperors[1]; the square character following generally the first, and the rustic the second.

In square capital writing the letters are generally of the same height; but F and L are commonly exceptions. The angles are right angles, and the bases and tops and extremities are usually finished off with the fine strokes and pendants which are familiar to all in our modern copies of this type of letters.

Rustic capitals, on the other hand, are, as the name implies, of a more negligent pattern, but as a style of writing for choice books they were no less carefully formed than the square capitals. But the strokes are more slender, cross-strokes are short and are more or less oblique and waved, and finials are not added to them. Being thus, in appearance, less finished as perfect letters, although accurately shaped, they have received the somewhat misleading title which distinguishes them. More than is the case with square capital writing, there is a greater tendency in certain rustic letters to rise above the line.

The fact that a large proportion of the surviving MSS. in capital letters of the best class contain the works of Virgil points to the same conclusion as that suggested by the discovery of comparatively so many copies of the Iliad of Homer in early papyri, and by the existence of the Bible in three of the most important Greek vellum codices which have descended to us: namely, that a sumptuous style of production was, if not reserved, at least more especially employed for those

[1] See *Exempla Scripturae Epigraphicae Latinae* (*Corpus Inscript. Lat.*), ed. Hübner, 1885.

books which were the great works of their day. Homer
in the Greek world, Virgil in the classical period of
Rome, and the Bible in the early centuries of the
Christian Church, filled a space to which no other books
of their time could pretend. And the survival of even
the not very numerous copies which we possess is an
indication both that such fine MSS. were more valued
and better cared for than ordinary volumes and that
they must have existed in fairly large numbers. With
regard to the works of Virgil and their sumptuous production, it will not be forgotten that Martial, xiv. 186,
singles out a MS. of this author to be decorated with
his portrait.

Of Square Capital writing of ancient date there is
very little now in existence, viz., a few leaves of a MS.
of Virgil, divided between the Vatican Library and
Berlin, which are attributed to the close of the 4th
century (Z. W. *Ex.* 14) [2]; and a few from another MS.
of the same poet, of the 4th or 5th century, preserved
in the library of St. Gall in Switzerland (Z. W. *Ex.* 14 *a*;
Pal. Soc. i. pl. 208). We take a specimen from a
facsimile of one of the latter:

IDALIAELVCOSVBIM
FLORIBVSETDVLCIAD
IAMQ·IBATDICTOPAR

VIRGIL.—4TH OR 5TH CENTURY.

(Idaliae lucos ubi m[ollis]— | Floribus et dulci ad— | Iamque
ibat dicto par[ens]—)

It is certainly remarkable that this large character
should still have been employed at the time to which
these fragments of square-capital MSS. are attributed,

[2] Zangemeister and Wattenbach, *Exempla Codicum Latinorum
litteris majusculis scriptorum*, Heidelberg, 1876, 1879.

so long after the classical period of Rome. The use of so inconvenient a form of writing, and one which covered so much material in the case of any work of average extent, would, it might be thought, have been entirely abandoned in favour of the more ready uncial character, or at least of the less cumbersome rustic capitals. Its continuance may be regarded as a survival of a style first employed at an early period to do honour to the great national Latin poet; and may, in some degree, be compared with the conservative practice in the middle ages of keeping to an old style of writing for Biblical and liturgical MSS. The same remark applies also to the comparatively late employment of Rustic Capital writing under similar conditions.

This latter style of writing is found in the earliest extant Latin MSS. In some of the papyrus fragments recovered at Herculaneum it is of a character copied closely from the lettering of inscriptions on stone or metal (Z. W. *Ex.* 1, 2); in others it is of a less severe style. We give a specimen from the fragments of a poem on the Battle of Actium (*Fragmenta Herculanensia,* ed. W. Scott, 1885), written in light, quickly-formed letters, which must have been very generally used for literary purposes at the period of the destruction of Herculaneum in A.D. 79.

POEM ON THE BATTLE OF ACTIUM.—BEFORE A.D. **79.**

(cervicibus . aspide . moll[em] | [somn]um . trahiturque . libidi [ne . mortis .] | brevis . hunc . sine . mor[sibus . anguis .] | [ten]ui . pars . inlita . parva . v[eneni.])

Here the words are separated from one another with the full point, as in inscriptions. Long vowels are also, in many instances, marked with an accent; in the case of long i, the form of the accent (if accent it be) is rather that of the letter itself, and the scribe may have intended to indicate the length of the vowel by doubling it.

Specimens of nearly all the existing vellum MSS. written in rustic capital letters are represented in facsimile in the *Exempla* of Zangemeister and Wattenbach, the publications of the Palæographical Society, and other works. The writing on this material is of a more careful type than that which we have seen in the last facsimile from a papyrus MS. The estimation of the age of the earliest of these MSS. is necessarily a matter of uncertainty, as we have no specimen to which a date can be approximately assigned before the end of the fifth century. But some of them may be placed earlier than that period. For example, the palimpsest fragments of the Verrine Orations of Cicero, in the Vatican Library (Z. W. *Ex.* 4), are generally assigned to the fourth century. But the MSS. which before all others approach nearest in the forms of their letters to those of inscriptions, are the two famous codices of Virgil, known as the "Codex Romanus," and the "Codex Palatinus" (Z. W. *Ex.* 11, 12; *Pal. Soc.* i. pl. 113-115). In these the style of lettering found in formal inscriptions of the first century of our era has been closely followed; and although no one has ever thought of placing the MSS. in so remote a period, yet it has been suggested that scribes may have kept up the style without degeneration for one or two centuries, and that they may therefore be as old as the third century. Others are of opinion that they are merely imitative, and that the Codex Romanus in particular, on account of the barbarisms of its text and the coarse character of the pictures with which it is illustrated, must be of a later date. These objections, however, are not conclusive, and taking the writing alone under judgment, there seems to be no reason for dating the MSS. later, at all events, than the fourth century.

The following facsimile is from the Codex Palatinus (*Pal. Soc.* i. pl. 115) :—

VOLVITVRATERODORTECTISTV
INTVSSAXASONANTVACVAS
ACCIDITHAECFESSISETIAMIO
QVAETOTAMIVCTV.CONCVSSIT

VIRGIL.——4TH CENTURY (?).

(Volvitur ater odor tectis tu[m]— | Intus saxa sonant vacuas — | Accidit haec fessis etiam fo[rtuna]— | Quae totam luctu concussit—)

In this writing the contrast of the thick and fine strokes is as strongly marked as in inscriptions on stone or metal. Shortness of horizontal strokes, smallness of bows, as seen in letter R, and general lateral compression are characteristic. The formation of the letter H is easily explained by referring to the same letter in the second line of the facsimile from the poem on the Battle of Actium. It recalls the formation of the common truncated h-shaped *eta* in Greek papyri. The points are inserted by a later hand.

Another famous MS. of Virgil in rustic capitals is that known as the "Schedæ Vaticanæ," which is ornamented with a series of most interesting paintings in classical style, no doubt copied from more ancient prototypes (Z. W. *Ex.* 13; *Pal. Soc.* i. pl. 116, 117). It is assigned to the 4th century.

But the first rustic MS. to which an approximate date can be given is the Medicean Virgil in the Laurentian Library at Florence (Z. W. *Ex.* 10; *Pal. Soc.* i. pl. 86). A note at the end of the Bucolics states that the MS. was read, pointed, and corrected by the "consul ordinarius" Asterius, who held office in the year 494.

Consequently, the text must have been written at or before that date. A specimen is here given :—

NONILLUMNOSTRIPOSSUNTAIUTARELABO
NFCSITRICORIB·AIEDIIS·HEDRUAICQ·BIBAAI
SITHONIASQ·NIUIS·HIEMISSUBEAAIUSA
NICSICUMANORIENS·ALTALIBERARETINUL

VIRGIL.—BEFORE A.D. 494.

(Non illum nostri possunt mutare labo[res.]
Nec si frigoribus mediis . Hebrumque bibam[us.]
Sithoniasque nives . hiemis subeamus a[quosae.]
Nec si cum moriens . alta Liber aret in ul[mo]).

Among the remaining older MSS. of this style the most important is the Codex Bembinus of Terence (Z. W. *Ex.* 8, 9 ; *Pal. Soc.* i. pl. 135) in the Vatican Library, a MS. of the 4th or 5th century, which takes its name from a former owner, Bernardo Bembo, in the fifteenth century, and which is valuable on account of its annotations.

This handsome but inconvenient style of literary writing could not be expected to last, even for *éditions de luxe*, for a very long period. There still survives, however, one very finely executed MS., the poems of Prudentius, in the Bibliothèque Nationale at Paris (Z. W. *Ex.* 15 ; *Pal. Soc.* i. pl. 29, 30), written with great skill, but thought not to be earlier than the 6th century. In the Turin Sedulius (Z. W. *Ex.* 16) of the 7th century the rustic letters have altogether passed out of the domain of calligraphy in its true sense, and are rough and mis-shapen. Lastly, we may notice a MS. which, on account of its contents and history, has attracted more than usual attention—the Utrecht Psalter, which is written in rustic capitals and yet can be scarcely older than the beginning of the 9th century. Copied from an ancient original which was illustrated with drawings, it seems that, in order to maintain the same relative arrangements of text and drawings, the scribe found it the simplest course to copy the actual character of the letters, the text thus filling the same space as the original and leaving the proper intervals for the insertion of the drawings. And yet the text was not so exactly copied as to be quite consistent with ancient usage; for titles are introduced in uncial letters—an intrusion which would have been quite impossible in the earlier and purer period of rustic capital writing. In a word, the form in which the Utrecht Psalter is cast must be regarded as accidental —a mere imitation of a style which had practically passed away.

Judging by the specimens which have survived, capital writing may be said to have ceased to exist as a literary hand for entire texts about the close of the fifth century. In the middle ages it survived, in both square and rustic styles, as an ornamental form of writing for titles and initials, and occasionally for a few pages of text. For example, in the Psalter of St. Augustine's, Canterbury, of the beginning of the 8th century, now one of the Cottonian MSS. in the British Museum, there are several prefatory leaves written in imitative rustic letters (*Pal. Soc.* i. pl. 19; *Cat. Anc. MSS.* ii. 12, 13), and in the Benedictional of Bishop Æthelwold (*Pal. Soc.* i. pl. 143) of the 10th century, and in a MS. of Aratus at Boulogne (*Pal. Soc.* i. pl. 96) written quite at the end of the 10th century, pages in the same style are to be found. In the profusely ornamented MSS. of the Gospels and other sacred texts of the period of the Carlovingian kings the bountiful use of capitals is a prominent feature of their decoration.

Uncials.

The second form of Majuscule writing employed as a literary hand for the texts of MSS. is that to which the name of Uncial has been given.[3] It is a modification of the square capital writing. As the latter was the

[3] See above, p. 117.

easiest form to carve on stone or metal, so was it more
simple, when writing letters with the reed or pen on a
material more or less soft, to avoid right angles by the
use of curves. Uncial, then, is essentially a round hand,
and its principal characteristic letters are the curved
forms a ꝺ ε ʜ ꝳ. The main vertical strokes generally
rise above or fall below the line of writing. This style
appears to have come into common use as a literary hand
at least as early as the fourth century. How much
earlier it may have been employed must remain uncertain ;
but as in the most ancient specimens it appears in a fully
developed shape, it is not improbable that it was used
for books even in the third century. The period of the
growth of the hand has been determined, from the
occurrence of isolated uncial forms in inscriptions, etc.,
to lie between the latter part of the second century and
the latter part of the fourth century.[4] From the fifth to
the eighth century it was the ordinary literary hand of
the first rank. In MSS. of the fifth and sixth centuries,
and particularly in those of the earlier century, the uncial
writing is exact, and is generally formed with much
beauty and precision of stroke ; in the seventh century
it becomes more artificial ; in the course of the eighth
century it rapidly degenerates, and breaks down into a
rough, badly-formed hand, or, when written with care, is
forced and imitative. As a test letter of age the letter
ꝳ has been selected, which in its earliest forms appears
with the first limb straight, or at least not curved inwards
at the bottom, as it is seen in later examples. And the
shape of the letter ε may also be of assistance for determining the period of a MS. : in the earlier centuries, the
cross-stroke is consistently placed high, but when the
hand begins to give way in its later stages the stroke
varies in position, being sometimes high, sometimes low,
in the letter. In fact, as is the case with the handwriting
of all periods and countries, the first examples of an

---

[4] Z. W. *Exempla*, p. 5. Uncials were used in Latin inscriptions in
Africa in the third century. The Makter inscription (*Pal. Soc.* ii.
pl. 49), which is certainly as early as the fourth century, is in uncials
with some small letters.

established hand are the purest and best; the letters are formed naturally, and therefore consistently.

Of MSS. in uncial writing there are still a not inconsiderable number extant, and the earliest and most important have been represented by facsimiles in various palæographical works. The palimpsest fragments of Cicero *De Republica* (Z. W. *Ex.* 17; *Pal. Soc.* i. pl. 160) in the Vatican Library are generally quoted as the most ancient example, and are assigned to the 4th century. The letters are massive and regular, and the columns of writing are very narrow. A few lines will give an idea of the amount of material which must have been required for the whole work, there being only fifteen such lines in each column, or thirty in a page.

quiBONANEc
puiarenecap
pellaresoleat
quodearum
rerumuide

CICERO, DE REPUBLICA.—4TH CENTURY.

(qui bona nec | putare nec ap | pellare soleat | quod earum | rerum vide[atur].)

Probably of a nearly equal age are the fragments of the Vercelli Gospels (Z. W. *Ex.* 20), a MS. which is traditionally said to have been written by St. Eusebius himself, who died A.D. 371, and which may safely be placed in the fourth century. In this MS. also we have another example of the early practice of writing the text in extremely narrow columns.

Among MSS. which are placed in the fifth century two of the most famous are the codices of Livy at Vienna and Paris (Z. W. *Ex.* 18, 19; *Pal. Soc.* i. pl. 31, 32, 183). The writing of the Viennese MS. is rather smaller than that of the other. It is also historically an interesting volume to Englishmen, as it is conjectured, from the occurrence of a note in it, to have belonged to the English monk, Suitbert, or Suiberht, one of the apostles to the Frisians, who became their bishop about the year 693. We select from it a specimen as a good example of uncial writing of the fifth century.

LIVY.—5TH CENTURY.

(—ri oppido posset ante ipsam Tempe in fau | cibus situm Macaedoniae claustra | tutissima praebet et in Tessaliam | opportunum Macedonibus decur | sum cum et loco et praesidio valido in)

For an example of uncial writing of the sixth century we are able to turn to a MS. which can be approximately dated—the Fulda MS. of the Gospels and other books of the New Testament, which was revised by Victor, Bishop of Capua, in the years 546 and 547, and is itself probably of about the same period (Z. W. *Ex.* 34).

Uenerunt adeum in hospi tium plures. Quibus exponebat testificans regnum di. Suadensq. eisdeibuexlegemosiei prophetisamaneusp

FULDA NEW TESTAMENT.—ABOUT A.D. 546.

(Venerunt ad eum in hospi | tium plures . Quibus | expon bat testificans | regnum dei . Suadens*que* | eis de Ie*su* ex lege Mosi et | prophetis a mane usq*ue*)

Even in this MS., as early as the middle of the sixth century, there is a certain falling off in ease and firmness of writing as compared with the earlier examples which have been quoted. But fine distinctions between the handwritings of different MSS. can only be satisfactorily studied by a comparison of the MSS. themselves, or of delicate photographic reproductions of them. The facsimiles here set before the reader, representing only brief passages and being simply in black and white, cannot serve for more than the elementary purposes of this book.

Our next facsimile illustrates writing of a century and a half later, and is taken from the great MS. of the Bible known as the Codex Amiatinus (Z. W. *Ex.* 35 ; *Pal. Soc.* ii. pl. 65, 66), in the Laurentian Library at Florence. It is one of three MSS. which were written by order of Ceolfrid, who became Abbot of Jarrow in Northumbria in 690 ; and it was taken by him on the journey to Italy, during which he died, in 716, for presentation to the Pope. The date of the MS. is therefore about the year 700. It should, however, be remarked that uncial writing of this type appears to have never gained favour in England ; and it is probable that the MS. was produced by Italian scribes brought over to this country.

ETCONLOQUEBANTUR
ADINUICEM DICENTES
QUODEST HOCUERBUM
QUIA INPOTESTATEETUIRTUTE
IMPERAT SPIRITIBUS
INMUNDIS ETEXEUNT

CODEX AMIATINUS.—ABOUT A.D. 700.

(Et conloquebantur | ad invicem dicentes | quod est hoc
verbum | quia in potestate et virtute | imperat spiritibus |
inmundis et exeunt)

The text is arranged stichometrically, and the characters are bold and in harmony with the large scale of
the MS., which measures nearly twenty inches in height
and contains more than a thousand leaves.

CHAPTER XIV.

Mixed Uncial and Minuscule Writing.

THE fact must not, however, be lost sight of that, after all, the majuscule forms of writing, both capital and uncial, which have been under discussion, represent only one class of the handwritings of the periods in which they were practised, namely, the literary hand, used in the production of exactly written MSS., and therefore a hand of comparatively limited use. By its side, and of course of far more extensive and general use, was the cursive hand of the time, which under certain conditions, and particularly when a book was being produced, not for the general market, but for private or limited circulation, would invade the literary domain of pure majuscule writing and show its presence by the intrusion of letters which are proper to the cursive alphabet.[1] Thus, some of the notes of scholars in the margins of early majuscule MSS., or sometimes a few inserted leaves of additions, are found written in a mixed style of negligently formed uncials and certain cursive forms in limited numbers. For instance, the notes of Bishop Victor in the Fulda codex, quoted above (p. 193), are thus written; and, as an example of the employment of this hand for additions to a text, a few lines from a MS. of the Chronicles of Eusebius of the 6th century, in the

In describing these mixed hands it is necessary to anticipate the discussion of the Roman cursive writing.

Bodleian Library (*Pal. Soc.* ii. pl. 130), are here given :—

usq·adconseundemquotienspersecutio
quibdesignatistemporibfactaest
regnauitpostpassionemdñiannoxxxuiiii
etaestannoimperiieiusxiiiinquapetrus&
apostoliglorioseoccubuerunt

CHRONOLOGICAL NOTES.—6TH CENTURY.

(usq*ue* ad cons*ulatum* eundem quotiens persecutio | —quib*us* designatis temporib*us* facta est | —regnavit post passionem dom*i*ni anno xxxviiii | —[o]rta est anno imperii eius xiii in qua petrus et | —apostoli gloriose occubuerunt)

Here the general character is a sloping uncial, but the letters b and d are cursive forms, and the cursive influence shows itself in the lengthening of vertical strokes.

The adaptation of this mixed hand, growing as it were by accident into a recognized style of writing, to more formal literary purposes would naturally follow. In the MS. of Gaius at Verona (Z. W. *Ex.* 24) of the 5th century, besides the ordinary uncial forms, the cursive-shaped d and s [2] are used. In the Florentine Pandects, written by many scribes, several cursive forms appear (Z. W. *Ex.* 54; *Pal. Soc.* ii. pl. 108) in one portion of the MS. And fragments of a Græco-Latin glossary on papyrus (*Comment. Soc. Gottingen.* iv. 156; *Rhein. Museum*, v. 301) are also written in mixed

---

[2] A curious instance of misunderstanding of the cursive or long s (ſ) by an ignorant scribe is afforded by the Harley MS. 5792, which contains a Græco-Latin glossary, written probably in France in the seventh century. The archetype from which the MS. was transcribed, evidently had this form of the letter in several places. The scribe of the Harley MS., not understanding it, copied it sometimes as an i without a dot (ı), sometimes as an i with a dot (i).—*Glossae Latinograecae*, etc., ed. Goetz and Gundermann, 1888, praef. xxii.

characters.[3] From these examples it appears that
secular MSS., such as those relating to law and grammar,
were not always subject in their production to the same
strict calligraphic rules as MSS. for church use or of a
specially sumptuous character. The scribe, writing
rather for the scholar than for the public reader or book-
collector, allowed himself a certain freedom and adopted
a style which he could write more rapidly; and yet at
the same time the preponderating element remained
uncial. In the following facsimile from the Pandects of
the Laurentian Library at Florence (*Pal. Soc.* ii.
pl. 108), probably of the end of the 6th or beginning
of the 7th century, it will be noticed that the cursive
forms are used at the ends of lines, generally the weak
point, so to say, of handwritings, where innovations
make their first appearance.

PANDECTS.—6TH-7TH CENTURY.

([proba]vi existimantis si quidem praeces | —[sp]onsalia durare
ea quamvis in domo | —[nupt]ae esse coeperit si vero non
praeces | —[ho]c ipso quod in domum deducta est | —[vide]ri
sponsalia facta quam sententia*m*)

---

[3] The same mixed style is found in Latin inscriptions of Northern
Africa; *e.g.* the Makter inscription (*Pal. Soc.* ii. pl. 49). It also
appears in the recently discovered inscription of Diocletian's edict,
"de pretiis venalium" of A.D. 301 (*Pal. Soc.* ii. pl. 127, 128). Even
in inscriptions in square capitals small letters sometimes intruded:
see an instance of a small b in an inscription of A.D. 104, given in
Letronne, *Inscriptions de l'Egypte,* 1842, 1848, atlas, pl. 31.

From the same MS. we give another specimen (Z. W.
Ex. 54) of a hand which employs the cursive forms
more generally, not only at the ends of lines, but pro-
miscuously with the uncial forms, and illustrates a
further stage of development.

PANDECTS.—6TH-7TH CENTURY.

(legum tramitem qui ab ur[be]— | temporibus ita esse con-
fu[sum]— | humanae naturae capacit[ate]— | [stu]dium sacra-
tissimis retro— | [con]stitutiones emendare)

But these examples represent the mixed hand in its
simpler stages. A reference to the early MSS. in
which it is employed by the writers of annotations
shows that the proportion of the uncial and cursive
forms depended a good deal on the taste or practice of
the writer. He was necessarily limited in the space
left for his notes, and was therefore constrained to use
a more formal kind of writing than his ordinary current
hand would have been, somewhat in the same way as
in annotating a printed book we, at the present day,
often employ a half-printing kind of writing, accommo-
dated to the narrow margins at our disposal. He
therefore naturally used a disconnected and not a cursive
form of writing; and the negligent uncial, referred to
above, seems to have been generally found most suitable
for the purpose, qualified, as already described, by an
admixture of cursive forms. It is the varying extent to
which these cursive forms were admitted by different
writers that here claims our attention. The marginal
directions for the artist in the Quedlinburg fragment of

an illustrated early Italic version of the Bible (Schum, *Theolog. Studien,* 1876) ; and ,the scholia and notes in such MSS. as the fragments of Juvenal in the Vatican (Z. W. *Ex.* 5), the Codex Bembinus of Terence (Z. W. *Ex.* 8; *Pal. Soc.* i. pl. 135), the Medicean Virgil (Z. W. *Ex.* 10; *Pal. Soc.* i. pl. 86), the Bible fragment at Weingarten (Z. W. *Ex.* 21), and others, exhibit the hand in various phases between the uncial and minuscule (or formal cursive) styles. In the scholia on the Bembine Terence, we have the hand in the fully developed condition, in which the minuscule element asserts itself so strongly that but few of the purely uncial forms remain, and to which the title of Half-uncial writing has been given. We find it employed as far back as the fifth century as a literary hand in the production of formally written MSS.

Half-Uncial Writing.

This writing, as will afterwards be seen, plays a very important part in the history of certain national hands. A modified form of the uncial, as just explained, and recommending itself no doubt from the greater ease with which it could be written than the more laborious pure uncial, it was quickly adopted as a book-hand ; and the not inconsiderable number of examples which are still extant prove how widely it was practised, at least within a certain area, chiefly comprising, it seems, Italy and Southern France. The earliest example appears to be the Fasti Consulares of the years 487-494 in a palimpsest at Verona (Z. W. *Ex.* 30). Of more importance is the MS. of St. Hilary at Rome, written before 509 or 510 (Z. W. *Ex.* 52 ; *Pal. Soc.* i. pl. 136). Other examples are the Sulpicius Severus of Verona, of the year 517 (Z. W. *Ex.* 32) ; a list of popes to 523, and carried on to 530, together with a collection of canons, in a MS. from Corbie (Z. W. *Ex.* 40-42; *Alb. Pal.*[4] 11) ; a similar MS. at Cologne (Z. W. *Ex.* 37, 38, 44); a

---

[4] *Album Paléographique, avec des notices explicatives par la Société de l'Ecole des Chartes.* Paris, 1887.

Bible commentary at Monte Cassino earlier than 569 (Z. W. *Ex.* 53); various MSS. at Milan, originally in the monastery of Bobio (*Pal. Soc.* i. pl. 137, 138, 161, 162); a MS. in the Libri collection (*Pal. Soc.* ii. pl. 10); a Hilary on papyrus at Vienna (*Pal. Soc.* ii. pl. 31); and several MSS. at Lyons, Paris, and Cambrai (*Alb. Pal.* 6-9, 11, 13)—of the sixth or seventh centuries.

As in this style of writing a large proportion of the forms of letters which are afterwards found in the minuscule hand of the Carlovingian period are already developed, it has also been called the Præ-Caroline minuscule. This title, however, being anticipatory, it is better to give the hand an independent name, and that of Half-uncial is sufficiently distinctive; unless indeed the still more exact title of Roman Half-uncial is preferable.

In the following specimen, taken from the MS. of St. Hilary on the Trinity in the Archives of St. Peter's at Rome, which, as a note records, was revised in the fourteenth year of Trasamund, King of the Vandals, that is, in A.D. 509-10, an almost complete alphabet is represented; and it will be seen that while the round style of uncial writing is still maintained, there are very few of the letters which are really uncials.

ST. HILARY.—BEFORE A.D. 509-10.

(damnationem fidei esse | —te aboletur per alteram— | rursus abolenda est cu[ius]— | episcopi manum innocente[m]— | [lin]guam non ad falsiloquium coe[gisti] —)

The most beautifully executed MS. of early date in this style of hand is the Biblical commentary of Monte Cassino, written before the year 569 (Z. W. *Ex.* 53). A specimen is here selected from it as a standard example of the perfect half-uncial which formed the model for certain forms of the national hands which will be described afterwards.

BIBLICAL COMMENTARY.—BEFORE A.D. 569.

(aboleret . natus ergo e — | ut quae primum fecer[at]— | crearet quia per erro[rem]— | mortua ut semper in—)

We must here break off our examination of the formal book-hands to take up that of the Roman Cursive writing which, as we have just seen, essentially affected the half-uncial, and which had an all-important influence in forming the later handwritings of Western Europe.

CHAPTER XV.

Roman Cursive Writing.

SOME of the earliest material which has survived for the study of Roman Cursive writing is found among the wall-inscriptions of Pompeii. These inscriptions have been divided into two classes : (1) those traced with the brush, generally in formal and not cursive capitals, and consisting of advertisements, recommendations of candidates, announcements of public games, of lost articles, of houses to let, etc. ; and (2) scrawls and scribblings, sometimes in charcoal, chalk, etc., but more generally scratched with a point (the so-called *graffiti*), and written in cursive letters, being quotations from poets, idle words, reckonings, salutations, love addresses, pasquinades, satirical remarks, etc. A few are of ancient date, but most of them range between A.D. 63 and the year of the destruction of the city, A.D. 79. Similar inscriptions have been found at Herculaneum, and in the excavations and catacombs of Rome. Most of them have been collected by Zangemeister in the *Corpus Inscriptionum Latinarum* of the Berlin Academy, vol. iv., which also contains a carefully compiled table of the forms of letters employed. Some of those found in Rome are represented in the *Roma subterranea Christiana* of De Rossi.

Contemporary with these wall-inscriptions are the

waxen tablets found in 1875 at Pompeii, in the house of L. Cæcilius Jucundus,[1] inscribed with documents in cursive writing, and ranging in date chiefly from A.D. 53 to 62. Of similar character are the waxen tablets, some of which are dated between A.D. 131 and 167, found in the ancient mining works of Verespatak in Dacia,[2] and published with a table of forms of letters in the *Corpus Inscriptionum Latinarum*, vol. iii. With these also must be grouped the tiles which have been found on various sites, scratched, before being baked, with alphabets, verses, or miscellaneous memoranda.[3]

The examples of Roman cursive writing which have been enumerated above represent the ordinary writing of the people for about the first three centuries of the Christian era. The letters are nothing more than the old Roman letters written with speed, and thus undergoing certain modifications in their forms, which eventually developed into the minuscule hand. These same original Roman letters written carefully became, as we have seen, the formal capital alphabets in use in inscriptions under the Empire and in the sumptuous MSS. of the early centuries of our era. It is probable that the wall-scribblings of Pompeii essentially represent the style of writing which had been followed for some two or three centuries before their actual date; for, in the other direction, the difference between the style of the Dacian tablets and that of the Pompeian period, although they are separated by a long interval, is not so marked as might have been expected.

If we turn to the Table of letters which are found in the *graffiti* of Pompeii and other Roman sites, we see how in the first century the original capital forms stand side by side with other modified forms which even at

---

[1] See above, p. 25. [2] See above, p. 24.

[3] See above, p. 15. Some of them are inscribed with memoranda of the brickfields. One found at Aquileia bears the warning of a severe taskmaster to some unfortunate workman: " Cave malum, si non raseris lateres DC; si raseris minus, malum formidabis." *Corp. Ins. Lat.* v., no. 8110 (176).

that date had begun to tend towards minuscules. In A the cross stroke falls, so to say, out of its horizontal position and hangs as a short middle stroke or entirely disappears. The slurring of the bows of B, in quick writing, produces the form of the letter resembling a stilted a, the waved stroke representing the bows and the loop the original upright mainstroke. This is the most complete transformation of any letter in the alphabet. C and G exaggerate the length. of the upper part of the curve. The letter D developes gradually the uncial form, which afterwards produced the minuscule, by lengthening the upper stroke of the bow, while the straight main-stroke, like that of the B, turns into a curve. The letter E is represented in two forms, the second being the double vertical-stroke letter used also in inscriptions and in the Faliscan alphabet. F in like manner takes the form of a long and a short stroke, both more or less vertical, the short stroke gradually degenerating into a curve. In the changes of H we see the origin of the minuscule in the shortening of the second main-stroke. Besides the normal capital form we have M represented by four vertical strokes, ||||, the first being longer than the rest; and so, too, N appears in the form of three strokes, |||. The hastily written O is no longer a circle, but is formed by two curves ; and, the natural tendency when writing with a hard point being to form concave rather than convex curves, the second curve of the letter also becomes concave. In the letter P we see the gradual wearing down of the bow into a mere oblique stroke; in R the slurring of the bows into a curved stroke; and in S the straightening of the lower curve and the development of the upper one into an oblique stroke.

In the alphabets of the Dacian tablets many of these modifications are seen to be carried still farther, as for example in the straightening of the exaggerated head-curve of C and G into the flat head which in the latter letter afterwards becomes so marked a feature. The similarity now existing between certain letters is also very striking, and it is obvious how easily one may be misread for another. A and R, B and D, C and O, C and P, C and T, E and U, bear, under various conditions, more or less resemblance to each other; and, to add to the difficulties of decipherment, linking and combination of letters was carried in the cursive hand of this period almost to an extreme.

The two following facsimiles are taken from the Pompeian *graffiti*. First we select the beginnings of four lines, two from Ovid (*Amor.* I. viii. 77) and two from Propertius (IV. v. 47), written in a style which we may call formal cursive, the normal shapes of the old letters being fairly maintained (*Corp. Insc. Lat.* iv. 1893, 1894, tab. xxv. 7).

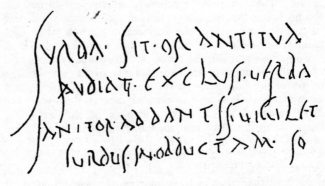

WALL-INSCRIPTION.—1ST CENTURY.

(Surda sit oranti tua [ianua laxa ferenti] | audiat exclusi verba [receptus amans] | ianitor ad dantis vigilet [si pulsat inanis] | surdus in obductem so[mniet usque seram])

Next is given a specimen of the more cursive style in which the normal shapes of the letters are considerably modified and the vertical-stroke forms of E and M are used. The shape of the O may also be noticed, being formed by two convex strokes as explained above. (*Corp. Insc. Lat.* iv. 1597, tab. vii. 1).

WALL-INSCRIPTION.—1ST CENTURY.

(communem nummum— | censio est nam noster— | magna
habet pecuni[am])

We now turn from the large hasty scrawls of the
plaster-covered walls of Pompeii and take up the delicate
specimens traced with the fine-pointed stilus on smooth
waxen surfaces.

In the waxen tablets found at Pompeii we have two
styles of writing : that of the deeds themselves, inscribed
on the waxen pages with the stilus in the decidedly
cursive character which may be compared with the facsimile of the wall-inscription just given; and that of the
endorsements and lists of witnesses written in ink upon
the bare wood of the pages which were not coated with
wax,[4] in a more formal character which may be compared
with the preceding facsimile. The following specimen
is a fragment of one of the tablets which record payments
made on account of sales by auction (*Atti dei Lincei*,
1875-6, p. 218, tav. 1), written in the full cursive style.

See above, p. 25.

POMPEIAN WAXEN TABLET.—1ST CENTURY.

(—[S]aturni[no]— | —[Scipi]one— | iv idus Novembr | —s
Umbricae Antiochidis se[rvus] | —[ea]m accepisse ab L.
Caec[ilio] | [Iucundo] sestertios nummos sescentos | [quadra-
gi]nta quinque [ob au]ctionem | . . . . | rebus
innisiticis v[enditis]— | ex qua summa—)

The handwriting is very firm and distinct, and the
letters are formed upon the same pattern as those of the
last facsimile. Nor is the hand complicated by the
linkings and monogrammatic arrangements of two or
more letters, which will be presently shown in another
example. Indeed, the letters are inscribed so distinctly
that there is no difficulty in deciphering the text when
once the forms are mastered.

Two facsimiles from the Dacian tablets of the second
century are now given. The first is taken from one of
the pages of a tablet recording the dissolution of a burial
club at Alburnus Major, or Verespatak, in the year 167.
It is written clearly, and the letters generally stand
distinct without much linking (Massmann, *Lib. aur.*
tab. 2; *Corp. Insc. Lat.* iii. 926-7).

DACIAN WAXEN TABLET.—A.D. 167.

(Descriptum et recognitum | factum ex libello qui propo | situs erat Alb*ur*no maiori ad statio | nem Resculi in quo scrip | tum erat id quot *infra scriptum* est | Artemidorus Apolloni magister | collegi Iovis Cerneni et Valerius | Niconis et Offas Menofili questo | res collegi eiusdem | posito hoc libello publice testantur | ex collegis *supra scriptis* ubi erant homine*s* liiii | ex eis non plus remasisse Albur*ni* quam quot homine*s* xvii :)

The facsimile represents the beginning of the deed written, in duplicate, in the left-hand compartment of the fourth page of the tablet, as described above (p. 26); the right-hand compartment being reserved for the names of the witnesses.

The second example is taken from the very perfect remains of a triptych, to which the witnesses' seals still remain attached. The contents refer to the purchase of a girl in the year 139 (*Corp. Insc. Lat.* iii. 936-7).

P

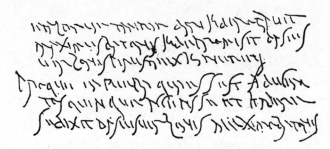

DACIAN WAXEN TABLET.—A.D. 139.

(et alterum tantum dari fide rogavit | Maximus Batonis fide promisit Dasius | Verzonis Pirusta ex Kaviereti | Proque ea puella quae *supra scripta* est ✳ ducen | tos quinque accepisse et habere | se dixit Dasius Verzonis a Maximo Batonis)

The writing here is more complicated than that of the other example, and it will at once be seen that the difficulty is not caused by any deficiency in the character of the hand, which is on the contrary particularly bold and well formed, but by the number of linked letters, or rather monograms, which occur. This system of linking dismembers the letters and leaves the initial stroke of a letter attached to its predecessor, while the rest stands quite separate, thus intensifying the natural disposition to write in disjointed strokes upon such a material as wax, and increasing the difficulty of reading. With such a condensed form of writing before us, we are tempted to speculate what would have been the cast of the hand-writing, derived from the Roman, of the middle ages and modern times, had waxen surfaces been the only, or principal, material to receive it. We should certainly have had no loops to our cursive letters and curves would have disappeared.

To complete the illustration of the early Roman cursive hand we give a few lines inscribed on a tile found at Silchester, probably of the 1st or 2nd century. They seem to be the material for a writing lesson, the teacher apparently first writing certain words as examples of the

formation of certain letters, and then dashing off the
"conticuere omnes" of Virgil.

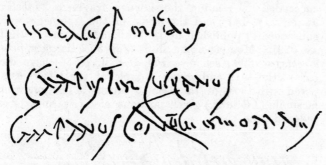

INSCRIBED ROMAN TILE.—1st or 2nd CENTURY.

(Pertacus Perfidus | Campester Lucilianus | Campanus conti-
cuere omnes)

The alphabet employed is identical with that of the
waxen tablets. It will be noticed that the initial C is
marked with an extra dash at the top in continuation of
the curve of the letter, and that the linked form of the
letters ER occurs several times.

Examples of the Roman cursive hand now fail us for
a period of some centuries. We have to wait till the
fifth century to find its representative in Italian deeds of
that period. But we must step aside to examine some
interesting fragments of papyrus, in Paris and Leyden,
inscribed in a character which is quite otherwise unknown :
a modification of the Roman cursive, cast in a mould
which stamps it with a strong individuality. The documents contained in them are portions of two rescripts
addressed to Egyptian officials; and they are said to have
been found at Philæ and Elephantine. The writing is
the official cursive of the Roman chancery, and is ascribed
to the 5th century. Both documents are in the same
hand. For a long time they remained undeciphered, and
Champollion-Figeac, while publishing a facsimile (*Chartes
et MSS. sur papyrus,* 1840, pl. 14), was obliged to admit

his inability to read them. Massmann, however, after his experience of the writing of the waxen tablets, succeeded in reading the Leyden fragment (*Libellus aurarius*, p. 147), and the whole of the fragments were subsequently published by De Wailly (*Mém. de l'Institut*, xv. 399). Mommsen and Jaffe (*Jahrbuch des gem. deut. Rechts*, vi. 398; see also *Pal. Soc.* ii. pl. 30) have discussed the text and given a table of the letters compared with those of the Dacian tablets. The following facsimile (*Lib. aur.*) gives portions of a few lines on a reduced scale.

IMPERIAL RESCRIPT.—5TH CENTURY.

(portionem ipsi debitam resarcire | nec ullum precatorem ex instrumento— | pro memorata narratione per vim con[fecto]— | sed hoc viribus vacuato)

The writing is large, the body of the letters being above three-quarters of an inch high. A comparison of the letters, as set out in the Table, with those of the alphabet of the waxen tablets leaves no room to question their connection, but at the same time shows the changes effected by the flourished style of the later hand and also by its more cursive formation with pen and ink upon papyrus, the natural slope of the writing inclining, under the altered conditions, to the right, instead of inclining rather to the left, or at least being upright, as in the waxen tablets. It is interesting to note the change in the shape of B, to suit the system of connecting letters practised in the more cursive style, from the stilted a-form of the tablets with closed bow, to an open-bowed letter somewhat resembling a reversed modern cursive *b*. The tall letters have developed loops; O and v-shaped U are small and written high in the line. The shapes of E, M, and N are peculiar; but the first is evidently only a quick formation, in a loop, of the old double-stroke E (‖), and the other two, although they have been compared with the Greek minuscule *mu* and *nu*, as if derived from those letters, appear to be nothing more than cursive shapes of the Latin capitals M and N.

This official hand, however, as already stated, is quite exceptional, and we turn to the documents on papyrus from Ravenna, Naples, and other places in Italy, dating from the fifth century, for examples of the less trammelled development of the Roman cursive into a bold straggling hand, which, however, is not wanting in effectiveness. The largest number are brought together by Marini (*I Papiri Diplomatici*), and other examples will be found in the works of Mabillon (*De Re Diplomatica*), Champollion-Figeac (*Chartes et MSS. sur papyrus*), Massmann (*Urkunden in Neapal und Arezzo*), Gloria (*Paleografia*); in the *Facsimiles of Ancient Charters in the British Museum*, iv. nos. 45, 46; and in *Pal. Soc.* i. pl. 2, 28, ii. pl. 51-53. The following facsimile is taken from a deed of sale of property in Rimini, now in the British Museum, drawn up at Ravenna in the year 572 (*Pal. Soc.* i. pl. 2). The papyrus roll on which it is inscribed is of great length, measuring as much as 8 ft. 6 in., and is a foot wide. The writing, not only of the deed itself, but also of the attestations, is on a large scale, which has been reduced to nearly half-size in the facsimile.

DEED OF SALE.—A.D. 572.

(quantum *supra scripto* emptori interfuerit— | mancipationique
rei *supra scriptae* dol[um]— | que esse vi metu et circumscrip
[tione]— | unciis superius designatis sibi *supra scriptus*)

As compared with the alphabet of the waxen tablets the
letters have here undergone a great alteration, which must
be chiefly attributed to the variations arising out of the
system of connecting the letters together *currente calamo.*
Most of the letters, indeed, have now assumed the shapes
from which the minuscules of the literary hand of the
Carlovingian period were directly derived.   The letter a
has no longer any trace of the capital in its composition ;
it is now the open u-shaped minuscule, derived no doubt
through an open uncial form (ᗛ ᗛ) from the parent
capital ; it is sometimes written in a small form high in
the line ; and it is to be noticed that it is always connected with the next following letter, and on this account
may be distinguished from the letter u, which is never thus
connected.   This link of the a no doubt has its origin in

the sweeping main-stroke of the early cursive letter as seen in the waxen tablets. The letter b has thrown away the bow on the left, as seen in the chancery hand of the fifth century, and has developed one on the right, and appears in the form familiar in modern writing. The letter e, derived from the ordinary capital, not from the two-stroke cursive letter, varies in form in accordance with the conditions of its connection with other letters, and affords a good illustration of the influence of linking-strokes in determining alterations of shape. Among the other letters the fully formed minuscule m and n are seen; long r is easily derived from the cursively-written letter of the waxen tablets; and s, having developed the initial down-stroke or tag, has taken the shape ſ, which it keeps long after.

The general application of the Roman cursive hand to the purposes of literature would hardly be expected; but a few surviving instances of its employment for annotations and even for entire texts are found in the notes written probably in the fifth century by the Arian bishop Maximin in the margins of a MS. at Paris containing the Acts of the Council of Aquileia; in a short Græco-Latin vocabulary on papyrus (the Greek words being written in Roman letters), perhaps of the 5th or 6th century (*Not. et Extr. des MSS.* xviii. pl. 18); in the grammatical treatise of the 6th century in the palimpsest MS. of Licinianus in the British Museum (*Cat. Anc. MSS.* ii. pl. 1, 2); and in the texts of the Homilies of St. Avitus at Paris, perhaps of the 6th century (*Pal. Soc.* i. pl. 68), the Ambrosian Josephus on papyrus, ascribed to the 7th century (*Pal. Soc.* i. pl. 59), and the Homilies of St. Maximus of Turin, also in the Ambrosian Library of Milan, of about the same period (*Pal. Soc.* ii. pl. 32); and in other MSS. From the survival of comparatively so many literary remains in this style of writing, it may be inferred that it was used as a quick and convenient means of writing texts intended probably for ordinary use and not for the market. As an example, we give a few lines from the MS. of St. Maximus.

HOMILIES OF ST. MAXIMUS.—7TH CENTURY.

([pa]trem specialiter exsuperantium— | [mi]nister in sacerdoti
comes in ma[rtyrio] — | [labo]re in cuius vultibus *sanctun*
quoque — | [cre]dimus et quasi in quodam speculo — | [imagi
nem contuemur facile enim cogn[oscimus])

For our present purpose we need not follow in thi
place the further course of Roman cursive writing. I
was still used in the legal documents of Italy for som
centuries, ever becoming more and more corrupt anc
complicated and illegible. Facsimiles of documents o
the eighth and ninth centuries are given by Fumagall
(*Delle Istituzioni diplomatiche*), by Sickel (*Monumenta
Graphica*), in the *Codex Diplomaticus Cavensis*, vol. i.
in the *Paleografia artistica di Montecassino*, tav. xxxiv.
xxxv., and by Silvestre (*Palæography*, i. pl. 137). The
illegible scrawl into which it finally degenerated in
notarial instruments of southern Italy was at length
suppressed by order of Frederic II. in the year 1220.[5]

---

[5] In the thirteenth century the Roman cursive was unintelligible.
Simon of Genoa, *Clavis Sanctionis* (1514, f. 37), says: "Ego vidi
Romæ in gazophilaciis antiquorum monasteriorum Romæ libros et
privilegia ex hac materia (*sc.* charta) scripta ex litteris apud nos non
intelligibilibus, nam figuræ nec ex toto Græcæ nec ex toto Latinæ
erant." And again, when speaking of papyrus (f. 47), he uses these
words: "Ego vidi Romæ in aliquibus monasteriis antiquissima
volumina ex eisdem litteris semi-græcis scripta ac nullis modernis
legibilia." See De Rossi, *Codd. Palatini Latini*, 1886, Introd. p. ci.

CHAPTER XVI.

LATIN PALÆOGRAPHY.—CONTINUED.

Minuscule Writing.—National Hands.

WE have now to investigate the very interesting subject of the formation of the national handwritings of Western Europe, derived from Roman writing. On the Continent the cursive hand which has just been noticed became the basis of the writing of Italy, Spain, and Frankland, and from it were moulded the three national hands which we know as Lombardic, Visigothic, and Merovingian. The common origin of all three is sufficiently evident on an inspection of the earliest charters of those countries.

In the book-hands elaborated by professional scribes from the cursive, with a certain admixture of uncial and half-uncial forms, we see the lines of demarcation between the three kinds of writing at length quite clearly defined. But it was only to be expected that particularly in the earlier stages there should be examples which it would be difficult to assign definitely to either one or other of these national divisions; and, as a matter of fact, the difference between a MS. written in France and another written in Italy is not always so strongly marked as to enable us to call the one decidedly Merovingian or the other decidedly Lombardic in its style.

We will examine the three hands in the order in which they have been above referred to, reserving the Merovingian for the last, as that form of writing leads on to the Caroline Minuscule, which eventually displaced all three.

Lombardic Writing.

That the national handwriting of Italy, founded on the old Roman cursive, should not have developed on the same lines throughout the country is attributable to political causes. The defeat of the Lombards in northern Italy by Charlemagne subjected it there to new influences, and checked its development in the direction which it continued to follow in the Lombard duchies of the south, and particularly in the monasteries of Monte Cassino near Naples and La Cava near Salerno. Therefore, although the title of Lombardic is given as a general term to the writing of Italy in the early middle ages, that title might be more properly restricted to its particular development in the south, covering the period from the ninth to the thirteenth century, and reaching its climax in the eleventh century.

In an example of the book-hand of Northern Italy in the seventh century, the Verona Augustine (Sickel, *Mon. Graph.* iii. 1), we find the half-uncial element very strong, and what would be termed the Lombardic element, the peculiar adaptation of certain cursive forms, rather subordinate. Again, in the Sacramentarium (MS. 348) of St. Gall (*Pal. Soc.* i. pl. 185), which belonged to Remedius, Bishop of Chur (A.D. 800-820), and which may therefore be placed at least as early as the beginning of the 9th century, if not at the end of the 8th century, the writing, though classed as Lombardic, is rather of the type which we should prefer to call modified Lombardic. In the facsimile here given, while the descent of the writing from the Roman cursive can pretty readily be traced, the national character of the hand is not very marked, and it is only the letters a (in the double-c form) and t which are absolutely Lombardic in shape.

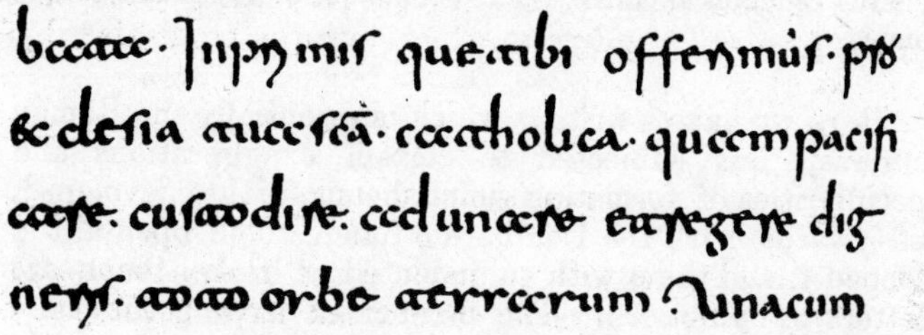

[handwritten Lombardic script facsimile]

([inli]bata : Inprimis que tibi offerimus pro | ecclesia tua
sancta . catholica . quam pacifi | care . custodire . adunare . et
regere dig | neris . toto orbe terrarum : Una cum)

To illustrate the Lombardic hand in one of its earliest
stages, written cursively, we take a few lines from a
deed of Grimoaldus IV., Duke of Benevento, of the year
810 (*Paleografia artistica di Montecassino—Longobardo-
Cassinese*, tav. xxxiv.).

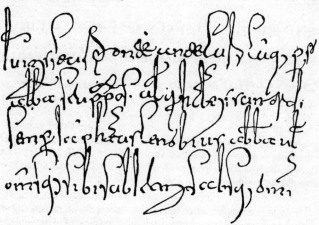

DEED FROM BENEVENTO.—A.D. 810.

(—*in*vitis seu sponte an*t*e cui*u*scum*que* perso[na] | —abb*atissam* seu p*repositos* vel q*ui* hab eis su̇nt ordi[nati] | —semp*er* ia*m* phatus cenobius abb*atissa* vel | —om*n*es*que* sibi subiectis absq*ue* om*n*i).

Here we have a writing which is essentially the Roman cursive, but subjected to certaiu exaggerations and peculiarities of formation which, being further developed, afterwards mark the Lombardic hand. The open a, the looped t, and the e with an indented or broken back are letters to be noticed. The manner of writing the letter a above the line in a zig-zag stroke commencing with a curve (*hab* in l. 2, and *phatus* in l. 3) is only an exaggeration of the practice which was referred to above in the remarks upon the Ravenna documents.

The next facsimile is from a MS. of Albinus Flaccus "De Trinitate," of the year 812, in the monastery of Monte Cassino (*Pal. art. di M. C.* tav. xxxvii).

ALBINUS FLACCUS.—A.D. 812.

(centum qua·lraginta tres hos divide— | triginta centum viginti remanent.— | egyptiorum . ad ipsas adice octo et fiun[t] | — triginta superat unus ipsum est ad— | Sic et ceteros annos p*er* aeras discurrentes—)

In this example the hand is formally written as a book-hand, with the characteristic shapes of the letters a, e, and t now quite·developed. And even at this early period there is discernible the tendency to give a finish to short vertical strokes, as in m, n, and u, by adding heavy oblique heads and feet. This style of ornamental finish was carried to its height in the course of the eleventh century, and had the result of imparting to Lombardic writing of that period, by the strong contrast of the fine and heavy strokes, the peculiar appearance which has gained for it the name of *broken* Lombardic. The facsimile which follows is a good specimen of this type. It is from a Lectionary written at Monte Cassino between the years 1058 and 1087 (*Pal. art. di M. C.* tav. xlv.).

LECTIONARY.—A.D. 1058-1087.

(nos et lavit nos | a peccatis no*st*ris in | sanguine suo.' et fe | cit no*stru*m regnum | sacerdotes deo et)

After this period the Lombardic hand declines in beauty and becomes more angular. A specimen of the later style is found in a commentary on monastic rules by Bernard, abbot of Monte Cassino from 1264 to 1282 (*Pal. art. di M. C.* tav. liii).

MONASTIC RULES.—A.D. 1264-1282.

(sum . id e*st* tributum q*uo*d ex debito debent ¦ sicut servi
domi*no* videlicet septem vicib*us* in ¦ die et semel i*n* nocte
psallere . *non* negli ¦ gant reddere . id e*st* reddant diligent*er* ¦
et studiose . debent enim habere a biblio[theca])

Visigothic Writing.

Visigothic is the title given to the national writing of
Spain derived from the Roman cursive. It runs a course
very close to that of the Lombardic, developing a book-
hand of distinctive character, which is well established
in the eighth and ninth centuries and lasts down to the
twelfth century. Its final disuse was due, as in the case
of the other continental national hands, to the advance
of the Caroline minuscule hand, which, however, as was
to be expected, could only displace the native hand by
degrees, making its presence felt at first in the north of
the Peninsula.[1] In the collection of photographic facsimiles *Exempla Scripturae Visigoticae*, edited by P.

---

[1] "Dans un des volumes acquis par nous se trouve le catalogue des
livres que le monastère de Silos possédait au commencement du xiiie
siècle.... Le redacteur du catalogue a pris soin d'avertir que
plusieurs des livres de son abbaye étaient écrits en lettres françaises
...... C'est une allusion à la révolution qui s'introduit au xiie
siècle, et peut-être dès le xie, dans les habitudes des copistes espagnols,
probablement sous l'influence des colonies françaises que notre grande
abbaye de Cluni envoya dans plusieurs diocèses d'Espagne."—Delisle,
Mélanges de Paléographie, p. 59.

Ewald and G. Loewe (Heidelberg, 1883), the course of
the Visigothic writing can be fairly followed. In the
cursive hand of the seventh century we find little variation from the Roman cursive; but almost immediately we
are in the presence of a half-cursive book-hand (*Ex.* 4)
which is attributed to the 7th or 8th century, and
which has already assumed a distinctive character, as
will be seen from the following facsimile. It comes
from a treatise of St. Augustine in a MS. in the Escurial.

ST. AUGUSTINE.—7TH OR 8TH CENTURY.

([qu]od scit medicus esse noxium sanitati | —medicus ergo ut
egr*um* exaudiat | —voluntatem . denique etiam ipsa | —accipit
propter quod ter d*ominum* rogabit | —mea nam virtus in in-
firmitate p*er*ficitur | —tur a te stimulus carnis quem accepisti)

In this specimen the old forms of the Roman cursive
letters are treated in a peculiar method, the inclination
of the writing to the left imparting a compressed and
angular character. The high-shouldered letter r and
the ordinary t are already in the forms which at a later
period are prominent in Visigothic MSS., and the letter
g is beginning to take the q-form which makes it the
most characteristic letter of the Visigothic alphabet.
It is interesting to notice the shapes of a and u (the
linking of the first letter which distinguishes it, as in

its Roman prototype, from the independently written u, still being observed), the forms of p, and the different changes of t when in combination with other letters—all referable to their Roman ancestors.

In many of the specimens of the eighth and ninth centuries we find a small evenly-written hand, in which the light and heavy strokes are in strong contrast, the inclination of the letters being still rather to the left. But we choose our next facsimile from a MS. which is of a rather more formal type, and is a more direct link in the development of the later style. It is from a MS. of the Etymologies of St. Isidore, in the Escurial, of the first half of the 9th century (*Ex.* 14).

ST. ISIDORE.—9TH CENTURY.

(sunt nova. Testamentum | au*tem* novu*m* . ideo nuncupatur . | quia innovat., non enim illu*m* | discunt . nisi homines reno-vati | ex vetustate p*er* gratiam et p*er*ti—)

The letters of the Visigothic hand are here fully developed; and at the same time the thickening or clubbing of the tall vertical strokes seems to indicate the influence of the French school. Attention may be drawn to the occurrence in the last line of the abbreviated form of *per* peculiar to the Visigothic hand, which in other countries would represent *pro*.

We advance some hundred years, and select our next facsimile from a Martyrology in the British Museum (*Pal. Soc.* i. pl. 95), which was written in the diocese of Burgos in the year 919.

MARTYROLOGY.—A.D. 919.

(iussit eum capite plecti: quum*que* | decollatus esset beatus Prota | sius.' ego servus Chri*st*i Philippus | abstuli cum filio meo furtim | nocte corpora san*cta*.' et in domo)

It will be seen that this specimen differs from the last one in being rather squarer in form of letters and in having the vertical strokes finer. There is, in fact, a decided loss as regards actual beauty of writing. The MS. is one which may be classed as a specimen of calligraphy, and therefore rather in advance of others of the same period which still retain much of the older character, and is dominated by the increasing influence of the French hand. In passing, the use of the conjunction *quum* in our specimen may be noticed, a practice of Visigothic scribes, while those of other nations employ the form *cum*.

The squareness and thinness of type which we have seen appearing in the above specimen increases in course of time, and is most characteristic of later Visigothic writing of the eleventh and early twelfth centuries. In this change, too, we may trace the same influence which is seen at work in other handwritings of Western Europe of that period.

Our last Visigothic facsimile is supplied by a MS. of the Commentary of Beatus on the Apocalypse, now in the British Museum (*Pal. Soc.* i. pl. 48), which was written in the monastery of St. Sebastian of Silos, in the diocese of Burgos, in the year 1109.

COMMENTARY ON THE APOCALYPSE.—A.D. 1109.

(ad hanc ęcclesiam pertrait . ut semper sibi | socios requirat . cum quos pręcipitetur | in geenna.' semper enim hęc mulier ętiam | ante adventum domini parturiebat | in doloribus suis . quę est antiqua ęcclesia | patrum et profetarum . et sanctorum et apostolorum)

Merovingian Writing.

The hands which have been classed as Merovingian, practised as they were over the whole extent of the Frankish empire, were on that account of several types; and, as has been already stated, the boundary line between the different national hands is not always to be accurately traced. First to consider the style of writing to which the name of Merovingian may *par excellence* be applied, we turn to the many official documents still in existence of the Merovingian dynasty which are to be found in facsimile in such works as Letronne's *Diplomata* (1848), the *Facsimile de Chartes et Diplomes Mérovingiens et Carlovingiens* of Jules Tardif (1866), the *Kaiserurkunden in Abbildungen* of von Sybel and Sickel (1880, etc.), and the *Musée des Archives Départementales* (1878). In these the Roman cursive is transformed into a curiously cramped style of writing, the letters being laterally compressed, the strokes usually slender, and the heads and tails of letters exaggerated. As an example we may take a section from a charter of Childebert III., in favour of the Abbey of St. Denis, of the year 695 (Tardif, *Monuments Historiques*, p. 28).

CHARTER OF CHILDEBERT III.—A.D. 695.

([sexcen]tus eum roganti pro ipso conposuisset et pro | —
[nonco]panti Hosdinio in pago Belloacense ad inte[grum] | —
per suo estrumentum delegasset vel fir[masset] | —ibidem ad
presens aderat interrogatum fuit | —sua in suprascripto loco
Hosdinio ipsius Hai[noni] | —[v]el firmasset sed ipsi Boc-
tharius clirecus in)

There is no difficulty in tracing the descent of the various forms of letters here employed from the parent stock, the Roman cursive. But, besides such shapes as those of the varying t and the high-written a and the coalescing form of the same letter in combination, as in the word *ad,* which at once arrest the eye, special notice may be taken of the narrow double-c shaped a, which is characteristic in this hand, and, in a less degree, of the u, worn down into a curved or sickle-shaped stroke —a form which is found in the book-hand, not only as an over-written u, but also as a letter in the body of the writing.

The book-hand immediately derived from this style of writing, which is, in fact, the same hand moulded into a set calligraphic style, appears in various extant MSS. of the seventh and eighth centuries. We select a specimen from a Lectionary of the Abbey of Luxeuil, written in the year 669.[2]

LECTIONARY OF LUXEUIL.—A.D. 669.

(hic est qui verbum audit . et continuo c[um gau] | dio accipit illud . non habet autem in s[e radicem] | sed est temporalis, facta autem tri[bulatione] | et persecutione . propter verbum . con[tinuo] | scandalizatur, qui autem est semina[tus])

[2] See *Notice sur un Manuscrit de l'Abbaye de Luxeuil,* by L. Delisle, in *Notices et Extraits des MSS.,* tome **xxxi.** ; and *Questions Mérovingiennes,* no. iii., by J. Havet (1885).

As an example of the same type of writing, but of later date, the following facsimile is taken from a MS. of Pope Gregory's *Moralia*, probably of the latter part of the 8th century, in the British Museum (Add. MS., 31,031; *Cat. Anc. MSS.* ii. pl. 33).

ST. GREGORY'S MORALIA.—8TH CENTURY.

(deseratur . Quia et frustra velociter currit— | veniat deficit. Hinc est enim quod de reprobis— | sustinenciam. hinc est enim quod de electis suis— | mansistis mecum in temtacionibus meis . hinc— | ad finem iustus perseverasse describitur)

Of other types of handwriting which were used within the limits of the Frankish empire and which must be considered under the present division, there are some which bear a close resemblance to the Lombardic style— so close, indeed, that many MSS. of this character have been classed as Lombardic. We are here, in fact, in presence of the same difficulties as have been noticed under the section dealing with Lombardic writing; and have to deal with examples, any classification of which, in face of their mixed character, cannot but be to some extent arbitrary.

The following specimen is from the Harley MS. 5041, in the British Museum, containing theological treatises, and homilies, of the end of the 7th century. It cannot be doubted that the volume was written in France, and in the character of individual letters it is of the Merovingian type, while in general appearance it has rather a Lombardic cast.

HOMILIES.—LATE 7TH CENTURY.

(Cum praees hominibus memento quia tibi est d*eu*s | iudicans homines scito quia ipse iudicaveris— | Qui locum p*r*edicationis suscipit ad altitudine | boni actionis ad excelsa transeat et eorum | qui sibi commissi sunt opera transcendat)

The letters which may be specially noticed are the a and the sickle-shaped u which were referred to above.

There are also a certain number of extant MSS. of the eighth and ninth centuries of a particular type, of which some were certainly written in France, while others appear to have been written in Italy. There seems then to be a doubt whether we should class this hand as Lombardic or as a variation of Merovingian. It certainly approached more nearly to the Lombardic style. It appears, for example, in the Paris MS. 3836, containing a collection of Ecclesiastical Canons, of the 8th century (*Pal. Soc.* i. pl. 8, 9); in some leaves of the early part of the 8th century added to a MS. of Homilies, etc., written at Soissons early in that century[3]; and, on the

---

[3] See *Notice sur un Manuscrit Merovingien de la Bibliothèque Royale de Belgique*, by L. Delisle, in *Notices et Extraits des MSS.*, tome xxxi. Mons. Delisle classes these leaves as Lombardic, and remarks : " Il nous fait voir combien l'emploi de l'écriture lombardique, importée chez nous par des moines italiens, devait être ordinaire dans les abbayes franques."

other hand, in the Harley MS. 3063, the commentary of
Theodore of Mopsuestia on the Pauline Epistles (*Cat.
Anc. MSS.* ii. pl. 35), of the 9th century, which, from
internal evidence seems to have been written in Italy.
We select a few lines from the Soissons MS.

SERMON OF ST. CÆSARIUS.—8TH CENTURY.

(aliis maledicere propter illud quod scriptu[m]— | regnum dei
possedibunt , Numquam iurar[e]— | vir multum iurans im-
plebitur iniquitat[e]— | de domo illius plaga . Quod autem
dicit de do— | plagam.' non de domo terrena sed de anima ei).

But it must not be forgotten that the Uncial and Half-
uncial styles were still employed for the production of
the greater number of literary MSS. ; and that the professional scribes, who were of course expert both in
those formal book-hands and in the more cursive characters
of the Merovingian, would naturally, when writing without special care or in a rough and ready style, mix the
characters of the different hands. Thus we are prepared
to find the influence of the uncial and half-uncial showing
itself in modifying the extravagances of the cursive

Merovingian, and, on the other hand, the cursive breaking
out among lines written in a more formal character.
Two very interesting MSS. in a variety of hands in
which these influences are marked have been described
by Monsieur Delisle: *Notice sur un Manuscrit Merovingien d'Eugyppius* (1875) written early in the 8th
century, and *Notice sur un Manuscrit Merovingien de la
Bibliothèque d'Epinal* (1878) of the Epistles of St.
Jerome, written in the year 744. The two following
facsimiles represent two of the many hands employed.

EUGYPPIUS.—8TH CENTURY.

(—e potuerit quod per serpentem dictum | —fructu ligni illius
vescerentur quia sci | —de*u*s propter dinoscentiam boni et ma |
—[bo]num creaturę suae creator invi | —[spir]itali mente
praeditus credere | —[cre]dere ipsi n*o*n possit . propterea
mu—)

Here we have a hand cast into a fairly simple form,
but in some words using more cursive letters than in
others.

In the next example the influence of the half-uncial
style is more evident, and the minuscule book-hand has
here advanced to that stage of development which only
required a master to mould it into the simple and elegant
form which it was soon to receive.

ST. JEROME.—A.D. 744.

(—ri oportet . ante tribunal Chr*isti* | —[co]rporis sui . prout
gessit . sive bonu*m* . | —te virgo . filia Sion . quia magna | —
[t]ua effunde sicut . aqua cor . con[tra] | —[man]us tuas . pro
remedium pecca[torum] | —[la]mentationem . et *n*ullo quide*m*)

Later examples of the eighth century continue to
show an advance towards the desired minuscule literary
hand which should take the place of the less convenient
uncial writing.

The Caroline Reform.

The period of Charlemagne is an epoch in the history
of the handwritings of Western Europe. With the
revival of learning naturally came a reform of the writing
in which the works of literature were to be made known.
A decree of the year 789 called for the revision of church
books; and this work naturally brought with it a great
activity in the writing schools of the chief monastic
centres of France. And in none was there greater
activity than at Tours, where, under the rule of Alcuin
of York, who was abbot of St. Martin's from 796 to 804,
was specially developed the exact hand which has received
the name of the Caroline Minuscule. Monsieur Delisle,
in his *Mémoire sur l'Ecole calligraphique de Tours au*

ix⁰ siècle (1885)⁴ enumerates as many as twenty-five MSS. of the Carlovingian period still in existence which, from the character of the writing, may be ascribed to the school of Tours or at least to scribes connected with that school.

Of the capital writing employed in the titles and other ornamental parts of such MSS. we need not concern ourselves; but, besides the minuscule hand, there is a hand, employed, in a sense, as an ornamental form of writing, which is characteristic of the school and is adapted from the Roman Half-uncial hand of the sixth century. We select a few lines from one of Monsieur Delisle's facsimiles, taken from a MS. at Quedlinburg.

SULPICIUS SEVERUS.—EARLY 9TH CENTURY.

(ne crevit et ampulla cum o | leo quod benedixerat super | constratum marmorem pa | vimentum caecidit et in | tegra est inventa)

If reference is made to the facsimiles of half-uncial writing above (p. 202) it will be seen how in this hand the sentiment of breadth in the older hand is maintained, as *e.g.* in the sweeping strokes of r and s, and in the width

---

⁴ *Extrait des Mémoires de l'Académie des Inscriptions et Belles-Lettres,* tome xxxii.

and curves of a and m. The shape of g is also to be
noticed ; and not less the employment of the capital **N**.

The habit of copying this fine bold type of early
writing undoubtedly contributed to the elegance of the
minuscule hand which was developed in the French
school. Of this hand the following example is selected
from the same MS. of Quedlinburg.

SULPICIUS SEVERUS.—EARLY 9TH CENTURY.

(ex uberib*us* caprarum aut ovium pas | torum manu praessis .
longa linea | copiosi lactis effluere.' Puer . sur | rexit incolomis.'
Nos obstupefacti | tantae rei miraculo . id quod ipsa | cogebat
veritas fatebamur . non)

We now leave for the present the further consideration
of this new style and devote the following chapter to an
examination of the early Irish and English schools of
writing, which followed a different line from that of the
continental national hands.

CHAPTER XVII.

Irish Writing.

THE origin and development of the early handwritings of our own Islands differ from those of the continental nations of Western Europe which have been examined in the last chapter. While on the continent the Roman Cursive hand formed the basis of the national forms of writing, in Ireland and England the basis was the Roman Half-uncial.

The foundation of the early Church in Ireland and the consequent spread of civilization naturally fostered the growth of literature and the development of a national school of writing; while at a later period the isolation of the country prevented the introduction of new ideas and changes which contact with neighbouring nations invariably effects. Ireland borrowed the types for her handwriting from the MSS. which the Roman missionaries brought with them; and we must assume that the greater number of those MSS. were written in the half-uncial character, and that there was an unusually scanty number of uncial MSS. among the works thus imported; otherwise it is difficult to account for the development of the Irish hand on the line which it followed.

In writing of the course of Greek Palæography we had occasion to notice the very gradual changes which came over the handwriting of Greece, confined as it was to a comparatively small district and to a single language. In Ireland this conservatism is still more strongly marked. The hand which the modern Irish scholar writes is

essentially, in the forms of its letters, the pointed hand
of the early middle ages; and there is no class of MSS.
which can be more perplexing to the palæographer than
Irish MSS. Having once obtained their models, the
Irish scribes developed their own style of writing and
went on practising it, generation after generation, with
an astonishing uniformity. The English conquest did
not disturb this even course. The invaders concerned
themselves not with the language and literature of the
country. They were content to use their own style of
writing for grants of land and other official deeds; but
they left the Irish scribes to go on producing MSS. in
the native characters.

The early Irish handwriting appears in two forms:
the round and the pointed. Of pure uncial writing we
have to take no account. There are no undisputed
Irish MSS. in existence which are written in that style;
although the copy of the Gospels in uncials, which was
found in the tomb of St. Kilian and is preserved at
Würzburg, has been quoted as an instance of an Irish
uncial MS. The writing is in ordinary uncial characters
and bears no indication of Irish nationality (Z. and W.,
Exempla, 58).

The round Irish hand is half-uncial, and in its characters
there is close relationship with the Roman half-uncial
writing as seen in the MSS. of Italy and France dating
from the fifth or sixth century. A comparison of the
earliest surviving Irish MSS. with specimens of this
style leaves no room to doubt the origin of the Irish
round hand; and, without accepting the traditional ascription of certain of them to St. Patrick or St. Columba
or other Irish saints, there can be no hesitation in
dating some as far back as the seventh century. We
may therefore place the period of the first development
of the Irish round hand somewhat earlier, namely, in
the sixth century, the Roman half-uncial MSS. of which
time evidently served as models.

Among the oldest extant Irish MS. of this character
is the fragmentary copy of the Gospels, of an early
version, in the library of Trinity College, Dublin (*Nat.*

MSS. Ireland, i. pl. 2 ; *Pal. Soc.* ii. pl. 33), which is to
be ascribed to the latter part of the 7th century. The
writing bears a very close resemblance to the continental half-uncial hand, but at the same time has the
distinct impress of its Irish nationality, indicated generally in a certain angular treatment of some of the
strokes which in the Roman half-uncial MSS. are
round.

GOSPELS.—LATE 7TH CENTURY.

([ami]cus meus supervenit de via a[d me] | et non habeo quod
ponam an[te illum] | ad ille deintus respondens [dicit no] | li
mihi molestus esse iam ostiu[m clusum] | est et pueri in cubi-
culo mecum [sunt] | non possum surgere et dare)

The MS. may be cited as a specimen of a style of
writing which was no doubt pretty widely used at the
time for the production of MSS. of a good class—a
careful working book-hand, which, however, did not
compete with the sumptuous style for which the Irish
scribes had by this time become famous. The same
kind of writing, but more ornamental, is found in a
Psalter (*Nat. MSS. Ireland,* i. pl. 3, 4) traditionally
ascribed to St. Columba, but probably also of the same
date as the Gospels just described.

No school of writing developed so thoroughly, and,

apparently, so quickly, the purely ornamental side of calligraphy as the Irish school. The wonderful interlaced designs which were introduced as decorative adjuncts to Irish MSS. of the seventh and eighth centuries are astonishing examples of skilful drawing and generally of brillant colouring. And this passion for ornamentation also affected the character of the writing in the more elaborately executed MSS.—sometimes even to the verge of the fantastic. Not only were fancifully formed initial letters common in the principal decorated pages, but the striving after ornamental effect also manifests itself in the capricious shapes given to various letters of the text whenever an opportunity could be found, as, for instance, at the end of a line. The ornamental round hand which was elaborated under this influence, is remarkable both for its solidity and its graceful outlines. The finest MS. of this style is the famous copy of the Gospels known as the "Book of Kells," now in the library of Trinity College, Dublin (*Nat. MSS. Ireland,* i. pl. 7-17; *Pal. Soc.* i. pl. 55-58, 88, 89), in which both text and ornamentation are brought to the highest point of excellence.

BOOK OF KELLS.—7th CENTURY.

(fecit . Se ipsum non p[otest sal] | vum facere si rex Israh[el
est des] | cendat nunc de cruce[et crede] ⱶ mus ei . Confidit in
do*mi*no [et nunc li] | beret eum si vult dixit)

Although tradition declares that the MS. belonged to
St. Columba, who died in the year 507, it does not
appear to be older than the latter part of the seventh
century.

It was a volume of this description, if not the Book
of Kells itself, which Giraldus Cambrensis, in the twelfth
century, saw at Kildare, and which he declared was so
wonderful in the execution of its intricate ornamental
designs that its production was rather to be attributed
to the hand of an angel than to human skill. The oftener
and the more closely he examined it, the more he found
in it to excite his admiration.[1]

Another MS. of Irish execution, which is of the same
character, but not nearly so elaborate as the Book of
Kells, is the copy of the Gospels of St. Chad, at Lich-
field (*Pal. Soc.* i. pl. 20, 21, 35). But the grand style of
round half-uncial writing which is used in these MSS.
was not adapted for the more ordinary purposes of
literature or the requirements of daily intercourse, and,
after reaching the culminating point of excellence in the
Book of Kells, it appears to have quickly deteriorated—
at all events, the lack of surviving examples would
appear to indicate a limit to its practice. The MS. of
the Gospels of MacRegol, written about the year 800,
now in the Bodleian Library, is a late specimen, in
which the comparative feebleness and rough style of the
writing contrast very markedlv with the practised
exactness of the older MSS.

---

[1] " Sin autem ad perspicacius intuendum oculorum aciem invitaveris
et longe penitius ad artis arcana transpenetraveris, tam delicatas et
subtiles, tam arctas et artitas, tam nodosas et vinculatim colligatas,
tamque recentibus adhuc coloribus illustratas notare poteris intri-
caturas, ut vere hæc omnia potius angelica quam humana diligentia
jam asseveraveris esse composita. Hæc equidem quanto frequentius
et diligentius intueor, semper quasi novis abstupeo, semper magis ac
magis admiranda conspicio."—*Topographia Hiberniæ*, ii. 38. See
Nat. MSS. Ireland, ii. pl. 66.

GOSPELS OF MACREGOL.—ABOUT A.D. 800.

(prophetas audiant illo[s]— | abracham sed si quis ex mo[rtuis]
— | [paeni]tentiam agent ait autem ill[i] | —*non* audiunt ne*que*
si quis ex mor[tuis])—

The pointed Irish nand was derived from the same
source as the round hand. On the continent we have
seen that the national cursive hands were but sequels
of the Roman Cursive subjected to varying conditions,
and were distinct from the literary or book hands which
were used contemporaneously by their side. The Irish
scribes had, or at least followed, but one model—the
Roman Half-uncial. The pointed hand is nothing more
than a modification of the round-hand, with the same
forms of letters subjected to lateral compression and
drawn out into points or hair-lines, and is a minuscule
hand. There cannot be much doubt that this style of
writing came into existence almost contemporaneously
with the establishment of a national hand. The round
hand no doubt preceded it ; but the necessity for a
more cursive character must have made itself felt almost
at once. The pointed hand, of an ornamental kind,
appears in some of the pages of the Book of Kells, a
fact which proves its full establishment at a much earlier
period. The Book of Dimma (*Nat. MSS. Ireland*,
i. pl. 18, 19) has been conjecturally ascribed to a period
of about the year 650, but can scarcely be older than the
eighth century. The first example to which a certain
date can be given on grounds of internal evidence which

R

are fairly conclusive is the Book of Armagh (*Nat. MSS. Ireland*, i. pl. 25-29), a MS. containing portions of the New Testament and other matter, written, as it seems, by Ferdomnach, a scribe who died in the year 844.

BOOK OF ARMAGH.—BEFORE A.D. 844.

([Id]eo dico vob*is* ne soliciti sitis animæ | quid manducetis aut corpori ve*st*ro qu*id* | induamini no*n*ne anima plus *est* quam æs | ca *et* corpus quam aësca vestimen*tu*m | respicite volatilia cæli q*uonia*m no*n* ser*unt* | neq*ue* congregant in horrea *et* pate*r* | ve*st*er cælestis pascit illa no*n*ne vos | magis plures estis illis)

There is a close resemblance between the writing of this MS. and that of the pointed hand written in England at the same period.

The MS. of the Gospels of MacDurnan, in the Lambeth Library (*Nat. MSS. Ireland*, i. pl. 30, 31) of the end of the 9th or beginning of the 10th century may be referred to as a specimen of the very delicate and rather cramped writing which the Irish scribes at this time affected.

In the eleventh and twelfth centuries the pointed hand took the final stereotyped form which it was to follow in the future, and had assumed the angular shapes which are henceforth characteristic of the Irish hand. As a good example of the early part of the twelfth century we select a passage from the Gospels of Mælbrighte (*Nat. MSS. Ireland*, i. pl. 40-42; *Pal. Soc.* i. pl. 212), written in the year 1138, and now in the British Museum.

GOSPELS OF MÆLBRIGHTE.—A.D. 1138.

(Penitentia*m et* remisionem peccato*rum in* om*nes* gen | tes
incipientib*us* ab ierusolima. Vos *autem* tes | tes estis horu*m*.
Et ego mitto p*ro*missum p*at*ris | mei in vos. Vos *autem* sedete
hic in civitate quo | adus*que* induamini virtute exalto. Eduxit |
autem eos us*que* in bethaniam. Et elevatis manib*us* | suis
bene*dixit* eis. Et *factum est* cum bene*di*ceret illis re | cessit ab
eis *et* ferebat*ur* in celum *et* ipsi adoran[tes])

In the writing of this MS. the old forms of letters
have undergone but little change, but yet they have
assumed the essential character of the Irish mediæval
hand. Attention may also be drawn to the use of certain
forms of abbreviation which are found almost exclusively
in Irish and English MSS.

But while the writing of Ireland remained untouched
by external influences, and passed on from generation to
generation with little .change, the influence which, in
revenge, it exercised abroad was very wide. We shall
presently see how England was almost entirely indebted
to Ireland for her national handwriting. In the early
middle ages Irish missionaries spread over the Continent
and founded religious houses in France and Italy and
other countries, and where they settled there the Irish
form of handwriting was practised. At such centres as
Luxeuil in France, Würzburg in Germany, St. Gall in

Switzerland, and Bobio in Italy, it flourished. At first, naturally, the MSS. thus produced were true specimens of the Irish hand. But thus distributed in isolated spots, as the bonds of connection with home became loosened and as the influence of the native styles of writing in their neighbourhoods made itself more felt, the Irish writers would gradually lose the spirit of their early teaching and their writing would become traditional and simply imitative. Thus the later MSS. produced at these Irish settlements have none of the beauty of the native hand ; all elasticity disappears, and we have only the form without the spirit.

English Writing.

The history of writing in England previous to the Norman Conquest takes a wider range than that of writing in Ireland, although, at least in the earlier periods, it runs on the same lines. Here we have to take into account influences which had no part in the destinies of the Irish hand. In England there were two early schools of writing at work : the one originating from Ireland, in the north, from which emanated the national hand, holding its own and resisting for a long time foreign domination ; the other, the school of the Roman missionaries, essentially a foreign school making use of the foreign styles which they brought with them but which never appear to have become naturalized.

We may commence with stating what little can be gathered regarding the foreign school from the few remains which it has left behind. That the Roman Rustic capital writing was made use of by the missionaries and was taught in their school, whose principal seat must have been at Canterbury, is proved by the occurrence of such specimens as those found in a Psalter of about A.D. 700, in the Cottonian collection, which belonged to St. Augustine's monastery at Canterbury (*Cat. Anc. MSS.* ii. pl. 12, 13), and in one or two charters, or, more properly, copies of charters. The Psalter just referred to also affords an example of the character which the foreign uncial assumed in this Canterbury school—an unmistakably local character, of which, however, so few specimens have survived that perhaps no better proof, negative as it is, could be found of the failure of the Roman majuscule styles of writing to make their way in the country. The celebrated copy of the Bible, the "Codex Amiatinus," [2] which was presumably written in Northumbria about the year 700, must not be taken as an example of native uncial writing. The style is quite foreign ; the MS. is probably the work of foreign scribes, and has none of the local cast which belongs to the Canterbury uncial hand. We must suppose that the Canterbury school of writing ceased to exist at a comparatively early period; and, as it had no influence upon the native hand, its interest for us is merely incidental.

The introduction of the foreign minuscule hand in the tenth century is due to later political causes and to the growth of intercourse with the Continent; and it must be considered as altogether unconnected with the early foreign school which has just been discussed.

Now, as to the native school of writing—

St. Columba's settlement in Iona was the centre from whence proceeded the founders of monasteries in northern Britain; and in the year 634 the Irish missionary Aidan founded the see of Lindisfarne (Holy Isle), which became a great centre of English writing. At first the writing was indeed nothing more than the Irish hand transplanted into new soil, and for a time the English style is scarcely to be distinguished from that of the sister island. But gradually distinctions arose, and the English school, under wider influences, developed more graceful forms and threw off the restraints which fettered the growth of Irish writing.

We have, then, first to follow the course of English writing on the same lines as that of Ireland, and to examine the two styles, the round and the pointed, which

---

[2] See above, p. 194.

here, as in Ireland, were adopted as national forms of writing. The round hand again is a half-uncial hand. Uncial writing, as we have seen, was excluded from Irish writing and therefore finds no place in the English school of St. Aidan's followers.

The earliest and most beautiful MS. of the English round half-uncial is the copy of the Lindisfarne Gospels, or the "Durham Book," in the British Museum (*Pal. Soc.* i. pl. 3-6, 22; *Cat. Anc. MSS.* ii. pl. 8-11), said to have been written by Eadfrith, Bishop of Lindisfarne, about the year 700.

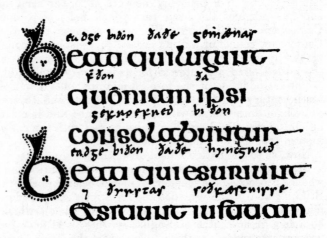

LINDISFARNE GOSPELS.—ABOUT A.D. 700.

(Beati qui lugunt | quoniam ipsi | consolabuntur | Beati qui esuriunt | et sitiunt iustitiam || *Gloss:* eadge biðon ða ðe gemænas | *for* ðon ða | gefroefred biðon | eadge biðon ða ðe hyncgrað | *and* ðyrstas soðfæstnisse)

This very beautiful hand leaves nothing to be desired in the precision and grace with which it is executed, and fairly rivals the great Irish MSS. of the same period.

The glosses in the Northumbrian dialect were added by Aldred, a writer of the tenth century.

The round hand was used for books, and, less frequently, even for charters, during the eighth and ninth centuries; but, although in very carefully written MSS. the writing is still solid, the heavy-stroke style of the Lindisfarne Gospels appears generally to have ceased at an early date. We give a specimen of a lighter character from a fragmentary copy of the Gospels which belonged to the monastery of St. Augustine, Canterbury, though not necessarily written there (*Pal. Soc.* i. pl. 8; *Cat. Anc. MSS.* ii. pl. 17, 18). It is probably of the end of the 8th century.

CANTERBURY GOSPELS.—LATE 8TH CENTURY.

(erue eum et proice abs te . | bonum tibi est cum uno oculo | in vitam intrare quam duos | oculos habentem mitti | in gehennam ignis)

In its original state this MS. must have been a volume of extraordinary magnificence, adorned with paintings and illuminated designs, and having many leaves stained, after the ancient method, a beautiful purple, a few of which still remain.

Other specimens of this hand are found in the Durham Cassiodorus (*Pal. Soc.* i. pl. 164), the Epinal Glossary (*Early Engl. Text Soc.*), and in some charters (*Facs. Anc. Ch.* i. 15, ii. 2, 3; *Pal. Soc.* i. pl. 10). One of the latest MSS. in which the hand is written in its best form is the "Liber Vitæ," or list of benefactors of Durham

(*Cat. Anc. MSS.* ii. pl. 25; *Pal. Soc.* i. pl. 238), which was compiled about the year 840.

For study of the pointed English hand there has survived a fair amount of material. This form of writing was used both for books and documents; but, as might be expected, it is chiefly seen in the latter. The *Facsimiles of Ancient Charters in the British Museum* and the *Facsimiles of Anglo-Saxon MSS.* (Rolls Series), besides many plates published by the Palæographical Society, contribute largely to our knowledge of the different varieties of the hand as practised in various parts of the country, and we are even able to distinguish certain forms as peculiar to certain districts. The period covered by existing documents in the pointed hand, properly so called, ranges from the eighth to the tenth century; later than this time, the changes effected in its structure by contact with southern influences mark a new departure. In the oldest specimens the writing generally exhibits that breadth of form and elegance of shape which we have noticed in other handwritings in their early stages. Then comes the tendency to lateral compression and fanciful variations from the older and simpler types. In illustration of the progress of this hand it will be convenient to select facsimiles from both books and documents in chronological order, the distinction between book-hand and cursive hand being not very marked, although here, as elsewhere, we must expect rather more care in the writing of books than in that of documents.

Our first example shall be selected from the remarkably handsome copy of Bede's " Ecclesiastical History," in the University Library of Cambridge, written probably not long after the year 730 and, it has been conjectured, at Epternach, or some such Anglo-Saxon colony on the Continent. The MS. is also famous as containing the original Anglo-Saxon of the song of Cædmon (*Pal. Soc.* i. pl. 139, 140).

[facsimile of Bede's Ecclesiastical History manuscript]

BEDE'S ECCLESIASTICAL HISTORY.—MIDDLE OF 8TH CENTURY.

([divi]nitus adiutus . gratis canendi— | et supervacui poematis facere— | [re]ligionem *pert*inent religiosa*m eius*— | [ha]bitu secular*i* us*que* ad tempora pr*o*— | carminum aliqu*ando* didicerat — | laetitiae causa decretum . ut)

Nothing could be finer of its kind than the broad, bold, style of this hand, and it requires no demonstration to explain its evolution from the perfect round hand of the early Irish and English scribes who could execute such books as the Book of Kells and the Lindisfarne Gospels.

We make an advance of some half-century and next take a few lines from a charter of Cynewulf, King of the Mercians, of the year 812 (*Pal. Soc.* i. pl. 11).

[facsimile of Mercian Charter manuscript]

MERCIAN CHARTER.—A.D. 812.

(Indictione v. Regni quoque gloriosissimi Me[rciorum]— |
eventōs verbi gratia placuit itaque reg[i]— | —eorum consen-
tientibus firmiter perager[e]— | hlincas vocitantur iuxta distri-
butionem— | —lond appellatur. Quam terram vide[licet])

The writing of this document is more laterally compressed than the preceding example, and is refined and
elegant. Many of the existing charters of Mercian
origin of this period are in this style, and prove the
existence of an advanced school of penmanship in the
Mercian kingdom. Comparing with those deeds other
finely written specimens which belong to the kingdom
of Kent, we are disposed to discern in the latter the
influence of the Mercian school.

In contrast with this elegant style of writing we find
a hand practised chiefly in Wessex, and less widely in
Kent, in which the letters are roughly formed and adopt
in some instances peculiar shapes. The following
specimen is taken from a MS. in the Bodleian Library,
which was written at Winchester, apparently before the
year 863, and contains collections relating to the paschal
cycle and other computations (*Pal. Soc.* i. pl. 168).

COMPUTATIONS.—MIDDLE OF 9TH CENTURY.

([Do]mino vere . *sancto* adqu*e* beatissimo ac | [a]postolico .
mihiqu*e* post d*omi*n*um* pluri | [m]u*m* . colendo . Papa Leoni .
Pascasinus | [epi]*scopus* Apostolatus v*es*tri scripta | [diacon]o
Panormitanæ Ecclesię . Silva | [no def]erente . *percipi* quæ
nuditati meæ)

It will be observed that in this MS., although the
writing is cast into a fairly regular mould as a book
hand, the letters are rather straggling in shape, as for
example in long s and r, and particularly in the t, the
bow of which terminates in a short thickened stroke
or dot.

The rugged nature of this southern hand is more
apparent in the less carefully written charters, as will
be seen from the following facsimile taken from a
Kentish charter of the year 858 (*Facs. Anc. Chart.* ii. 33).

KENTISH CHARTER.—A.D. 858.

([Pas]singwellan hancque livertatem | —tum liventer largitus
sum | —[dominati]one furisque conprehensione | —[se]cura
et inmunis permaneat)

The change which took place in the English pointed
hand in the course of the tenth century is very marked,
and towards the close of the century the influence of
the French minuscule hand begins to assert itself, and
even, under certain conditions, to usurp the place of the
native hand. Characteristic is the disposition to flatten
the upper part of the round portion of such letters as
a and q, and, so to say, cut it off at an oblique angle.
This will be seen in an example selected from a charter
of Æthelstan of the year 931 (*Facs. Anc. Chart.* iii. no. 3),
a good instance of a carefully written document which,
while exhibiting the new forms just referred to, retains
much of the graceful character of the earlier century.

CHARTER OF ÆTHELSTAN.—A.D. 931.

(to ottes forda ; ðonon to wudumere— | Si autem quod absit .
aliquis diabol[ico]— | examinationis die . stridula cla[ngente]
— | qui á satoris pio sato . filius perd[itionis]— | atque inventę
voluntatis scedula . An[no])

With this we may compare the writing of a Latin
Psalter of about the year 969 (*Pal. Soc.* i. pl. 189),
having an interlinear Anglo-Saxon gloss of the early
part of the 11th century. The text is written with
regularity in well-formed minuscules; but the influence
of the foreign school can be detected in the fluctuations
of certain forms, as *e.g.* in the letter s, the round shape
being more generally used than the long Saxon letter.

PSALTER.—ABOUT A.D. 969.

(qui faciad bonu*m* non e*st* usq*ue* ad unu*m* | [Domi]n*us* de cẹlo prospexit sup*er* filios | hominum.' ut videad si est intelle | gens aut requirens deum | [O]m*ne*s declinaverunt simul inutiles || *Gloss :* þa do god ua oþ on anne | drihten of heofena besceawaþ ofer bear | manna þ*æt* geseo gif is ynderstan | dende oþ͞ðe secende drihten | ealle fram ahyldan ætgædere unnyt)

This is not the place to discuss the establishment of the foreign minuscule hand as an independent form of writing in England. This subject will engage our attention when the history of that form of writing will be treated as a whole and its progress throughout the different countries of Western Europe will be taken into one view. It is enough at present to notice the fact that foreign minuscules generally take the place of the native hand in the course of the tenth century for Latin texts, while the Saxon writing still held its own for texts in the vernacular. Thus, in charters of this period we find the two styles standing s*i*de by side, the body of the document, in Latin, being written in the foreign minuscule hand, and the boundaries of the property conveyed, expressed in Anglo-Saxon, being in the native hand. This foreign invasion naturally made its chief impression in the south, if we may judge from the fact that three important MSS. of English origin, which still survive, and which are written in the continental style, viz. the charter of King Eadgar to New Minster, Winchester, of the year 966 (*Pal. Soc.* i. pl. 46, 47), the Benedictional of Bishop Æthelwold of Winchester, earlier than the year 984 (*Pal. Soc.* i. pl. 142, 144), and a MS. of the Office of the Cross in the British Museum (*Pal. Soc.* i. pl. 60), which, though not quite so early, falls in the first years of the next century, A.D. 1012-1020, were all executed in the southern royal city.

The beginning of the eleventh century is an epoch of decided change in the native minuscule hand. It cannot any longer be called a pointed hand. The body of the letters becomes squarer, and the strokes above and below the line become longer than before. In a word, the writing has by this time lost its compactness ; and the change must be attributed to exterior influence, the sentiment of the foreign style of the period being instilled into the native characters. This change is well illustrated by a MS. of the Anglo-Saxon Chronicle of about the year 1045 (*Pal. Soc.* i. 242).

ANGLO-SAXON CHRONICLE.—ABOUT A.D. 1045.

(*and* his broðor eac eadmund æþeling eal[dor]— | æt sæcce . swurda ecgum . embe brunna[nburh]— | clufon . heowon heaþo-linda . hamora la[fum]— | weardes . swa him geæþele wæs . fram cn[eo]— | campe oft . wiþ laþra gehwæne land eal[godon])

The same characteristics are seen in the series of charters of this century. From one of these, dated in 1038 (*Facs. Anc. Ch.*, iv. no. 20), we select a few lines. The writing is very neat and uniform. It is interesting to notice the survival, in an altered shape, of the fashioning of the top of the letter a into a point by an oblique stroke, which was noticed above as characteristic of the tenth century. Here the top stroke, made independently of the body of the letter, is generally a hair-line nearly horizontal. The practice of marking the letter y with a dot, as seen in this facsimile, is a survival from about the sixth century, when it appears to have been first followed in uncial MSS. for the purpose of distinguishing the Y from V.

CHARTER.—A.D. 1038.

(begen þa to eallon gebroþran *and* bædon— | heom ealle
togædere endemes *þæt* he hit— | þa gyrnde he *þæt* he moste
macian forna[ngen]— | *and* se arce*bisceop* eadsige let hit eall
to heora— | wolde *þæt* scip ryne sceolde þærinne licgea[n]— |
willan . *and* se abbo*d* let hit eall þus. *and* se hire[d]— | *sancte*
augustine . þis is eall soð gelyfe se þe— | eallon a on ecnysse .
amen).

This is a favourable specimen of the charter-writing
of the period. Many of the surviving documents are
written in a far rougher style, but in all cases the
lengthening of the main strokes, as well as deterioration in the forms of letters, marks the hand of the
eleventh century.

With the Norman Conquest the native English minuscule hand disappeared as an official hand. The conquerors brought their own form of writing; and the
history of later charters and legal and official documents
written in England is the history of the law-hand—
the hand used in the courts of law and for legal business generally. The native hand had already practically
disappeared as the handwriting of the learned. There
remained only books composed in the native tongue in
which to employ the native form of writing : and there

it continued, for a certain time, to survive, more and more, however, losing its independent character, and being evermore overshadowed and displaced by the new writing of the continental school, until at length the memory of the old hand survives only in the paradoxical employment of the letter y to represent the old Saxon long thorn þ, particularly in writing the definite article, *ye* for þe.   We break off, then, with the period of the Norman Conquest as virtually marking the end of the English hand of the Anglo-Saxon type.

CHAPTER XVIII.

The Literary or Book-Hand in the Middle Ages.

WE have now examined the various national handwritings of Western Europe, as they were developed within
the borders of different countries. We have seen how
they had their origin in different styles of Roman writing, and how they followed their own lines and grew
up in different forms under different conditions. And
yet, with all their variations from one another, they
followed one general law of development, passing from
the broad simple style in the early periods through
stages of more artificial calligraphy to eventual degeneration from their first standards. We have now to
gather the threads together and follow the course of the
handwritings of Western Europe along a new line. One
form of handwriting had been developed, which by its
admirable simplicity recommended itself at once as a
standard hand. The Caroline Minuscule, which we have
already seen brought to perfection at Tours and at other
monastic centres of France, spread quickly throughout
the confines of the Frankish empire, and extended its
influence and was gradually adopted in neighbouring
countries. But at the same time, with this widespread
use of the reformed hand, uniformity of character could

S

not be ensured. National idiosyncrasies show themselves
as manifestly in the different handwritings of different
peoples as they do in their mental and moral qualities;
and, although the Caroline minuscule hand forms the
basis of all modern writing of Western Europe, which
thus starts with more chance of uniformity than the old
national hands which we have been discussing, yet the
national character of each country soon stamps itself
upon its handwriting. Thus in the later middle ages we
have again a series of national hands, clearly distinguish-
able from each other, although in some degree falling
into groups.

First we follow the course of the minuscule hand as
a book hand, reserving the examination of the more
cursive styles used for legal and other documents for a
later chapter.

In a former chapter we have examined the development and final moulding of the Caroline minuscule
hand, and we left it established as the literary hand of
the Frankish empire. Its course through the ninth
and tenth centuries, particularly on the Continent, can
be traced with fair precision by means of the excellent
facsimiles which have been published during recent
years. Its general characteristics during the ninth
century, at least in the better written examples, are
these: the contrast of fine and heavy strokes is marked,
there is a tendency to thicken or club the stems of tall
letters, as in b, d, h; the letter a is often in the open
form (α), and the bows of the letter g are often left
unclosed, somewhat after the fashion of the numeral 3.
In the tenth century, the strokes are usually of a less solid
cast; the clubbing gradually disappears; the open a (in
its pure form) is less frequently used, and the upper bow
of g closes. No fixed laws can, however, be laid down for
distinguishing the MSS. of the two centuries, and the
characteristics which have been named must not be too
rigidly exacted. As in all other departments of our
subject, practice and familiarity are the best guides.

In illustration of the finest style of writing of this
class in the ninth century, we may take a few lines

from the Gospels of the Emperor Lothair, executed in the middle of the century in the Abbey of St. Martin of Tours and now preserved in the Bibliothèque Nationale in Paris (*Album Paléogr.* pl. 22). For such a book the most skilful writers were of course employed, and the handwriting was formed in the most accurate and finished style of the new school.

GOSPELS OF LOTHAIR.—MIDDLE OF 9TH CENTURY.

(Ait paralytico . tibi dico | surge . et tolle lectu*m* | tuu*m* . et vade in domu*m* | tuam ; Et confestim | surgens coram illis | tulit in quo iacebat | et abiit in domum sua*m*)

This MS. shows scarcely any advance upon the style of the MS. of Quedlinburg quoted above (p. 235). We may notice the prevalent use of the open-bowed g to which reference has been made as characteristic of this time; but an instance of the open a does not happen to occur in the facsimile. The general style of the writing, however, is quite typical of the ninth century. Greater variety is seen in a MS. containing commentaries of St. Augustine, written by order of Bishop Baturich of Ratisbon in 823, and now in the Royal Library of Munich (*Pal. Soc.* i. pl. 123).

s 2

(facsimile of manuscript text)

COMMENTARY OF ST. AUGUSTINE.—A.D. 823.

(sic et vos maneatis in eternum : quia talis est— | eius dilectio
est ; Terram diligis : terra eris ; d— | quid dicam . deus eris :
Non audeo dicere ex m— | audiamus : ego dixi dii estis . et
filii excelsio— | vultis esse dii et filii altissimi, Nolite diligere—)

The writing here is in some respects rather archaic,
and may be quoted as an example produced outside the
direct influence of the French school, but at the same
time conforming generally to the new style of the
period.

Next we select two specimens from two MSS. of
Lyons, the one a commentary of Bede, written before
852 ; the other containing works of St. Augustine,
written before 875 (*Album Paléogr.* pl. 20).

(facsimile of manuscript text)

COMMENTARIES OF BEDE.—BEFORE A.D. 852.

(uxoris eius abigail interventa et muneribus— | decem dies
mortuo nabal ipse accipit uxore[m]— | de iezrahel . data uxore
sua michol falti fil— | Zipheis prodentibus saul descendit
cont[ra]— | ipse nocte descendens dormientibus cun[ctis]—)

This MS. is more carelessly written than the preceding,
and shows in the general character of the letters a
falling off from the earlier models of the Caroline minuscule hand and rather an advance towards the more
meagre style of writing of the next century, when the
graceful contrast of heavy and fine strokes is gradually
lost. The survival of the old high-shouldered letter r
may be noticed in the word *mortuo* in the second line.

ST. AUGUSTINE.—BEFORE A.D. 875.

(ullo appetitu significandi pręter se aliquid aliu[d]— | nosci
faciunt . sicuti est fumus significans ignem— | volens signifi-
care id facit . sed rerum experta[rum]— | adversione et nota-
tione cognoscitur. Ignem— | si fumus solus appareat., Sed
et vestigium tr—)

This MS., while it is later than the other, is written
in rather better style, but a facsimile of only a few lines
can hardly make this very evident.

The two specimens may be taken as typical examples
of the ordinary French minuscule book-hand of this
time.

The very gradual change which came over the writing
of the tenth century as compared with that of the ninth
century is well illustrated by a MS. in the British

Museum, containing the commentary of Rabanus Maurus upon Jeremiah (*Pal. Soc.* ii. pl. 109), which, from internal evidence, could not have been written earlier than the year 948.

RABANUS MAURUS.—AFTER A.D. 948.

(—suo ut ponat terra*m* tua*m* in solitudine*m* . civitates | —*que* habitatore. Iste *est* ut dixim*us* verus nabucho[donosor] | adversarius n*oste*r diabolus quasi leo rugiens cir[cuit] | —in quas religandus e*st* . et ne mitta*tur* exorat . | —levavit de quo dictum *est*. Omnium inimicorum suorum)

The not infrequent occurrence of the open a and the general regularity of the writing would have inclined us to place this MS. within the ninth century, had not its approximate date been clearly ascertained. It may be the work of an old man who had not grown out of the training of his younger days. At all events it is an interesting instance of an older style of writing surviving into a new generation, and emphasizes the difficulty of accurately assigning MSS. of the period of the ninth and tenth centuries to their true positions—a difficulty which is enhanced by the comparatively few MSS. of the tenth century which bear dates.

In illustration of the ordinary minuscule hand of the Caroline type in this century, we may take a facsimile from a Sacramentary of Corbie in the Bibliothèque Nationale (Delisle, *Cabinet des MSS.* pl. 31).

[facsimile of manuscript text]

SACRAMENTARIUM.—10TH CENTURY.

(Nos tibi sem*per* et ubi*que* gratias agere— | pater om*nipotens*
aetern*æ* de*us*. Honoru*m* auc[tor]— | [distri]butor omni*um*
dignitatu*m* . *per* qu*em* profic[iunt] [univer] | sa . *per* qu*em*
cuncta firmantur . Am[plificatis] | sem*per* in melius natur*æ*
rationalis)

It will be seen that the letters are not so well formed
and are less graceful in stroke than in the earlier
examples. They are also rather squarer and are more
slackly written. Comparing this example with the
facsimile from the Gospels of Lothair (p. 259), a single
glance is enough to satisfy the eye of the change which
the lapse of a century can effect in a style of handwriting.
It is true that the Lothair Gospels are written in the
finest style of the ninth century, and this example is an
ordinary one of the tenth century, and the contrast
between two MSS. of the two centuries would not in all
cases be so marked. For the present purpose, however,
strong contrast is a first object.

All the specimens which we have given of this class
of Caroline minuscule writing represent the normal
hand of the Frankish empire. Another style, however,
was also followed in the eastern districts, which developed later into the hand which we recognize as
German. The special characteristic of this style is the
sloping of the letters and a certain want of finish,
which, perhaps, may be due to distance from the influence of the French centres of Caroline writing. A
MS. of this class is the Fulda Annals at Leipzig, written

at the close of the ninth century but before the year 882 (Arndt, *Schrifttafeln*, pl. 44).

[facsimile of manuscript text]

([tes]tatus est quod illi non inficientes quasdam assercion[ibus] | racionum verisimilium quibus geste rei qualitatem [muni] | re nisi sunt obposuerunt easque litteris conpræhe[nsas] | ut legati apostolici suggesserunt per gundharium agr[ippine] | colonie et theotgaudum treverensem gallie be[lgice]))

And another example of the same period, but written in a rougher manner, may be selected from a MS. of Canons, in the Library of St. Gall, of about the year 888 (*Pal. Soc.* i. pl. 186).

[facsimile of manuscript text]

(episcopo apamie syrię. Euphranta religiosis[simo]— | [Ty]-anorum. Theodoro religiosissimo episcopo hiero[polis] | — Bosporio religiosissimo episcopo neocesarię | | [r]eligiosissimo episcopo bostre Philippo religi[osissimo] | — mirorum . Theodoto religiosissimo episcopo sele[tie])

In both these examples is apparent the lack of sense of grace which is so marked a failing in mediæval German writing.

It will here be convenient to follow briefly the progress of the continental minuscule hand, as practised in France and Germany, into the eleventh century, before touching upon the course which it took in England. In that century lies the period in which the handwritings of the different countries of Western Europe, cast and consolidated in the new mould, began to assume their several national characters, and which may be said to be the starting-point of the modern hands which employ the Roman alphabet. In the course of the century many old practices and archaisms which had lingered are cast off, and general principles are more systematically observed. The words of the text are now more generally separated from one another; abbreviations and contractions are more methodical; and the handwriting makes a palpable advance towards the square and exact character which culminates in the MSS. of the thirteenth century.

The general characteristics of the writing of the first half of the century are shown in the following facsimile from a MS. of Saints' Lives at Paris (*Cabinet des MSS.*, pl. 32).

LIVES OF SAINTS.—11TH CENTURY.

(etiam dominica quę advenerat nocte ac die— | [vesper]tinam pene horam quarti a transitu diei quę— | [habe]batur . magno concursu fidelium multa*que* de— | [frequen]tabatur . ita ut noctu et interdiu congregat—)

In a later and more compressed style is a MS. of the Life of St. Maurillus, at Paris, written about the year 1070 (*Cabinet des MSS.*, pl. 34).

LIFE OF SAINT MAURILLUS.—ABOUT A.D. 1070.

(—tur ad urbe*m* . Quo cu*m* sine mora venisset . et pace— | tuta
regredi cepisset ⁊ antequa*m* ad pontem leug*e* p*er*— | loci ipsius
ut benedictionib*us* p*re*sulis firmari mere[rentur] | devotius
p*re*stolabant*ur* . Int*er* quos ⁊ parentes cui*us*dam pu[eri]— |
[ni]mia infirmitate extempore gravatu*m* secus via*m* p*er*)

And of a bold type of the close of the century is the
next facsimile, from a Bible written at Stavelot in the
Low Countries between the years 1094 and 1097, and
now in the British Museum (*Pal. Soc.* ii. pl. 92).

BIBLE.—A.D. 1094—1097.

([con]tritione tua ? Insanabilis est dolor tuu[s Prop] | ter mul-
titudinem iniquitatis tu*e* et pr[opter] | dura peccata tua feci
h*e*c tibi . Propter[ea omnes] | qui comedunt te devorabuntur .
et univ[ersi ho] | stes tui in captivitatem ducentur . et qu[i]])

When examining the early English forms of writing
in use before the Norman Conquest, we noticed the

result of the introduction of the continental minuscule
hand in England as a general form of writing, for
Latin texts, in the course of the tenth century. The
character which the English scribes impressed upon
this imported style is that of roundness—a character
which indeed continued to mark the Latin writing
of MSS. executed in England for a long time. No
better example of this round English hand could be
quoted than the Benedictional of Æthelwold, Bishop of
Winchester from A.D. 963 to 984 (*Pal. Soc.* i. pl. 142).
The MS. is not only a valuable example of English
writing of this period, but is also famous for the interesting drawings which it contains.

BENEDICTIONAL.—A.D. 963—984.

(virginitate manente . nova | semper prole fecundet . fidei
[spei] | et caritatis vos munere repleat | et suae in vobis
benedictionis d[o]na infundat . Amen)

It is interesting to notice that, while the letters are of
the foreign type, there is a strongly-marked English
character in the writing which is unmistakable, even if
it were not known that the scribe was an Englishman.
And the difficulty which English scribes appear to have
experienced in laying aside their native style when
writing the continental minuscule hand is remarkably
well illustrated by a MS. of Pope Gregory's " Pastoral
Care," in the Bodleian Library, which is probably of the
beginning of the eleventh century (*Pal. Soc.* ii. pl. 69).

imaginibuſ deliberando cogitatur;
itaq· eſt quia priuſ foramen in pariete·
cernitur· & tunc demum occulta
demonſtrat·. quia nimirum uniuſcui̅
nuſ ſigna forinſecuſ. deinde ianua

DE CURA PASTORALI.—EARLY 11TH CENTURY.

(imaginibus deliberando cogitatur ; | —itaque est quia prius
foramen in pariete | —cernitur .' et tunc demum occulta | —
demonstratur .' quia nimirum uniuscuius | —[p]rius signa
forinsecus . deinde ianua)

The thoroughly Anglo-Saxon form of the letter t will
be observed, as well as the compromise between the
flat-headed Saxon g and the 3-shaped French minuscule
which the scribe has effected in his rendering of the
letter. But in the course of the century, and consequent
on a closer intercourse with the Continent, the foreign
minuscule, as written by English scribes, lost all such
marks of the native writer and developed, on the lines
of the writing of the Æthelwold Benedictional, into a
beautifully exact hand, with correct forms of letters, and
distinguished by the roundness which has been described.

In a work of limited scope, such as the present one,
it is impossible to do more than select a certain number
of specimens to illustrate the different hands of the
successive centuries of the middle ages. Dating from
the twelfth century onwards, the number of existing
MSS. is comparatively large, and the varieties of handwriting to be found in them are numerous, each country
at the same time having its own style and developing
individual peculiarities. But there is not space to illustrate the writing of each individual country. The most

that can be done, in order to give an idea of the main line of development from century to century, is to place before the reader a few facsimiles of typical MSS. of the different periods, which may serve as a general, though imperfect, guide; and in making this selection we shall depend mostly upon MSS. of English origin, as being probably of more practical value to those who will make the chief use of this book.

The twelfth century was a period of large books, and of forms of handwriting on a magnificent scale. The scribes of the several countries of Western Europe seem to have vied with each other in producing the best types of book-writing of which they were capable, with the result that remarkable precision in the formation of the letters was attained, and that the century may be named as excelling all others for the beauty of its MSS. in general. Great advance was made at this period towards the compressed and angular style which marks the writing of the later middle ages as compared with the rounder hands of the centuries immediately succeeding the Caroline reform.

The following facsimile is a good example of the bold style of writing which is found in numerous MSS. of English origin in this century. It is taken from a commentary of Bede upon Ezra, which was written at Cirencester not long after the year 1147 (*Pal. Soc.* ii. pl. 72).

BEDE ON EZRA.—AFTER A.D. 1147.

([de]cebat om*n*imodis ut dom*us* | qu*ę* d*o*minici figura*m* corporis | erat habitura .' eo annoru*m* | numero condere*tur* in ieru*s*ale*m* | qu*o* dieru*m* n*u*mero ipsu*m* d*o*m*i*ni | corpus in utero virginis sac*r*o)

The handsome appearance of this English hand of the twelfth century can hardly be surpassed. It certainly bears most favourable comparison with the other hand-writings of Northern Europe of the same date; and we must go to Italy to find anything so fully pleasing to the eye.

In this calligraphic style the growth of upstrokes from the base of the main strokes in the form of hair-lines lends an ornamental effect to the writing. It is the beginning of a practice which, when carried farther, tends to cause confusion in the decipherment of the short-stroke letters i, m, n, u, when two or more of them happen to come together. The form of the general mark of abbreviation and contraction, the short oblique curve, may also be noticed as very general in MSS. of English origin in this century.

As an example of French writing of this period we select a facsimile of a MS. of Valerius Maximus, written in the year 1167 (*Cabinet des MSS.*, pl. 37).

VALERIUS MAXIMUS.—A.D. 1167.

([Cor]neli*us* scipio cu*m* plurimis *et* clarissi | mis familię suę cognominib*us* ab | undaret . in servile*m* serapio*n*is ap | pella-tione*m* vulgi sermone impact*us* | *est* *quod* hui*usce* no*min*is vic-timario *quam* simi[lis])

And to illustrate the less elegant style of the German hand of this time, we take a few lines from a MS. of Origen's Homilies, of the year 1163 (Arndt, *Schrifttaf.*, pl. 51).

HOMILIES OF ORIGEN.—A.D. 1163.

(gra*tia*m et participatione*m* dei appellantur dii⁚ de q*uibus* | et alibi scriptura dic*it*. Ego dixi dii⁚ estis . et iterum | d*eus* stetit in synagoga deor*um*. Sed hi quamvis capa | ces sint d*e*i . et hoc nomine donari p*er* gra*tia*m vide | antur . nullus tame*n* deo similis invenitur)

We may be content with these three specimens to represent the writing of Northern Europe. In the south a different style prevailed. The sense of grace of form which we perceive in the Lombardic writing of Italy is maintained in that country in the later writing of the new minuscule type, which assumes under the pens of the most expert Italian scribes a very beautiful and round even style. This style, though peculiarly Italian, extended its influence abroad, especially to the south of France, and became the model of Spanish writing at a later time. We select a specimen from a very handsome MS. of Homilies of the first half of the 12th century (*Pal. Soc.* ii. pl. 55), written in bold letters of the best type, to which we shall find the scribes of the fifteenth century reverting in order to obtain a model for their MSS. of the Renaissance. The exactness with which the writing is here executed is truly marvellous, and was only rivalled, not surpassed, by the finished handiwork of its later imitators.

fuerat traditurus· Ut quem secun
presidem post se facere disponeb
eundem faceret plenum atq; per
habentem in se et dignitatem qua
celleret · et potestatem qua cunc

HOMILIES.—12TH CENTURY.

(fuerat traditurus. Ut quem secun[dum] | presidem post se
facere disponeb[at] | eundem faceret plenum atque per[fectum] |
habentem in se et dignitatem qua [pre] | celleret . et potes-
tatem qua cunc[tis])

It will of course be understood that this was not the
only style of hand that prevailed in Italy. Others of a
much rougher cast were also employed. But as a typical
book-hand, which was the parent of the hands in which
the greater proportion of carefully written MSS. of
succeeding periods were written in Italy, it is to be
specially noticed.

The change from the grand style of the twelfth
century to the general minuteness of the thirteenth
century is very striking. In the latter century we reach
the height of the exact hand, in which the vertical
strokes are perfectly formed but are brought into
closer order, the letters being laterally compressed, the
round bends becoming angular, and the oblique strokes
being fined down into hair-lines. In the second half of
the century there appears to have been a great demand
for copies of the Bible, if we are to judge by the large
number of surviving examples, and the minuteness with
which many of them are written enabled the scribes to
compress their work into small volumes, which stand in
extreme contrast to the large folios so common in the
preceding century. An interesting example of the
transitional hand of the end of the twelfth century, in
which the writing is reduced to a small size, but yet is

not compressed with the rather artificial precision of some fifty years later, is found in a MS. of the *Historia Scholastica* of Petrus Comestor, written for Elstow Abbey in the year 1191 or 1192.

HISTORIA SCHOLASTICA.—A.D. 1191-2.

(martirium ⁘ dix*it* iacobo. Pate*r* . da m*i*hi remissione*m*. At | ille paru*m*per deliberans . ait . Pax t*i*bi ⁘ *et* osculat*us est* eu*m*. | Et sim*u*l ambo capite truncati su*n*t. Petru*m* autem | apprehensu*m* misit *h*erodes *in* carcerem . q*u*ia *in* dieb*us* azimo|ru*m* *n*on licebat aliq*ue*m occidere. *Et* p*re*ter custodes car | ceris ⁘ tradidit eu*m* custodiend*um* quatuor q*u*aternionib*us* milit*um*.)

As a good illustration of the perfect style of the book-hand of the first half of the thirteenth century, we next select some lines from a Bible, written at Canterbury between the years 1225 and 1252 (*Pal. Soc.* i. pl. 73), which exhibits great regularity and precision in the compressed writing.

BIBLE.—A.D. 1225-1252.

([fir]mamento. Et *factum* est ita. Vocavit*que* firma | mentum
deus celum. Et f*actu*m est vesp*ere* *et* ma | ne dies sec*undus*.
Dixit vero deus. Congregentur | aque que sub celo sunt in locum
unum : | *et* appareat arida . factum*que* est ita. Et vocavit d*eus* |
aridam terram : congregationes*que* aquar*um* | appellavit maria.
Et vidit deus q*uod* *esset* bon*um* | *et* ait. Germinet terra herbam
virentem *et* | facientem. semen *et* lignum pomifer*um* faci[ens])[1]

And of a still more ornamental type, of the second
half of the century, is a Lectionary of the year 1269,
which was written by an English scribe, John of
Salisbury, at Mons in Hainault (*Pal. Soc.* ii. pl. 113).

LECTIONARY.—A.D. 1269.

(—cussione mirifica tremen | do palpitasse . Cuius mox | manu
tenuit . et eum pa | tri viventem atq*ue* inco | lumen dedit.
Liquet pe | tre quia hoc miraculu*m* | in potestate non habuit ‖
nono . fuit lib*er* | iste scriptus. | Iohannes de | salesburi
scrip[sit])

These two specimens have been selected as presenting
the style of book-writing of the thirteenth century in
its most decided form. There is no mistaking the
period to which they belong. Variations from this high
standard are of course to be found in the more ordinary
MSS. written with less exactness ; but in all writing of

---

[1] The oblique double hair-lines above the words "Vocavitque" and
" firmamentum " (lines 1 and 2) are marks of transposition.

this time, whether formal or cursive, the rigidity, which is its strong characteristic, never fails to impress the eye almost at the first glance.

With the fourteenth century we enter on a new phase in the history of Latin palæography; and the latter part of this century and the following century are a period of gradual decadence from the high standard which had been attained in the twelfth and thirteenth centuries. As if wearied by the exactness and rigidity of the thirteenth century, handwriting now becomes more lax, the letters fall away in beauty of shape, and in those MSS., such as biblical and liturgical works, in which the old form of writing still remains prevalent, it degenerates into an imitative hand. At this period also, and including the latter part of the thirteenth century, we have numerous instances of the cursive or charter-hands being employed in the production of books as well as for documents. In England particularly a large number of law MSS., which date from the reigns of Edward I. and Edward II., are written in the charter-hand. But we here confine our attention to the more formal styles.

As a specimen of a class of writing which is not un-common in the first half of the century, when the reminiscence of the teaching of the thirteenth century still remained and exercised a restraining influence, we may give a few lines from a MS. of the *Legenda Aurea* of Jacobus de Voragine, which was written at Paris in 1312 (*Pal. Soc.* i. pl. 222). Comparing this hand with the specimens of the previous century, the advance is apparent in the decreasing regularity of the strokes generally and in certain changes in the formation of some of the letters. For example, the letter a, which in the twelfth and thirteenth centuries normally has an open upper bow, now generally appears with the bow closed ; and the vertical stroke of the letter t, which at an earlier date, in the best specimens, does not rise above the transverse, now betrays an increasing dis-position to do so.

[facsimile of Legenda Aurea manuscript text]

LEGENDA AUREA.—A.D. 1312.

(testamenti .' occidental*is* autem n*on* facit | festum de *sanctis*
veteris testamenti . eo q*uod* ad infe | ros descend*er*unt . preter-
quam de innocentib*us* | ex eo q*uod in* ip*s*is singulis occis*us* e*st*
Christus .' et de | machabeis . su*n*t a*u*te*m* quatuor *rationes*
quare | *ecclesia* de istis machabeis l*icet* ad inferos | descend-
erint [2] solempnizat . prima e*st* propter pre)

Next, we will take a specimen from a liturgical MS.,
a Psalter written in England about the year 1339 (*Pal.
Soc.* i. pl. 99), in which the formal style of an older date
is retained.

[facsimile of Psalter manuscript text]

PSALTER.—ABOUT A.D. 1339.

[2] Original termination *unt*, corrected into *int* by an underwritten
deleting dot.

([I]uravit *domin*us *et* non penite | bit eum: tu es sacerdos in | et*ernum* secu*nd*um ordine*m* melchisedec [3] | [D]ominus a dextris | tuis : *con*fregit *in* die ire sue reges.)

Apart from the actual shapes of the letters in which indications of the true date are to be detected, there are forms of decoration employed which would not be found in writing of the preceding century.

A formal French style of writing of the latter half of the century is well represented in a MS. of the "Grandes Chroniques" which was copied about the year 1377, and which illustrates the constantly increasing debasement of the individual letters from the old standard, although the setting and general run of the text are sufficiently regular (*Album Paléogr.* pl. 42).

GRANDES CHRONIQUES.—ABOUT A.D. 1377.

(une lampe de voirre qui devant so*n* tombel | ardoit chai da- venture sus le pavem*ent* . le | voirre qui assez legierem*ent* brise de sa na | ture entra en la duresce du pavem*ent* sanz | nulle froisseure *et* sanz nulle corrupcion | aussi *com*me il eust fait en plain mui de fa | rine b*ie*n bulettee . Ses freres qui sore*nt* la | desloiaute quil avoit faite assamblerent | leurs oz *et* distrent que ho*m*me de si gr*ant* felo*n*)

[3] The syllable *dec* is written at the end of the l:ne below.

As a contrast to this, we select a facsimile of a not uncommon type of the English hand of about the same time, which has a slightly cursive element in it, and which developed into the ordinary hand of the fifteenth century. It is taken from a chronicle of English history, written about the year 1388 (Brit. Mus., Harl. MS. 3634).

CHRONICLE.—ABOUT A.D. 1388.

(Et ecce subito princeps iunctis manibus et erectis | in celum oculis deus gratias inquit tibi ago de | cunctis beneficiis tuis tuam pietatem omnibus vo | tis expostulo ut mihi concedas veniam delic | torum eorum que contra te nequiter perpetravi sed et a cunc | tis mortalibus quos scienter sive ignoranter offen | di remissionis gratiam tete corde posco Cum | hec dixisset in plena fide catholica spiritum exala[vit])[4]

Finally, to close the facsimiles of the handwritings of the fourteenth century, we take a few lines from a copy of Horace, written at Cremona in the year 1391 (*Pal. Soc.* i. pl. 249), in the fine exact hand of Italian type which is found in so many surviving MSS. of the hundred years between 1350 and 1450, and even later—the direct descendant of the beautiful hand of the twelfth century, which is illustrated above (p. 272) by a facsimile from a MS. of homilies of that period.

---

[4] This passage describes the death of the Black Prince.

𝕹 atalis hore seu tyrannus
𝕳 esperic capricornus unde /
𝖁 truq; nrm incredibili modo
𝕮 onsentit astrum te iouis impio
𝕿 utela saturno irsulgens
𝕰 ripuit: uolucris q; fati

(Natalis hore seu tyrannus | Hesperie capricornus unde |
Utrum*que* no*strum* incredibili modo | Consentit astrum te
iovis impio | Tutela saturno refulgens | Eripuit . volucris*que*
fati)

The course of the fifteenth century witnessed the final
dissolution of the mediæval minuscule book-writing.
When printing was at length established, MS. books
were no longer needed and only survived as specimens
of calligraphy, especially in the Italian school. In this
century there is, necessarily, an ever-increasing number
of varieties of hands. The charter-hand is now very
generally used for books as well as for documents. And
while the formal minuscule hand is still employed for
liturgical and other books, and under certain conditions
is written with great exactness, it generally betrays an
increasing tendency to slackness and to malformation or
exaggeration of individual forms of letters : there is, in
a word, an artificiality about it by which it is to be distinguished from the purer style of two hundred years
before. Between MSS. in the cursive charter-hand and
the formal minuscule book-hand, there is that large mass
of MSS., all more or less individual in their characteristics, which are written with a freedom partaking of the
elements of both styles—an ordinary working hand,
which has no pretensions to beauty of form, and which,

in course of time, grows more and more angular, not
with the precise angular formation of letters as in the
thirteenth century, but with the careless disregard of
curves which accompanies rapid writing. And finally,
in the latter part of the century we find those different
styles of handwriting which were so markedly peculiar
to the several countries of Western Europe, and which
formed the models for the types of the early printers.

We cannot here do more than select a few specimens
to illustrate the general styles of the many varieties of
handwritings of this century.

The first is from a MS. containing a treatise on
the Passion, by an Austin friar named Michael de
Massa, which was written at Ingham, in Norfolk, in the
year 1405 (*Pal. Soc.* ii. pl. 134).

TREATISE ON THE PASSION.—A.D. 1405.

([exo]ravit us*que* in passionis finem.' *quando* corpus Chr*i*s*t*i
de | positum tuit de cruce . *et* sepultum in sepulcro. Un | de
subsecute sunt mulieres que c*um* ipso uen*er*ant de galilea *et*
vi | derunt monumentum . *et* quemadmodum positu*m* | erat
corpus I*es*u. Luce' xxiii. P*r*ima pars que inci | pit in die
ven*er*is ante d*om*inicam in passione.)

The writing is in the formal square literary hand,
maintained chiefly in liturgical books from the earlier
style, but is entirely wanting in the old regularity. The
forms of the letters are weak and debased, and the
general character is irregular and imitative.

Of the same class of writing, but of rather later date
and taken from a liturgical MS., is the following facsimile from a selection of Psalms written for Humphrey,
Duke of Gloucester, who died in 1446 (Brit. Mus., Royal
MS., 2 B. 1).   This is the common hand of the liturgies
of English origin throughout the fifteenth century, and
it maintains a monotonous uniformity for a comparatively
long period.

PSALMS.—BEFORE A.D. 1446.

(Sicut unguentum in capite.' quod des | cendit in barbam bar-
bam aaron | Quod descendit in oram vestimenti ei*us* | sicut
ros hermon qui descendit in monte*m* sio*n* | Quoniam illic
mandavit dominus be | nediccionem: *et* vitam usq*ue* in secu-
lum.)

As a contrast to this formal book-hand we next select
a specimen from a MS. of the chronicle of Robert of
Avesbury, written, in a small half-cursive hand founded
on the charter-hand, in the first quarter of the fifteenth
century (Brit. Mus., Harley MS. 200).

R. DE AVESBURY.—EARLY 15TH CENTURY.

([vin]culum quo ip*se et* nos noscim*ur* adinvicem fore coniuncti
necno*n* ob [sp*cci*alem] | affectionem *et* sinceram dilectionem
quas erga p*er*sonam suam [sup*er*] | om*n*es alios de sang*ui*ne
no*st*ro m*er*ito gerim*us et* habem*us* ac p*ro* eo [q*uod* ip*se*] | qui
alio*s* principes in str*e*nuitate precellit meli*us* qua*m* aliquis
[alius] | poterit maliciam dictor*um* rebelliu*m* p*er* dei gra*ti*am
refrenare mero [metu] | ac no*st*ra pura *et* spontanea voluntate
diligenti *et* mat*ur*a deliber[acione] | p*re*habita in hac parte
dedim*us* concessim*us et* pr*e*senti carta no*st*ra co[nfirmavimus])

This style of hand and a more hurried and angular
form of the writing shown above (p. 278) in the facsimile
from the chronicle of about the year 1388 were very
generally used in England for MSS. of ordinary literature in the fifteenth century, always becoming more
slack and careless as time progressed.

Turning to foreign countries, we first give a specimen
of a common class of handwriting found in MSS. of the
Netherlands and northern Germany at this period.
There is a marked angularity and pointed style in the
forms of the letters, besides their individual shapes,
which impart to the general character of German and
Flemish writing its peculiar cast. The facsimile is taken
from a MS. of St. Augustine, *De Civitate Dei*, which
belonged to Parc Abbey near Louvain, and was written
in 1463 (Brit. Mus., Add. MS. 17,284).

ST. AUGUSTINE.—A.D. 1463.

([P]romissiones dei que facte su*n*t ad abraha*m* cui*us* | s*e*mi*ni*
et gente*m* israheliticam secu*n*dum carne*m*, et omnes | gentes
debe*ri* secu*n*dum fidem deo pollicente didicimus | que*m*admo-
du*m* complean*tur* per ordine*m* tempo*rum* pro | curre*n*s dei
civitas indicavit. Q*uonia*m ergo superi | or*is* libri us*que* ad
regnu*m* david factus e*st* finis: | nu*n*c ab eode*m* regno q*uantum*
suscepto op*er*i sufficere)

More strongly marked is the German character in the
next facsimile, from a MS. of the Epistles of St. Jerome,
written at Lippe in the year 1479 (Arndt, *Schrifttaf.*, 59).

ST. JEROME.—A.D. 1479.

(lectulo decumbentes . longaq*ue* egrotaci[one]— | notario cele-
riter scribenda dictavim*us*.— | sed ne tibi in p*r*incipio amici-
ciarum aliq[uid]— | [vide]remur negare Ora nobiscum a do*m*i*n*o
— | duodecim menses, quibus iugi labore— | sim aliquid dig-
nu*m* vestre scribere volu[ntati])

The handwritings of northern and eastern France of
the fifteenth century run on the same lines as those of
other countries, sometimes following the set square style,
more often developing varieties based upon the cursive
charter-hand of documents. Among the latter there is
one which should be specially noticed. It is found particularly in MSS. derived from French Flanders and
Burgundy, and afforded a pattern of type to the early
printers. It is a heavy, sloping, and pointed hand,

which is in very common use for general literature, particularly in the middle and latter part of the century. The following specimen of this kind of writing is taken from a volume of *Miracles de Nostre Dame* written for Philip the Good, of Burgundy, about the middle of the century (*Album paléogr.*, pl. 43).

MIRACLES DE NOSTRE DAME.—ABOUT A.D. 1450.

(—[q]ui bien chantoit et hault Eru | —[qu]el la vierge marie preserva de | — [A]nice que lon nomme orenmort | — en auvergne fut Iadis une | —quilz aloyent tous les samediz)

Lastly, we give a specimen of a hand of the Italian Renaissance, a revival of the style of the eleventh or twelfth century, and a very successful imitation of a MS. of that period. It was this practice, followed by the scribes of the Renaissance, of reverting to that fine period of Italian writing (see p. 272) to find models for the exquisitely finished MSS. which they were compelled to produce in order to satisfy the refined taste of their day, that influenced the early printers of Italy in the choice of their form of type. The facsimile is from a MS. of Sallust, written at Florence in the year 1466 (*Pal. Soc.* ii. pl. 59).

SALLUST.—A.D. 1466.

negocia transferunt.   Quod si hominibus bonar*um* | rerum
tanta cura esset : quanto studio aliena ac | nihil profutura mul-
to*que* etiam periculosa petu*n*t: | neq*ue* regerentur á casibus,
magis q*uam* regerent casus .' | et eo magnitudinis procederent.'
ubi pro morta | libus gloria eterni fierent.   Nam uti genus
homi | num compositum ex corpore et anima est .' ita res)

It is unnecessary to pursue the history of the Latin
minuscule literary hand beyond the fifteenth century.
Indeed, after the general adoption of printing, MS.
books ceased to be produced for ordinary use, and the
book-hand practically disappears in the several countries
of Western Europe.   In the comparatively small number
of extant literary MSS. of a later date than the close of
the century it is noticeable that a large proportion of
them are written in the style of the book-hand of the
Italian Renaissance—the style which eventually superseded all others in the printing press.   The scribes of
these late examples only followed the taste of the day
in preferring those clear and simple characters to the
rough letters of the native hands.

The English Book-hand in the Middle Ages.

A handbook of Palæography which is intended chiefly
for the use of English students would be incomplete

without a special examination of the styles of writing employed by English scribes of the later middle ages when writing in English.

We have already followed the course of English minuscule writing down to the period of the Norman Conquest. From that date, as we have seen, the foreign hand became the recognized literary hand and was employed for Latin literature; and the old Saxon hand was discarded. With the native English, however, it naturally continued in use; and eventually, after its cessation as a separate style of writing, a few special Saxon forms of letters, the g, the thorn (þ and ð), and the w, still survived to later times. But it must be remembered that, as we have seen above, the influence of the foreign minuscule had already begun to tell upon the native hand even before the Conquest. In the eleventh century the spirit of the change which marks the general progress of the handwriting of Western Europe is also visible in the cast of Anglo-Saxon writing, and after the Conquest the assimilation of the native hand to the imported hand, which was soon practised in all parts of the country, naturally became more rapid. In some English MSS. of the twelfth century we still find a hand which, in a certain sense, we may call Anglo-Saxon, as distinguished from the ordinary Latin minuscule of the period; but, later, this distinction disappears, and the writing of English scribes for English books was practically nothing more than the ordinary writing of the day with an admixture of a few special English letters. On the other hand, it is observed that there was a tendency to prefer the use of charter-hand for English books, and in many MSS. of the late fourteenth and early fifteenth centuries we find a kind of writing, developing from that style, which may be called an English hand, in the sense of a hand employed in English MSS.

To illustrate the handwriting of the twelfth century referred to above, we select a specimen from a copy of the Anglo-Saxon Chronicle written about the year 1121 (Skeat, *Twelve Facsimiles*, pl. 3), in which the writing may still be called Saxon as regards the forms of letters employed.   At the same time, it has the impress of the general character of twelfth century writing.

[facsimile of Anglo-Saxon Chronicle script]

ANGLO-SAXON CHRONICLE.—ABOUT A.D. 1121.

(tællon . sægdon þet hi hit dyden for ðes mynstres holdscipe. |
syððon geden heom to scipe . ferden heom to elig betæhtan | þær
þa ealla þa gærsume þa denescæ menn wændon þet hi | sceoldon
ofer cumen . þa frencisca men þa todrefodon | ealle þa munekes .
beleaf þær nan butan án munec he | wæs gehaten leofwine
lange . he læi seoc in þa secræman)

A rough but strong hand of the beginning of the thirteenth century, founded on the charter-hand of the time, is employed in a MS. of homilies in the Stowe collection of the British Museum (*Pal. Soc.* ii. pl. 94).

[facsimile of Homilies script]

HOMILIES.—EARLY 13TH CENTURY.

(ne so ʒeap . ne swa witti to donne ᷡit tu scalt don . [bute ᷡu habbe] | ᷡese strengþe of god ⸴ ne miht tu non god don . Ðu [miht isien sum] | wel wis clerec . ᷡe wisliche him selven naht ne wisseᷡ [and þincþ ᷡat he] | hafᷡ inohʒ on his witte ᷡe he cann . ne ᷡese streng[þe ne besekᷡ nauht at] | gode for ᷡi he belæfᷡ among ᷡan ᷡe non god ne [cunnen . And hem] | he is ilich of werkes . alswa lihtliche oᷡerhwile he)

And a very pretty and regular hand of the same period appears in a copy of " The Ancren Riwle," or rule for anchoresses, in one of the Cottonian MSS. (*Pal. Soc.* ii. pl. 75), which may be compared with the Latin facsimile of that time given above (p. 273).

THE ANCREN RIWLE.—EARLY 13TH CENTURY.

(elle . þer ho lai i prisun fowr þusent | ʒer *and* mare ho *and* hire were baᷡe | *and* demde al hire ofsprung to leapen | al after hire . to deaᷡ wiᷡuten ende | Bininge *and* rote of al þis ilke reow | ᷡe ⸴ was a lute sihᷡe þus . Ofte as mon ‖ [pa] triarches . *and* a muche burh forb | earnd . *and* te king *and* his sune | *and* te burhmen isleine . þe wum | mon ilad forᷡ.   Hire fader *and* | hire breᷡre utlahes makede | se noble princes as ho weren . þus eo[de])

Following on the same lines as the Latin hands, the transition from the stiff characters of the thirteenth century to the more pliant style of the fourteenth century is seen in the " Ayenbite of Inwyt," or Remorse of Conscience, written in the year 1340 by Dan Michael, of Northgate, in Kent, an Augustinian monk of Canterbury, in heavy minuscules of the charter-hand type (*Pal. Soc.* i. pl. 197).

AYENBITE OF INWYT.—A.D. 1340.

(workes of wysdom to þe zone ‡ alsuo þe worke[s]— | wor guod-
nesse is ase zayþ sanyt Denys to lere— | þet him naȝt ne costneþ ‡
þet ne is naȝt grat guo[dnesse]— | se zcve yefþes spret him
zelve ine oure hert[en]— | streames . þervore hi byeþ *propre-
liche* ycleped ye[fþes]— | welle . hy byeþ þe streames . And þe
oþer scele is—)

Next, as a contrast, we take a few lines from a
Wycliffite Bible of the latter part of the fourteenth century, written in a square hand akin to the formal writing
as seen in Latin liturgical MSS. (*Pal. Soc.* i. pl. 75).

WYCLIFFITE BIBLE.—LATE 14TH CENTURY.

(for to have wirschipi*ng* þe þrittenþe day | of þe moneþ adar .
þat is seid bi voyce of | sirie : þe first day of mardochius, þer-
fore | þese þingis don aȝein*us* nychanore . *and* of þe | tymes þe
cytee weeldid of ebrues ‡ and | I i*n* þese þingis schal make an
eende of | word, *and* soþeli ȝif wel *and* as it acordiþ to)

Of the latter part of the fourteenth century, perhaps
about the year 1380, is a MS. of the Vision of Piers
Plowman, in the Cottonian collection (*Pal. Soc.* ii. pl. 56),
written in a set minuscule hand, partly formed upon the
charter-hand of the time. This specimen may be compared with the facsimile from the chronicle of about
the year 1388 above (p. 278).

PIERS PLOWMAN.—LATE 14TH CENTURY.

(Have me excused quod clergie . bi crist but in [scole] | Schal
no swich motyng be mevet . for me bu[t þere] | For peres love
þe plouhman . þat enpungned[e me ones] | Alle kyne cunnynges .
and alle kyne craftes | Save love and leute . and lownesse of
herte | And no tixt to take . to preve þis for trewe)

And of about the same date, but written in a more
careless style, and partaking rather of the character of
the fifteenth century, is the original MS. of Hereford's
Wycliffite translation of the Old Testament, at Oxford
(*Pal. Soc.* ii. pl. 151), which is probably of the year
1382.

WYCLIFFITE BIBLE.—A.D. 1382.

(rereden up to hevene, *and* þe holi lord god herde | anoon þe
vois of he*m*, he reme*m*bride not þe | sy*n*nes of he*m* . ne ȝaf
he*m* to þ*er* enemys ꞉ but | purgide he*m* i*n* þe hond of isaie þe
holi pr*o*phete | he þrew dou*n* þe tentis of assiries : *and* hem
to | broside þe au*n*gil of þe lord, forwhi ezechie | dide þat ple-
side to þe lord . *and* strongli he wente)

Early in the fifteenth century, in some of the more
carefully written MSS., a hand of the charter-hand type,
but cast in a regular and rather pointed form, is
employed. Such is the writing of a copy of Occleve's
poem *De Regimine Principum* in the Harleian collection
(*Pal. Soc.* ii. pl. 57).

OCCLEVE.—EARLY 15TH CENTURY.

(Yit so*m*me holden oppynyou*n* and sey | Þat none ymages schuld
imaked be | Þei erren foule *and* goon out of þe wey | Of trouth
have þei scant sensibilite | Passe ov*er* þat now blessed trinite |
Uppon my maistres soule m*er*cy have | For him lady eke þi
m*er*cy I crave)

And to illustrate two other varieties of the writing of
this century, we select the following :—

(i.) Some lines from a MS. of Bokenham's Lives of
Saints, written in the year 1447 in a formal hand (*Pal.
Soc.* ii. pl. 58).

LIVES OF SAINTS.—A.D. 1447.

(Of þe sevene wych be clepyd lyberal | So profoundly þat greth ner smal | Was no clerk founde in þat cuntre | What evere he were or of what degre | But þat she wyth hym coude comune | What shuld I speke of hyre fortune | Wych was ryht greth for as I seyd before | A kyngys doughtyr she was bore)

(ii.) A passage from a MS. of Chaucer's "Legend of Good Women" (Skeat, *Twelve Facs.*, pl. 10), written in the pointed charter-hand of the middle of the century.

CHAUCER.—15TH CENTURY.

(Madame quod he, it is so long agoon | That I yow knewe, so charitable and trewe | That never yit, syn that the worlde was newe | To me, ne founde y better noon than yee | If that ye wolde, save my degree | I may ne wol nat, werne your requeste | Al lyeth in yow, dooth wyth hym, as yow liste | I al foryeve, withouten lenger space)

CHAPTER XIX.

Cursive Writing.

THE history of the Cursive Writing of Western Europe in the middle ages covers as wide a field as that of the literary hand. Practically, however, a full knowledge of the peculiarities of the different official hands of Europe is not so necessary and is not so easily attainable as that of the various kinds of literary MSS. Each country has naturally guarded its official deeds with more or less jealousy, and such documents have therefore been less scattered than the contents of ordinary libraries. While, then, the student will find it of chief advantage to be familiar with the history of the book-hands of all countries—as in his researches, which, in most instances, will be connected with literary matters, his labours will lie among MS. books—he will be generally content with a slighter acquaintance with the official handwritings of foreign countries, for the study of which the available material is limited. An intimate knowledge, however, of the official and legal hands of his own country is as necessary to him as the knowledge of the literary hands, if he wishes to be in a position to make use of the vast mass of historical information to be extracted from the official and private records which lie ready to hand in the national repositories.

In this chapter, then, it is not practically necessary to examine the several forms of the cursive handwritings of the continent, but we propose to deal more largely with the official and legal hands of our own country.

In following the history of Roman cursive writing and of the national hands which sprang therefrom we traced the rise of the cursive writing of Western Europe in its three distinct forms of Lombardic, Visigothic, and Merovingian. We do not propose to follow the later cursive developments of these different forms; but there are two great series of official documents which, on account of their extent and political importance, it is necessary to examine a little more closely in regard to the styles of writing which were employed in their production. These are the documents which issued from the Papal Chancery and from the Imperial Chancery of the middle ages.

In the Papal Chancery a form of writing was developed which, from its likeness, in some respects, to the Lombardic cursive, has been named *Littera Beneventana.* It was, of course, derived from the Roman chancery hand, but took a different line from that followed by the writing found in the cursive documents of Ravenna. The peculiar letters which belong to it are the a made almost like a Greek ω, the t in form of a loop, and the e in that of a circle with a knot at the top. These letters also take other forms when linked with other letters. Specimens of it are in existence dating from the end of the eighth century; and facsimiles are to be found in various palæographical collections, and especially in the great work of Pfluck-Harttung, *Specimina selecta chartarum pontificum Romanorum,* 1885-1887. The following facsimile is taken from a bull of Pope John VIII., of the year 876, written on a very large scale, which is here greatly reduced (Pf.-Hart., tab. 5). The artificial nature of the writing can be detected in the construction of some of the letters. For example, tall strokes are not necessarily made by one sweep of the pen: it will be seen that that of the second d in the first line is distinctly formed in three pieces, the two upper ones being evidently added to the lowest one.

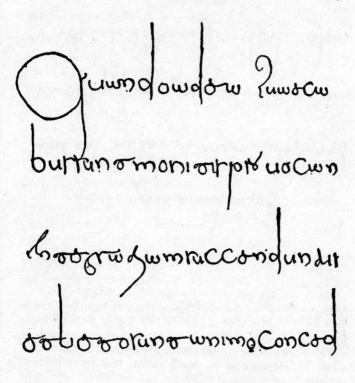

BULL OF JOHN VIII.—A.D. 876.

(Quando ad ea quae ca[tholicorum]— | bus sunt monitis pro
vocan[da] | —ente gratiam succenduntur— | et leto sunt animo
conced[enda—)

This hand continued to be practised down to the
beginning of the twelfth century, becoming in its later
stages peculiarly angular and difficult to read. We give
a facsimile of this late style from a bull of Urban II., of
the year 1098 (Pf.-Hart., tab. 47).

BULL OF URBAN II.—A.D. 1098.

([emenda]verit . potestatis honorisque sui dignita[te]— |
corpore ac sanguine dei et domini redemptoris— | eidem loco
iusta servantibus sit pax— | premia eternę pacis inveniant)

The peculiar forms which the long r and the t and
other letters assume in combination will be specially
noticed.

This kind of writing, however, did not remain supreme
throughout the period of its existence noted above. In
the course of the eleventh century the writing of the
Imperial Chancery became the ordinary hand for papal
documents also. This hand was at that period, as we
shall presently see, the ordinary minuscule, derived from
the Caroline minuscule, mixed, however, for some time
with older forms. In the twelfth and thirteenth centuries, and subsequently during the later middle ages,
the papal hand follows the general lines of the development of the established minuscule, cast, it must be remembered, in the mould of the symmetrical Italian style.

A very peculiar and intricate style adopted at a late

period for papal documents may here be just mentioned.
This is the so-called *Littera Sancti Petri* or *Scrittura
bollatica*, a character which appears to have been invented for the purpose of baffling the uninitiated. It
first appeared in the reign of Clement VIII., A.D. 1592—
1605, and was only abolished in our own time, in 1879.[1]

As the special form of writing developed in the Papal
Chancery is to be traced back to the Roman cursive as
practised in Italy, so the writing of the Imperial Chancery is derived from the same cursive, as practised in
France and represented by the facsimile of the Merovingian hand of the year 695 given above (p. 227).

Facsimiles of the early Imperial Chancery writing are
to be found scattered in various works; but a complete
course may be best studied in Letronne's *Diplomata*, in
Sickel's *Schrifttafeln aus dem Nachlasse von U. F. von
Kopp* (1870), and especially in the recent work of von
Sybel and Sickel, *Kaiserurkunden in Abbildungen* (1880,
etc.). In the earliest documents, commencing in the

---

[1] A very interesting paper, giving much information with
regard to papal documents, in a condensed form, was contributed
to the *Revue des Questions Historiques*, tom. xxxix., 1886, with
the title *Les Eléments de la Diplomatique Pontificale*, by Count
de Mas Latrie. In the *Bibliothèque de l'Ecole des Chartes*,
series 4, tome iv. (1858), Monsieur Delisle has also written a
valuable paper, *Mémoire sur les Actes d'Innocent III.*, in which
some points of palæographical interest are brought out. In the
thirteenth century, the leaden papal seal (*bulla*) was attached by
silken threads (red and yellow) to a bull which conferred or confirmed rights and was of a permanent nature; it was attached by
a hempen string to a bull which conveyed orders and was of a
temporary nature. Certain distinctive marks in the text of the
documents gave at a glance the clue to their character. In
(1) *silken* bulls, the intial letter of the pope's name was drawn in
open work, in (2) *hempen* bulls it was solid; in (1) the pope's
name was written in elongated letters, in (2) in ordinary letters;
in (1) a large majuscule letter began the word following the
words *servus servorum Dei*, in (2) the letter was an ordinary
majuscule; in (1) the mark of contraction was looped, in (2) it
was straight; in (1) the letters *ct* and *st* occurring in the middle
of words, as *dictus, justus*, were separated by a space and connected by a link above, as *dic˜tus, jus˜tus*, in (2) they were written
in the ordinary way.

seventh century and continuing to the middle of the eighth century, the character is large, and in the earlier part of this period is not so intricate as afterwards. The writing then grows into a more regular form. The following specimen represents the style of the close of the eighth century, as found in a document of Charlemagne of the year 797 (*Facs. Ecole des Chartes*).

DEED OF CHARLEMAGNE.—A.D. 797.

(adscribitur quod pro contemplatione servitii | [fil]ius noster cum aliquibus dei infidelibus ac nostris | —ex ipsis in nostra praesentia convicti et secundum | —cui et nos omnes res proprietatis suae iuxta eius)

In the ninth century a small hand of increasing regularity and gradually falling into the lines of the Caroline minuscule is established; but while the influence of the reformed hand is quite evident, old forms of letters are retained for some time, as might be expected in a style of writing which would, in the nature of things, cling to old traditions more closely than would that of the literary schools. And so it progresses, affected by the changes which are seen at work in the literary hands, but still continuing to maintain its own individuality as a cursive form of writing. As an illustration of a middle period, we select a few lines from a deed of the Emperor Henry I., written in the year 932 (*Kaiserurkund.*, tab. 22).

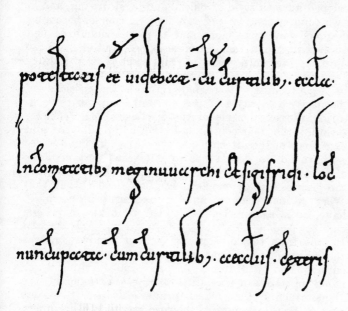

DEED OF THE EMPEROR HENRY.—A.D. 932.

(potestatis *esse* videbat*ur* . *cum* curtilib*us* . ecclesia— | in comitatib*us* meginuuarchi et sigifridi . loc[a]— | nuncupata . cum curtilib*us* . aecclesiis . cẹteris)

In this writing of the Imperial Chancery, as indeed in all other cursive styles derived from the Roman cursive, the exaggeration of the heads and tails of letters is a marked feature. And this exaggeration continued inherent in this hand and was carried over into the national official hands of France and Germany and Italy, which are but later developments of it. In England we see the influence of the hand of the Imperial Chancery in the official hand which the Normans brought with them and established in the country.

Each of the nations, then, of Western Europe developed its own style of official and legal writing, and in each country that writing ran its own course, becoming in process of time more and more individualized and distinct in its national characteristics. But at the same time, as we have seen in the case of the literary hand, it was subject to the general law of change; in each country it passed through the periods of the large bold style of the eleventh and twelfth centuries, the exact style of the thirteenth, the declining style of the fourteenth, and the angular style and decadence of the fifteenth century. With its later career we have not to do, except to note that certain forms of it still linger in law documents, as for example in the engrossing of modern English deeds; and that every ordinary current hand of modern Europe might have been as directly descended from the old legal cursive hand as the modern German is. What saved Europe from this diversity of current handwriting was the welcome which was given to the beautiful Italian cursive hand of the Renaissance, a form of writing which stood in the same relation to the book-hand of the Renaissance as the modern printer's *Italics* (the name preserving the memory of their origin) do to his ordinary Roman type. As the Italian book-hand of the Renaissance was not infrequently adopted at the end of the fifteenth and beginning of the sixteenth centuries as a style of writing for the production of select MSS. in England and France and other countries beyond the borders of Italy, so the Italian cursive hand at once came into favour as an elegant and simple style for ordinary use. In the sixteenth century and even later an educated Englishman could write two styles of current writing, his own native hand lineally descended from the charter-hand, and the new Italian hand; just as a German scholar of the present day can write the native German and the Italian hands. And in concluding these remarks it is worth noting that the introduction and wide acceptance of the Italian hand has constituted a new starting-point for the history of modern cursive writing in Western Europe. As the Roman cursive was adopted and gradually became nationalized in different forms in different countries ; and, again, as the reformed minuscule writing of Charlemagne's reign was taken as a fresh basis, and in its turn gradually received the stamp of the several national characteristics of the countries where it was adopted; so the Italian hand of the Renaissance has taken the impress of those same characteristics, and specimens are easily distinguished, whether written by an Englishman or a German, by a Frenchman or an Italian or a Spaniard, as the case may be.

English Charter-hand.

As already stated, the handwriting employed in England for official and legal documents after the Norman Conquest was the foreign hand introduced by the conquerors, and generally of the cursive type. An exception might be found in the few charters issued by William the Conqueror in the language of the people, which presumably were written by English scribes and are in the native hand. But these documents are so few that they are hardly to be considered as affecting the principle of the introduction of a new order of things in the issue of official and legal instruments.

But while we find it convenient to treat the cursive or charter-hand as a separate branch of mediæval English writing apart from the literary or book-hand, it must not be forgotten that both are derived from the same stock, that each influences the other and occasionally crosses its path (we have already seen how often the cursive hand was employed in a more or less modified form for literary purposes), and that the same laws of progress and change act contemporaneously upon both the one and the other. We shall accordingly have to note the same course of development and decadence in the cursive hand as we have followed in the set literary hand.

The official hand of the first hundred years succeeding the Conquest does not very materially alter. In the few surviving charters of the early kings of the Norman line it appears in a rough and angular character with the exaggeration of long limbs which we have noticed in the earlier hands derived from the Roman cursive. In such documents as the Pipe Rolls the writing is more careful and formal; in the great volume of Domesday, while it still retains the official cast, it has a good deal of the literary style of lettering, perhaps from the fact of the work being drawn up in form of a book. The character into which it soon settled for royal charters may be exemplified by the following specimen drawn from a grant of Henry II. to Bromfield Priory in the year 1155 (*Pal. Soc.* ii. pl. 41).

CHARTER OF HENRY II.—A.D. 1155.

(Comes Andegavie . Archiepiscopis . Episcopis . Abbatibus . Comitibus . | —suis totius Anglie ᛭ Salutem . Sciatis me pro | —dedisse . et Carta mea Confirmasse . Ecclesiam | —[per]tinentiis suis . Priori . et Monachis ibidem deo)

In this class of deeds the profuse employment of large letters is very striking; and it should be noticed that the long strokes are drawn out into fine hair-lines, and, as is seen in one or two instances in the facsimile, are occasionally provided with an ornamental spur near the top of the stem, which thus has the appearance of being cloven.

In the next example of the official hand, from the charter of King John to the borough of Wilton, of the year 1204 (*Pal. Soc.* i. pl. 214), the writing is a little more regular and cloven stems are more frequent.

CHARTER OF KING JOHN.—A.D. 1204.

(forisfactura*m* . sicut carte Regis . Henrici . proavi nostr[i]— | testant*ur* . Tes*tibus* . Gileberto fil*io* Petri Com*itis* Essexi*e* . Ricardo Co[mite]— | Nievill*a* . Roberto de vet*e*ri ponte . Petro de Stoka— | Cicestre*nsis* Electi . Apud Oxoni*am* . xxi . die April*is*)

A style of the charter-hand very common at the end of the twelfth and beginning of the thirteenth century— rather squarer in its forms of letters and less exaggerated than the official hand of the period—is shown in the following facsimile. It is taken from a deed of the Hospital of St. John of Jerusalem, written at Ossington in Nottinghamshire in the year 1206 (*Pal. Soc.* ii. pl. 117).

[facsimile of charter script]

CHARTER OF THE HOSPITALLERS.—A.D. 1206.

(Notum sit Omnibus presentibus et futuris Quod Ego frater
Rober[tus]— | [Hospi]talis Ierosolymitani in Anglia de com-
muni assensu et voluntate fratrum— | Carta confirmavimus
Roberto filio Ivonis de Wicham et— | Croftum que fuerunt
Ivonis patris eius in Wicham . et unam p[ortionam]— | super
Benecroftewelle . et aliam portionem terre ad Wirmode— | Bosci
ad frithwude . et unam Gairam terre super Hagenegate)

Except for its being rather looser in the formation of
its letters and more subject to flourishes, there is no
great difference between this writing and the ordinary
book-hand of the period ; and it is to be observed that
not infrequently the style of writing employed in
monastic charters is rather of the literary than of the
legal type, that is, it is more set than cursive.

This preference of the more exact style of writing is
conspicuous in many of the charters of the thirteenth
ȝentury—the period when, as we have seen above, a
more minute character was practised, contrasting strongly
with the bold writing of the preceding century. Under
this restrictive influence, a highly decorative class of
documents was produced, in which the scribe exercised
with effect his powers of penmanship in fanciful ornamentation of the capitals and the stems of tall letters.
A specimen of this style is given from a lease of land to
Abingdon Abbey, of the year 1230 (*Pal. Soc.* ii. pl. 99).

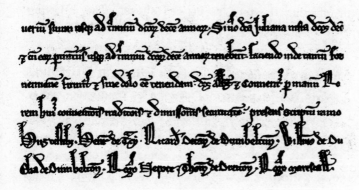

LEASE TO ABINGDON ABBEY.—A.D. 1230.

[Estov]erium suum usque ad terminum dictorum decem anno-
rum. Si vero dicta Iuliana infra dictos dec[em]— | et cum
eorum pertinentiis usque ad terminum dictorum decem annorum
tenebunt . faciendo inde tantum for[insecum]— | [con]ven-
tionem firmiter et sine dolo esse tenendam⁚ dictus Abbas et
Conventus per manum Ro[geri]— | [maio]rem huius conven-
tionis traditionis et dimissionis securitatem⁚ presens scriptum
in mo[dum]— | Hiis testibus. Henrico de Tracy. Ricardo
Decano de Dumbeltuna. Willelmo de Dic[lesduna]— | Elia
de Dumbeltona Rogero Nepote. Thoma de Dreitona. Rogero
Marescallo.)

Nothing can be prettier, as specimens of calligraphy,
than these delicately written charters of the thirteenth
century, which, moreover, are scarcely ever broader than
the hand, and in their little compass present so many
pleasing varieties of the penman's handiwork.

But the true cursive hand was more generally employed in the majority of legal and official deeds of
the period. In the course of the reign of Henry III.,
while the letters generally retain the stiffness characteristic of writing of the thirteenth century, a certain
amount of looping of the tall stems is gradually established—an advance upon the earlier practice of notching

or cleaving the tops, as noticed above. The following specimen is taken from a charter of Bitlesden Abbey, of the year 1251 (*Pal. Soc.* ii. pl. 118).

CHARTER OF BITLESDEN ABBEY.—A.D. 1251.

(Wal*ter*us miserac*i*one divina Norwicen*sis* Ecclesie minis*ter* hum[ilis]— | —*pat*ris dom*i*ni Iohannis Regis no*n* viciatam no*n* cancellatam nec in— | —Monachis *et* monasterio de Bittlesdena concessam in hac forma— | —[Com]itib*us* . Baronib*us* Iustic*iariis* . Vicecom*itibus* . om*n*ibus amicis *et* fidelibus sui[s] — | —Ernoldus de Bosco fecit deo *et* monachis de ordine Cistercie[nsi]— | —[or]dinis Cistercien*sis* . *et* de tribus carucatis *terre* in syresham qu*e* vocat*ur*)

At this period, under a more extended system of linking the letters together and the consequent establishment of a really current hand, many of the older forms of letters become modified. The looping of tall letters has already been referred to. The top stroke of the letter a is gradually more bent over, and already in several instances touches the lower bow and forms a closed loop; i, m, n, and u, when two or more come together in a word, are composed of uniform strokes; and, above all, the small round s becomes more frequent, and is finished off in a closed loop below. This form of the latter letter, as we shall see, afterwards became exaggerated, the loop growing to a disproportionate size.

The official hand of the reign of Edward I., as seen in

his charters, is in a regular and rather broad style, showing a further development in the open order of the letters, and the tendency to roundness characteristic of the fourteenth century.

CHARTER OF EDWARD I.—A.D. 1303.

(Aquit*anie* Omnibus ad quos presentes litter*e* perven*er*int | — [fi]delis n*os*tri Henrici de Lacy Comitis Lincolni*e* concessi-m*us* | —[quant]um in nobis est dilectis nobis in Ch*r*isto Abbati *et* Conven[tui] | —[cu]m *pertin*entiis in Mora que vocat*ur* Inkelesmore continentem | —longitudine per medium More illius ab uno capite)

In the specimen here given from a charter of the year 1303 (*Pal. Soc.* i. pl. 254), a further development is to be noticed in the looped a and s referred to under the last facsimile. Here also is to be seen a new change in the formation of the tall letters : the spur or flourish on the left side at the top of the stem is in some instances dispensed with (*e.g.* in b in the second *nobis* and *Abbati*, in line 3), leaving the letter provided with a simple curve or loop on the right instead of a cloven top.

Further progress in these particulars is seen in the official hand of the period of Edward II., as exemplified by the following specimen from a writ of Privy Seal of the year 1310 (*Facs. of National MSS.*, no. 27).

WRIT OF PRIVY SEAL.—A.D. 1310.

(Edward par la grace de dieu / Roi Dengle[terre]— | mons[ire]
Aymer de Valence Counte de Penbroke ⁝— | la ville seint Johan
de Perche / et noz autres— | Escoce ⁝ nous ont fait saver que noz
enemys— | iour en autre / Chasteux / villes / et terres)

But, on the other hand, an equal rate of development
of the new forms is not to be found contemporaneously
in all documents. Charters written in the king's courts
would be the work of the more expert scribes trained in
the newest style ; elsewhere the changes need not be so
regular or so rapid. In a grant from the Bishop of
Norwich to Flixton Priory, of the year 1321 (*Pal. Soc.*
i. pl. 254), the old form of tall letters with cloven tops is
still followed.

GRANT OF THE BISHOP OF NORWICH.—A.D. 1321.

(Iohannes permissione divina Norwycensis Episcopus / volu[n-
tate]— | —[Trin]itatis Norwycensis necnon de licencia speciali
domini nostri— | —[c]arta nostra / confirmavimus / pro nobis et
successoribus nost[ris]— | —[B]ungeye / ac Religiosis Mulieri-
bus // Emme Priorisse— | —iuxta Bungeye nostre Dyoceseos :
que ad nos et Ep[iscopatum]— | —[eius]dem loci pertinebat
temporibus preteritis . Habend[um]))

But there are late forms among the letters, which,
besides the general character of the writing, mark the
document as one of the fourteenth century.

The progress made in the latter part of the century is
very marked. Towards its close the letters begin to
take angular forms, without, however, all at once assuming the universal angularity which belongs to the
fifteenth century. The following is a specimen of a
rather rough style of the period, from a licence granted
by Croyland Abbey in the year 1392 (*Pal. Soc.* i.
pl. 257).

DEED OF CROYLAND ABBEY.—A.D. 1392.

([Conven]tus Omnibus ad quos presentes littere pervenerint |
—et licenciam dedisse . pro nobis et successoribus | —[Wil-
lel]mo Spenser et Iohanni Waldegrave de | —gardina . Sexa-
ginta et unam acras terre | —[de]nariatam et unam oblatam
redditus cum)

In this hand will be remarked the exaggerated loop of the round s, and the reversed or o-shaped e. The forms of these and of other letters may be compared with those of the facsimile of the set book-hand from the chronicle of 1388 (p. 278 above).

As a specimen of carefully written charter-hand of the last year of the fourteenth century, we may select a few lines from an official document of Henry IV., of the year 1400 (*Pal. Soc.* ii. pl. 160).

LETTERS OF HENRY IV.—A.D. 1400.

(quod do*mi*nus *Ricardus* nu*per* Rex Angl*ie* seco*n*dus post con-questum apud | —de sa *grace* espe*ci*ale *par* assent *et* accord de toutz *seignur*s espiri[tuelx] | —[demur]antz en Irland- qils reviendront en Englet*erre* illoeqes | —[nientc]ontresteant- le-statut ent fait lan du regne n*os*tre dit *seignur* | —v*est*ris in hac parte speci*aliter* providere Susscepim*us et* ponim*us* | —[moran]do in p*ro*tecc*ion*em tuic*ion*em *et* defensiones n*os*tras spe*ci*ales)

By this time the letters have become pointed and angular; and through the course of the fifteenth century this is their general character, with an ever-increasing tendency to careless formation. The following is a specimen of an ordinary rough hand of the reign of Henry V., from an official deed relating to a pledge of crown plate, of the year 1415 (*Pal. Soc.* i. pl. 258).

PLEDGE OF PLATE.—A.D. 1415.

(Ceste endenture fait p*a*rentre Richard Cou[rtenay]— |
Gardein de ses ioialx dune part *et* Robert— | *present* viage as
parties doultre la meer— | p*a*r vertu *et* com*m*aundement dez
le*t*tres pat[entes]— | signe p*a*r lez mains de Tresorer den-
gleterre— | pois*ant* ensemble iij unce*s* i q*u*arterone pr*is* del)

Although, however, the letters are roughly formed,
there is still a certain simplicity in the general character
of the writing, which later iu the century gives place to
more elaborate flourishes and to more fanciful shaping
of the letters.

To illustrate the charter-hand of the middle and latter
part of the century, we must be content to select the
two following specimens, which may serve to give some
indication of its later development ; but a really adequate
idea of the changes effected in the course of the fifteenth
century can only be gained by examination of a series of
documents.

The first is taken from a lease, in English, of the year
1457, written at Canterbury (*Pal. Soc.* i. pl. 260). The
old tradition of dotting the y here shows itself in the
careless little curved stroke which flies above the line
and is quite separated from the letter to which it belongs.
In the word *Payinge* in the second line this stroke might
at first sight be taken to mark the i.

LEASE.—A.D. 1457.

(of annunciacioun of oure lady next comynge aftir— | and
fully to be endid Payinge yerely the seid Ali[sandre]— | Suc-
cessours in hand . halfe yere afore . that is to— | next suyinge
xxiij. s. iiij d. by evene porciouns The— | and staves . and
Seyleclothes duringe the seid terme— | as of yrounwerke
Tymberwerke . and helyng of the)

The second, in a much more pointed hand, is from a
charter of John de Vere, Earl of Oxford, to Notley
Abbey, granted in 1485 (*Pal. Soc.* i. pl. 260).

GRANT TO NOTLEY ABBEY.—A.D. 1485.

(predictam . prefato Abbati et Conventui durante min[ori]— |
nulla proficua terrarum nec maritagium eiusdem perce-
perunt— | dedi et concessi ac do et concedo prefato Petro
Abb[ati] — | reddituum reversionum et serviciorum . ac
aliorum possessionu[m]— | nuper de Stoke Lysle in Comitatu
Oxoniensi . qui de me— | dicti Willelmi . et racione minoris
etatis . Iohannis)

It is not the design of this work to pursue the history
of Latin Palæography beyond the end of the fifteenth
century; and the examination of the literary hand was
accordingly brought to a close when it had reached that
limit. With regard, however, to the cursive form of
writing which has just been passed in review and which
was not superseded by the printing press, as was the
case with the set literary style, it will not be out of place
to lay before the reader a few specimens of later
varieties, among which some were elaborated in certain
of the law courts and became the styles peculiar to
those courts.

The ordinary class of charter or cursive hand in the
reign of Henry VIII. was a rather coarse development
of the style of the fifteenth century. The following
specimen, taken from an ordinary conveyance of the year
1530 (Brit. Mus., Add. Ch. 24,843), may suffice as an
illustration.

DEED.—A.D. 1530.

(Sond ac Georgio Taylour omnia illa terras te[nementa]— |
—[i]acentia et existentia in Wescote in parochia de Dorkyng
— | —[conc]essione et feoffamento Roberti Borne de Dorky[ng]
— | —Maydeman aliam vero medietatem inde nuper— | —[ap-
par]entis ac filii et heredis Alicie nuper uxoris mee ia[m]— | —
predicta terras et tenementa redditus et servicia cum suis per-
t[inentiis])

In most of the English cursive handwriting of the first half of the sixteenth century a certain heaviness of style was the fashion; but afterwards this gave place to a lighter and more elegant character, which was fully established by the reign of Elizabeth, and was most commonly used from that time onwards far into the seventeenth century, and then gradually toned down into a form modified by the Italian letters of the ordinary current hand of the day. The following specimen is taken from a deed of the year 1594 (Brit. Mus., Add. Ch. 24,798).

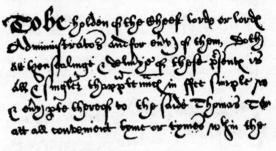

DEED.—A.D. 1594.

(To be holden of the Cheefe lorde or lord*es*— | Administra-tour*s* and for *every* of them, Doth— | att thensealinge *and* deliver*ye* of these *present*es is— | all *and* singul*er* thap*pur*tenau*nce*s in Fee simple w[ithout]— | *and* every *parte* thereof to the saide Thomas Tan[ner]— | att all convenient tyme or tymes wi*th*in the—)

In this hand we hav∍ a good fluent style to which none of the cursive writing of previous centuries had attained in England. In fact the close of the sixteenth century may be referred to as the epoch of the rise of the modern current hand, as distinguished from the more slowly written and more disjointed cursive writing of the middle ages.

Lastly, in taking leave of this ordinary style, we select a specimen of a form which it assumed early in the seventeenth century, from a deed of the year 1612 (Brit. Mus., Add. Ch. 24,000).

DEED.—A.D. 1612.

(pown*des* of good and lawfull mony— | himselfe fully satis-fied, And therof— | And in considerac*i*on of twoe hun[dred] — | confirmed, and by thease *presentes* d[oth]— | [A]ll that the Mannor of Butlers s[cituate]— | [M]esuage or Mannor howse of Butle[rs])

Now to turn to the peculiar official legal hands referred to above. From the earliest times succeeding the Norman Conquest there were, as we have seen, cer-tain styles followed, though not uniformly, for particular official documents; and a series of examples of these during the several reigns may be found in the public records. But it was not until the sixteenth century that a perfected system of particular styles for certain courts was finally established.

Without regarding the class to which has been given the name of " secretary,"[1] and which is in fact the hand which has been illustrated by the two preceding fac-similes, there are two main styles which practically cover the varieties enumerated in the special works on the subject, viz., the Chancery hand and the Court hand. The former was used for records under the great seal; the latter was employed in the courts of King's Bench

[1] Wright, *Court Hand Restored,* ed. Martin, 1879, p. xii.

and Common Pleas, for fines and recoveries, placita, etc. These two kinds of writing do not vary very materially; both may be described as fanciful renderings of the ordinary law hand. The Chancery hand, of the pattern found in its developed form in the sixteenth century, appears in an incipient stage in the latter part of the fourteenth century, and is therefore of an earlier origin than the Court hand, which indeed is rather a modification of the Chancery hand itself. It will be enough to select one or two examples of each style in order to give a general idea of their character.

First we take a few lines from an exemplification of a Chancery decree of the year 1539 (Brit. Mus., Add. Ch. 26,969) in illustration of the Chancery hand of the reign of Henry VIII.

EXEMPLIFICATION.—A.D. 1539.

(revencion*um* Corone no*s*tre quoddam decretum— | —xxiiij die Novembris Anno regni d*omi*ni Regi[s]— | —[reve]ncion*um* Corone sue Et *pro*tulit ib*ide*m quand[am]— | —[*ver*]ba This Indenture made the— | —the grace of god of Englond and Fraunce— | —Englond Betwene Raf Burell doctor in— | — [C]ountie of Leicester of the oon *pa*rtie and)

Next, an example is taken from a grant of wardship and marriage of the year 1618, which illustrates the form which the hand had assumed in the reign of

James I. (Brit. Mus., Add. Ch. 28,271), a form altogether of the modern type which continued in practice to quite a recent date.

GRANT OF WARDSHIP.—A.D. 1618.

(quous*que* eadem Maria Gwynet executor— | —vel ha*b*uerint Et hoc absq*ue* compoto seu aliq[uo]— | —contingat pre*dictum* Georgiu*m* Gwynet ante[quam]— | —Maria Gwynet executores sive assign*ati* sui— | hered*ibus* masculis eiusdem Georgii Gwynet tu[nc]— | —presentes dam*us et* concedim*us* prefate Marie Gwy[net])

In these two examples of the Chancery hand it will be seen that the chief characteristic is a fanciful angular and upright treatment of the letters without deviating from the setting of ordinary writing.

With the Court hand the treatment is different. While the shapes of the letters (with the exception of e, which in this style is in the circular form) are practically the same as in the Chancery hand, the cast of the writing is quite altered by lateral compression, which cramps and narrows the letters in an exaggerated manner.

Our first example of the Court hand is of Henry VIII.'s reign, and is taken from a final concord, or foot of a fine, of the year 1530 (Brit. Mus., Add. Ch. 23,539).

FINAL CONCORD.—A.D. 1530.

(Hec est finalis concordia *facta* in Cur*ia* *domini* Regis— |
domini Hiber*nie* a conquestu vicesimo primo coram Robert[o]
— | Inter AntoniumWyngfeld Militem Iohan*nem* Audele[y] |
et Reginaldum Dygby Armig*erum* deforc*ientes* de Maneri[o]
— | predic*tum* Maneri*um* cum pertine*ntiis* esse Ius ipsius
Humfri*di* et)

Next we select a passage from an exemplification of
a plea of Elizabeth's reign, dated in the year 1578 (Brit.
Mus., Add. Ch. 25,968).

EXEMPLIFICATION.—A.D. 1578.

(fac*it* I*deo* cons*ideratum* est quod pred*ictus* Iohan*nes* Collyn
recup*eret* | —[misericordi]a *et cetera* Et s*uper* hoc pred*ictus*
Iohan*nes* Collyn pet*it* breve | —[Trinit]atis in tres septimanas
et cetera Ad quem diem hic | —[u]ltimo p*re*terito h*a*bere fecit
p*re*fato Iohan*ni* Collyn | —[presenc]iu*m* duxim*us* exemplifi-
cand*a* In cuius rei testimoniu*m*)

There is practically no great difference in style between
these two specimens. The latter is perhaps to some extent the better hand and shows a very slight advance
on the other; but the forms of the letters are so stereotyped in this class of writing that the space of nearly
half a century which lies between the two documents
has impressed but little trace of change on the later
one.

Lastly, to show further how very gradual was the
alteration wrought by time in the character of the Court
hand, an example is taken from a final concord of the
reign of Charles II., bearing the date of 1673 (Brit.
Mus., Add. Ch. 25,871), nearly a century and a half after
the date of the final concord above, of the time of
Henry VIII., with which it is to be compared.

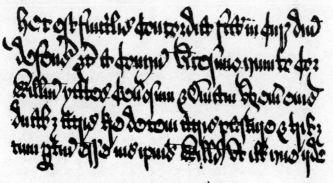

FINAL CONCORD.—A.D. 1673.

(Hec est finalis Concordia f*a*cta in Cur*ia* domini— | defens*oris*
et cetera a Conqu*estu* vicesimo quinto Cor[am]— | Will*elmum*

Yates Generosum *et* Dinam uxorem eius— | duabus acris terre decem acris pasture *et* tribus— | cum pertinentiis esse ius ipsius Willelmi ut illa que iide[m])

The more recent date of this document is to be recognized by the coarser style of the writing and by the broken appearance of the letters, which is effected by their more strongly defined angularity.

The Court hand continued in practice down to the reign of George II.; the Chancery hand still survives in the modern engrossing hands employed in enrolments and patents.

ADDENDA.

Page **49.**—A metal pen, about two inches long, shaped and slit after the fashion of a quill-pen, was recently found by Professor Waldstein in the so-called tomb of Aristotle at Eretria.—*Nineteenth Century*, May, 1891.

Greek Palæography.—Since the sheets of this volume passed through the press, Monsieur Omont has published his *Facsimilés des plus anciens Manuscrits Grecs en onciale et en minuscule de la Bibliothèque Nationale du ive au xiie siècle* (Paris, 1892). Among the plates are facsimiles of the Codex Sarravianus of the Old Testament, pl. 2 (referred to above, p. 152, l. 20, as an Octateuch) ; of the Codex Ephraemi, pl. 3 (above, p. 152, l. 19); of the Pauline Epistles from Mount Athos, pl. 4 (above, p. 154, l. 1); of the Codex Claromontanus, pl. 5 (above, p. 154, l. 22, and p. 181, l. 19) ; of the Coislin Octateuch, pl. 6 (above, p. 154, l. 9) ; of a series of MSS. in late uncial writing, 8th-11th centuries, pl. 8 to 21 (to be added to the lists on pp. 157, 158); and of an Evangelistarium in large ornamental round-uncials of the 12th century, pl. 22.

To the MSS. mentioned under the head of **Greek Writing in Western Europe** (p. 181) we can now add references to the following facsimiles in M. Omont's series :—Pauline Epistles, in Greek and Latin, the Codex Sangermanensis of St. Petersburg, 9th century, pl. 5 *bis* ; a Latin-Greek Psalter, Coislin MS. 186, 8th century, pl. 7; a Latin-Greek Glossary, MS. Latin 7651, 9th century, pl. 23 ; and a Psalter, Arsenal MS. 8407, 9th century, pl. 24.

Systems of Dating.—It may be of practical use to add a few words on the different systems observed in dating manuscripts.

Mediæval Greek MSS. are dated sometimes by the year of the indiction, sometimes by the year of the world according to the era of Constantinople, sometimes by both indiction and year of the world.

The Indiction was a cycle of fifteen years, which are severally styled Indiction 1, Indiction 2, etc., up to Indiction 15, when the series begins afresh. The introduction of this system is attributed to Constantine the Great. From the circumstance of the commencement of the indiction being reckoned variously from different days, four kinds of indictions have been recognized, viz. :—

i. The Indiction of Constantinople, calculated from the 1st of September, A.D. 312.

ii. The Imperial or Cæsarian Indiction (commonly used in England and France), beginning on the 24th of September, A.D. 312.

iii. The Roman or Pontifical Indiction (commonly used in dating papal bulls from the ninth to the fourteenth century), beginning on the 1st of January (or the 25th of December, when that day was reckoned as the first day of the year), A.D. 313.

iv. The Indiction used in the register of the parliament of Paris, beginning in October.

The Greeks made use of the Indiction of Constantinople.[1]

To find the indiction of a year of the Christian era, add 3 to the year (because A.D. 1 = Indiction 4), and

---

[1] An independent mode of reckoning the commencement of the indiction was followed in Egypt under the later Roman Empire. The indiction there began normally in the latter half of the month Pauni, which corresponds to about the middle of June; but the actual day of commencement appears to have been variable and to have depended upon the exact period of the rising of the Nile.—*Catalogue of Greek Papyri in the British Museum,* pp. 197, 198.

divide the sum by 15 : if nothing remains, the indiction will be 15 ; if there is a remainder, it will be the number of the indiction. But it must not be forgotten that the Indiction of Constantinople begins on the 1st of September, and consequently that the last four months of a year of the Christian era belong to the next indiction year.

The year of the Creation of the World was calculated, according to the era of Constantinople, to be B.C. 5508. The first day of the year was the 1st of September.

To reduce the Mundane era of Constantinople to the Christian era, deduct 5508 from the former for the months of January to August ; and 5509 for September to December.

A chronological table, showing the corresponding years of the Mundane era, the Christian era, and the Indiction, from A.D. 800 to A.D. 1599, will be found in Gardthausen's *Griechische Palaeographie*, pp. 450-459.

Latin MSS. are dated in several ways : by the year of the Christian era or of other eras, by the year of the indiction, by the regnal year of the reigning sovereign or pontiff, by the year of episcopate, etc. In England it was the general practice to date charters and other legal documents by the saint's day or festival on which, or nearest to which, the deed was executed, and the regnal year of the reigning sovereign.

The year of the Christian era, as now observed, is of the same form as the Julian year, which was settled by C. Julius Cæsar in A.U.C. 708, the first year of the system running from the 1st of January to the 31st of December, A.U.C. 709.

The Christian era is according to the calculation of Dionysius Exiguus (A.D. 533), who reckoned the birth of Our Lord, which took place in the 28th year of Augustus, as falling in A.U.C. 754, that is, dating from the time when the Emperor took the name of Augustus. The early Christians, however, placed the birth of Our Lord four years earlie, calculating the 28th year of Augustus from the date of the Battle of Actium (A.U.C.

723), and thus beginning the Christian era in A.U.C. 750.

The Dionysian year is supposed to have commenced on the 25th of March.

But the commencement of the year has been reckoned from different days in different countries :—

In England and Ireland, from the sixth century to 1066, it was reckoned from Christmas Day, or from the 25th of March ; after the Norman conquest to the year 1155, from the 1st of January ; and between 1155 and 1751, from the 25th of March.

In Scotland, down to the close of 1599, it was reckoned from the 25th of March. The 1st of January was the first day of the year 1600.

In France, the year began variously in different dioceses and districts : on Christmas Day, Easter Eve, or the 25th of March. The 1st of January first began the year in 1564.

In Germany, the year anciently began on Christmas Day. The 1st of January began the year in 1544.

In Italy, generally, the year was reckoned from Christmas Day ; the 1st of January was adopted in 1583. In Tuscany, however, the 25th of March was the first day, down to 1751, which commenced with the 1st of January ; and in Venice, before 1522, when the 1st of January was altogether adopted, the legal year began on the 1st of March, and the civil year on the 1st of January.

In Spain, the year began, in Aragon before 1350 and in Castile before 1383, on the 1st of January ; and in those years and subsequently, down to 1556, at Christmas. In 1556 the 1st of January was adopted.

In Portugal, the Spanish system was followed before 1420 ; and in 1420 and subsequently, down to 1556, the year began at Christmas.

The era of Spain is reckoned from the 1st of January, B.C. 38, that is, the year following the conquest of Spain by Augustus. This era was adopted in Africa, Spain, Portugal, and the South of France. Its use was abandoned in Catalonia in 1180, and in Spain generally in

1350 and 1383; in Portugal, in 1420. To reduce a year of the era of Spain to one of the Christian era it is therefore necessary to subtract 38 from the number.

The Julian calendar was followed down to the sixteenth century. The Julian calculation of the solar year was 365 days and 6 hours; but this exceeds the real amount by 11 minutes and 12 seconds. Consequently, by 1582 the revolution of the true year had become unduly retarded by rather more than ten days. In this year, Pope Gregory XIII. reformed the calendar and introduced the "New Style." Ten days were omitted from the year 1582, viz. from the 5th to the 14th of October, inclusive, the 5th being counted as the 15th. The Gregorian calendar was generally adopted in Roman Catholic countries at once, or within a few years; in Protestant countries it was generally adopted to begin in the year 1700, in some at a later period, and in England not till 1751. In countries under the Greek Church the "Old Style" of the Julian calendar is still followed.

By Act of Parliament of 24 George II., 1751, "An Act for regulating the Commencement of the Year and for correcting the Calendar now in use," the practice of commencing the legal year on the 25th of March was discontinued, and the 1st of January was adopted; and the Gregorian calendar took the place of the Julian. The year 1751, which had commenced on the 25th of March, was brought to a close on the 31st of December. The year 1752 began on the next day, the 1st of January, and ran to the 31st of December, but was reduced by 11 days in the month of September, by omitting the nominal 3rd to the 13th, and calling the day after the 2nd the 14th.

The reason why *eleven* days were now omitted instead of *ten*, as in the year 1582, is that the "New Style" required that every hundredth year which is not a fourth hundredth should be counted as an ordinary year and not as a Leap-year, the first year to be so treated being 1700, in which the 29th of February was unwritten.

The year 1800 being the second hundredth year so treated, the "New Style" differs to the amount of *twelve* days from the "Old Style" in the present century.

Full particulars of the various systems of dating will be found in Sir H. Nicolas's *Chronology of History,* and in J. J. Bond's *Handy-Book of Rules and Tables for verifying Dates.*

LIST OF
PRINCIPAL PALÆOGRAPHICAL WORKS
USED OR REFERRED TO.

Taylor (I.), *The Alphabet*, 2 vols., London, 1883, 8vo.

Kirchhoff (A.), *Studien zur Geschichte der griechischen Alphabets*, 4th ed., Gütersloh, 1887, 8vo.

Astle (T.), *The Origin and Progress of Writing*, London, 1803, 4to.

Berger (P.), *Histoire de l'Ecriture dans l'Antiquité*, Paris, 1891, 8vo.

Géraud (H.), *Essai sur les Livres dans l'Antiquité*, Paris, 1840, 8vo.

Egger (E.), *Histoire du Livre depuis ses origines jusqu'à nos jours*, Paris, 1880, 8vo.

Birt (T.), *Das Antike Buchwesen*, Berlin, 1882, 8vo.

Quantin, *Dictionnaire de Diplomatique Chrétienne* [vol. 47 of Migne's *Encyclopédie Théologique*], Paris, 1846, 8vo.

Wattenbach (W.), *Das Schriftwesen im Mittelalter*, 2nd ed., Leipzig, 1875, 8vo.

Blass (F.), *Palaeographie* [article in I. von Müller's *Handbuch der klassischen Altertums-Wissenschaft*], 2nd ed., Munich, 1892, 8vo.

Westwood (J. O.), *Palæographia Sacra Pictoria*, London, 1844, 4to.

Silvestre (J. B.), *Universal Palæography*, ed. F. Madden, 2 vols., London, 1850, 8vo., and 2 vols. (plates) fol.

Palæographical Society, *Facsimiles of MSS. and Inscriptions,*
   ed. E. A. Bond, E. M. Thompson, and G. F. Warner,
   1st Series, 3 vols., London, 1873-1883, 2nd Series, 1884,
   etc., in progress, fol.

*Catalogue of Ancient Manuscripts in the British Museum,
   Part i., Greek; Part ii., Latin,* ed. E. M. Thompson and
   G. F. Warner, London, 1881, 1884, fol.

Vitelli (G.) and Paoli (C.), *Collezione Fiorentina di facsimili
   paleografici Greci e Latini,* Florence, 1884, etc., in progress, fol.

Montfaucon (B. de), *Palæographia Græca,* Paris, 1708, fol.

Wattenbach (W.), *Anleitung zur griechischen Palaeographie,*
   2nd ed., Leipzig, 1877, 4to.

Gardthausen (V.), *Griechische Palaeographie,* Leipzig, 1879,
   8vo.

*Notices et Textes des Papyrus Grecs du Musée du Louvre et
   de la Bibliothèque Impériale* [in *Notices et Extraits des
   MSS. de la Bibliothèque Impériale,* tome xviii., part 2],
   ed. W. Brunet de Presle, Paris, 1865, 4to. and atlas.

Catalogue of Greek Papyri in the British Museum, ed. F. G.
   Kenyon, London, 1893, 4to. and atlas.

Peyron (B.), *Papiri Greci del Museo Britanico di Londra e
   della Biblioteca Vaticana,* Turin, 1841, 4to.

Leemans (C.), *Papyri Graeci Musei Lugduni-Batavi,* 2 vols.,
   Leyden, 1843, 1885, 4to.

Wilcken (U.), *Tafeln zur aelteren griechischen Palaeographie,*
   Leipzig and Berlin, 1891, fol.

Mahaffy (J. P.), *On the Flinders-Petrie Papyri* [Royal Irish
   Academy, *Cunningham Memoirs,* no. viii.], Dublin, 1891,
   4to.

*Mittheilungen aus der Sammlung der Papyrus Erzherzog
   Rainer,* Vienna, 1886, etc., in progress, fol.

Papyrus Erzherzog Rainer: Führer durch die Ausstellung,
   Vienna, 1892, 8vo.

Sabas, *Specimina Palaeographica codicum Graecorum et Slavo-
   nicorum,* Moscow, 1863, 4to.

Wattenbach (W.), *Schrifttafeln zur Geschichte der griechischen Schrift*, Berlin, 1876-7, fol.

Wattenbach (W.), *Scripturae Graecae Specimina*, Berlin, 1883, fol.

Wattenbach (W.) and Velsen (A. von), *Exempla Codicum Graecorum litteris minusculis scriptorum*, Heidelberg, 1878, fol.

Omont (H.), *Facsimilés des plus anciens Manuscrits Grecs en onciale et en minuscule de la Bibliothèque Nationale du iv⁰ au xii⁰ siècle*, Paris, 1892, fol.

Omont (H.), *Facsimilés des Manuscrits Grecs datés de la Bibliothèque Nationale du ix⁰ au xiv⁰ siècle*, Paris, 1890, fol.

Omont (H.), *Facsimilés des Manuscrits Grecs des xv⁰ et xvi⁰ siècles reproduits en photolithographie d'après les originaux de la Bibliothèque Nationale*, Paris, 1887, 4to.

Martin (A.), *Facsimilés des Manuscrits Grecs d'Espagne, gravés d'après les photographies de Charles Graux*, 2 vols., Paris 1891, 8vo. and atlas.

Lehmann (O.), *Die tachygraphischen Abkürzungen der griechischen Handschriften*, Leipzig, 1880, 8vo.

Allen (T. W.), *Notes on Abbreviations in Greek Manuscripts*, Oxford, 1889, 8vo.

———

Mabillon (J.), *De Re Diplomatica*, Paris, 1709, fol.

Tassin and Toustain, Benedictines, *Nouveau Traité de Diplomatique*, 6 vols., Paris, 1750-1765, 4to.

Kopp (U.), *Palaeographia Critica*, 4 vols., Mannheim, 1817-1829, 4to.

Wailly (N. de), *Eléments de Paléographie*, 2 vols., Paris, 1838, 4to.

Delisle (L.), *Mélanges de Paléographie et de Bibliographie*, Paris, 1880, 8vo. and atlas.

Wattenbach (W.), *Anleitung zur lateinischen Palaeographie*, 4th ed., Leipzig, 1886, 4to.

Chassant (A.), *Paléographie des Chartes et des Manuscrits du xi⁰ au xvii⁰ siècle*, 8th ed., Paris, 1885, 8vo.

Prou (M.), *Manuel de Paléographie Latine et Française,* Paris, 1891, 8vo.

Gloria (A.), *Compendio delle lezioni teorico-pratiche di Paleografia e Diplomatica,* Padua, 1870, 8vo. and atlas.

Arndt (W.), *Schrifttafeln zum Gebrauch bei Vorlesungen,* Berlin, 1874 (2nd. ed., 1876), 1878, fol.

Pertz (G. H.), *Schrifttafeln zum Gebrauch bei diplomatischen Vorlesungen,* Hanover, 1844-1869, fol.

Wattenbach (W.) and Zangemeister (C.), *Exempla Codicum Latinorum litteris majusculis scriptorum,* Heidelberg, 1876, 1879, fol.

Champollion-Figeac (A.), *Paléographie des Classiques Latins,* Paris, 1839, fol.

Chatelain (E.), *Paléographie des Classiques Latins,* Paris, 1884, etc., in progress, fol.

Zangemeister (C.), *Inscriptiones parietariae Pompeianae* [in *Corpus Inscriptionum Latinarum,* vol. iv.], Berlin, 1871, fol.

Massmann (J. F.), *Libellus Aurarius sive Tabulae Ceratae,* Leipzig, 1841, 4to.

Mommsen (T.), *Instrumenta Dacica in tabulis ceratis conscripta aliaque similia* [in *Corpus Inscriptionum Latinarum,* vol. iii., part 2], Berlin, 1873, fol.

Petra (G. de), *Le Tavolette Cerate di Pompei* [in *Atti della R. Accademia dei Lincei,* series ii., vol. iii., part 3], Rome, 1876, 8vo.

Marini (G.), *I Papiri diplomatici,* Rome, 1805, fol.

Champollion-Figeac (A.), *Chartes et Manuscrits sur papyrus de la Bibliothèque Nationale,* Paris, 1840, fol.

Letronne (J. A.), *Diplómes et Chartes de l'époque Mérovingienne sur papyrus et sur velin,* Paris, 1845-1866, fol.

Tardif (J.), *Archives de l'Empire: Facsimile de Chartes et Diplómes Mérovingiens et Carlovingiens,* Paris, 1866, fol.

Delisle (L.), *Le Cabinet des Manuscrits de la Bibliothèque Nationale,* 3 vols. and plates, Paris, 1868-1881, fol.

Album Paléographique avec des notices explicatives par la

Société de l'Ecole des Chartes, ed. L. Delisle, Paris, 1887, fol.

Recueil de Fac-similés à l'usage de l'Ecole des Chartes, Paris, 1880, etc., in progress, fol.

Musée des Archives Départementales, Paris, 1878, fol.

Delisle (L.), *Etudes Paléographiques et Historiques sur un papyrus du vime siècle renfermant des homilies de St. Avit et des écrits de St. Augustin,* Geneva, 1866, 4to.

Delisle (L.), *Notice sur un Manuscrit Mérovingien contenant des fragments d'Eugyppius,* Paris, 1875, fol.

Delisle (L.), *Notice sur un Manuscrit Mérovingien de la Bibliothèque d'Epinal,* Paris, 1878, fol.

Delisle (L.), *Notice sur un Manuscrit Mérovingien de la Bibliothèque Royale de Belgique* [in *Notices et Extraits des MSS.,* tome xxxi.], Paris, 1884, 4to.

Delisle (L.), *Notice sur un Manuscrit de l'Abbaye de Luxeuil* [in *Notices et Extraits des MSS.,* tome xxxi.], Paris, 1886, 4to.

Delisle (L.), *Mémoire sur l'Ecole calligraphique de Tours au ixe siècle* [in *Mémoires de l'Académie des Inscriptions,* tome xxxii.], Paris, 1885, 4to.

Delisle (L.), *Mémoire sur d'anciens Sacramentaires* [in *Mémoires de l'Académie des Inscriptions,* tome xxxii.], Paris, 1885, 4to.

Delisle (L.), *L'Evangéliaire de Saint Vaast d'Arras et la Calligraphie Franco Saxonne du ixe siècle,* Paris, 1888, fol.

Sickel (T.), *Monumenta Graphica medii ævi ex archivis et bibliothecis Imperii Austriaci collecta,* 4 vols., Vienna, 1858-1882, 4to. and atlas.

Sickel (T.), *Schrifttafeln aus dem Nachlasse von U. F. von Kopp,* Vienna, 1870, fol.

Sybel (H. von) and Sickel (T.), *Kaiserurkunden in Abbildungen,* Vienna, 1880, etc., in progress, 4to. and atlas.

Pflugk-Harttung (J. von), *Specimina selecta Chartarum Pontificum Romanorum,* Stuttgart, 1885-1887, fol.

Monaci (M.), *Facsimili di antichi Manoscritti,* Rome, 1881-3, fol.

Monaci (E.) and Paoli (C.), *Archivio Paleografico Italiano,* two series, Rome, 1882-1890, fol.

Foucard (C.), *La Scrittura in Italia sino a Carlomagno,* Milan, 1888, fol.

Bibliotheca Casinensis, ed. L. Tosti, 4 vols., Monte-cassino, 1873-1880, in progress, 4to.

Tabularium Casinense, 2 vols., Monte-cassino, 1887, 1891, in progress, 4to.

Paleografia Artistica di Montecassino, Monte-cassino, 1876, etc., in progress, fol.

Codex Diplomaticus Cavensis, ed. M. Morcaldi, 6 vols., Naples, 1873, etc., in progress, 4to.

Ewald (P.) and Loewe (G.), *Exempla Scripturae Visigoticae,* Heidelberg, 1883, fol.

Rodriguez (C.), *Bibliotheca Universal de la Polygraphia Española,* Madrid, 1738, fol.

Merino (A.), *Escuela Paleographica,* Madrid, 1780, fol.

Muños y Rivero (J.), *Paleografia Visigoda,* Madrid, 1881, 8vo.

Facsimiles of National Manuscripts of England (Ordnance Survey), ed. W. B. Sanders, 4 parts, Southampton, 1865-1868, fol.

Facsimiles of National Manuscripts of Scotland (Ordnance Survey), ed. C. Innes, 3 parts, Southampton, 1867-1871, fol.

Facsimiles of National Manuscripts of Ireland (Ordnance Survey), ed. J. T. Gilbert, 4 parts (in 5 vols.), Dublin and London, 1874-1884, fol.

Facsimiles of Ancient Charters in the British Museum, ed. E. A. Bond, 4 parts, London, 1873-1878, 4to. and fol.

Facsimiles of Anglo-Saxon Manuscripts (Ordnance Survey), ed. W. B. Sanders, 3 parts, Southampton, 1878-1884, fol.

Skeat (W. W.), *Twelve Facsimiles of Old English Manuscripts,* Oxford, 1892, 4to.

Walther (J. L.), *Lexicon Diplomaticum abbreviationes syllabarum et vocum . . . . exponens,* Göttingen, 1747, fol.

Mommsen (T.). *Notarum Laterculi* [in Keil's *Grammatici Latini*, vol. iv.], Leipzig, 1864, 4to.

Chassant (A.), *Dictionnaire des Abréviations Latines et Françaises*, 5th ed., Paris, 1884, 8vo.

Wright (A.), *Court-Hand restored*, ed. C. T. Martin, London, 1879, 4to.

Martin (C. T.), *The Record Interpreter*, London, 1892, 8vo.

Nicolas (Sir H.), *The Chronology of History* [in Lardner's *Cabinet Cyclopædia*], London, 1845, 8vo.

Bond (J. J.), *Handy-Book of Rules and Tables for verifying Dates*, London, 1869, 8vo.

———— ————

Full lists of palæographical works, Greek and Latin, will be found in the Introductions by Monsieur Omont to his *Facsimilés des Manuscrits Grecs datés de la Bibliothèque Nationale* and by Monsieur Delisle to the *Album Paléographique ;* and a series of articles on palæographical publications which annually appear have been written by Professor Wattenbach in the *Jahresberichte der Geschichtswissenschaft* since 1879 (II. Jahrgang).

INDEX.

A.

D.

DACIA, waxen tablets from, 24, 26, 204.

Dalmatia, charm on lead from, 17.

Damascus, a centre of paper commerce, 43.

Dating of MSS., systems of, 322–326.

δέλτος, δελτίον, δελτίδιον, tablets, 20.

Demetrius, will of, on papyrus, 133.

διαβάτης, a pricker, 53.

Diæresis, marks of, 73.

διαστολή, a dividing comma, 72.

"Dimma, Book of," 241.

Dioscorides, MS., 153.

διφθέραι, papyrus, 28; skins, 35.

διπλῆ, a paragraph mark, 68.

Diploma, a folded sheet, 63.

Diptycha, duplices, δίπτυχα, δίθυροι, a two-leaf tablet, 20.

Diræ, imprecations, on lead, 16.

Distinctiones, marks of punctuation, 70.

Dodona, oracular leaden plates found there, 16.

"Durham Book." *See* Lindisfarne Gospels.

E.

EDWARD I., King of England, charter of, 307.

Edward II., King of England, writ of Privy Seal, 308.

ἔγκαυστον, ink, 50.

Egyptians, ancient: their alphabet, 1–4; their use of linen as a writing material, 14; of potsherds, 14; of wooden tablets, 18, 19; of papyrus, 27; of skins, 34; of red ink, 51; their manufacture of papyrus, 30–33.

εἰλητάριον, εἴλητον, ἐνείλημα, ἐξείλημα, a roll, 54, 55.

ἐκφυλλοφορία, ostracism with leaves, 13.

England: writing before the

Norman conquest, 244–256; early foreign school, 244, 245; native northern school, 245; local styles, 249–251; foreign influence, 253; mediæval MSS. 266–270, 273, 274, 276, 278, 280–282, 285–292; cursive or charter-hand and court-hand, 301–320.

Ennius, invention of shorthand signs attributed to, 84.

Ephraem, St., MS., 167.

ἔπος, a measured line of writing, 78.

Erechtheum, at Athens, memoranda of accounts, 19, 28.

ἐσχατοκόλλιον, the last leaf of a papyrus roll, 31.

Euclid, MS., 163.

Eugyppius, MS., 232.

Eumenes of Pergamum, reputed inventor of parchment or vellum, 35.

Euripides, fragments of plays, 112, 120.

Euthalius of Alexandria, his stichometrical arrangements in the Bible, 80, 82.

Evangelistarium, 157.

Exclamantes, catch-words, 62.

Explicit, derivation of, 59.

"Exultet" rolls, 60.

F.

FLACCUS, Albinus, MS., 220.

Folium, φύλλον, the leaf of a codex, 63.

Forulus, a chest for rolls, 57.

France: ancient and mediæval MSS., 259–263, 265, 270, 275, 276, 277, 284.

Frontes, the edges of a roll, 56.

Fulda, MSS. connected with, 194, 264.

G.

GATHERINGS. *See* Quires.

Germanicus, charms used to destroy him, 16.

Germany: mediæval MSS., 264, 283.

Pompeian Wall-Inscriptions. Before A.D. 79.	Pompeian Waxen-Tablets. Before A.D. 76.	Dacian Waxen-Tablets. 2nd Century.	Imperial Rescript. 5th Century.	Ravenna Deed. A.D. 572.
a				
b				
t				
u				
x				
y				
z				

LATIN CURSIVE ALPHABETS.

F. S. Weller.